WHAT I WISH I KNEW ABOUT MONEY AT 25

Alex Gardener

This book is dedicated to all my nieces, nephews, cousins, friends, and family members who liked to listen to me ramble on for hours about financial stuff. You're the reason this book exists.
I can't thank you enough.

Table of Contents

Foreword: I Wish I Had a Time Machine

Alright. It's confession time. For this entire book, I'm going to tell you *not* to do this or *never* to do that. The truth is:

I've done **all** those things.

I've made a **ton** of financial mistakes in my adult life. I made them because I was chasing some fantasy version of my life that I thought would make me feel successful. I was a sitting duck for any person, company, or organization that sought to part a fool from his money. Ambition is a double-edged sword. I had the drive but didn't have the knowledge. The result is that I drove myself into financial brick walls and crashed over and over again. It's a wonder I'm still in one piece.

If you are like me, your drive, ambition and your passion **aren't the problems.** You have plenty of that and you know enough about money to be dangerous- to *yourself.* I had to learn about finances from the school of hard knocks. I was my own worst enemy when it came to building my wealth, but I didn't know any better. All I knew was that sitting around doing nothing would never fix anything.

I'm writing this book because I wish I could **redo** all my dumb financial decisions. Since time machines haven't been invented yet, I'll do the next best thing. I'm warning **you** in hopes that you'll listen to me and learn from my mistakes.

I don't know if any of you play video games, but this book is like the gaming guides they used to make. It shows you how to get past difficult areas and how to play the game so that you get through with the least amount of difficulty. Personally, I tended to avoid those guides. I *liked* difficult things. The more difficult, the better. I actually *preferred* to die a million times in the pursuit of accomplishing something on my own. It was extremely frustrating but very rewarding when I finally won on *my* terms. However, anytime you approach a problem that way, you usually learn **too late** that there was a far easier solution that would have made the game more enjoyable. You also fail repeatedly because you use a losing strategy based on your limited knowledge of how the game works. The tool you needed to succeed was likely in front of your face the whole time. You just didn't *realize* how significantly the tool would have helped you beat the game.

That's what sucks about the game of life. By the time you realize that your life could have been easier or more enjoyable, you're middle-aged. You can't redo a relationship that you screwed up or redo an opportunity that you failed at because you gave a half-assed effort. You just have to live with it. It's true that these failures will ultimately make you stronger. However, it's harder to deal with when you know that the person that held you back was yourself.

I know what it's like to be in your shoes. You want to be successful. You were promised success if you followed the rules. That didn't happen, so now you're looking for a way to get the success you were promised. Unfortunately, there are schemes and tricks that are *so* good and *so* convincing that you'll spend **all** your money chasing them. If you do that for 10 years as I did, the result will be that you gain AND lose *over and over again*. Your successes will be negated by your failures. When you finally take the time to question your life, ten years will have passed and you'll spend months deciding if you'll even *go* to your high school reunion.

Your **net** result for all your hard work and sacrifice will be **ZERO**.

It doesn't matter how smart you think you are. These companies spend millions of dollars studying people like you. They know what buttons to press. It doesn't matter how hard a test is if you have the cheat sheet, right? Well, these companies know **everything about you** and they know what will motivate you to sign the dotted line. It typically involves you getting excited about money, fame, or status long enough for you to commit to a terrible contract that lasts for several years.

If you think that this is the kind of book where some financial guru looks down on you and enlightens you with the knowledge from their finance degree at Harvard, **you couldn't be more wrong**. I am an average guy that grew up broke and *stayed* broke until his early thirties. It took me that long to understand how this money thing really worked. None of the stuff I learned at school or college prepared me for the real world. I only started learning that stuff when I worked at the bank and some of the higher-ups liked me enough to tell me how it *actually* worked.

They looked at me as if I were a basketball player furiously practicing with a tennis ball. They knew I had the right attitude and a good amount of ambition, but they could **clearly** see that I was going about things the **wrong way**. When they handed me the appropriate tools, it made everything **so much easier**. After that, I knew where to look and didn't need their constant guidance.

It is my hope that this book will be a tool that changes your life. I know that most of you only need to be pointed in the right direction. I'm confident that you'll figure out the rest once you know the basics. There's a whole lot about money and investing that we won't go into, but you'll probably discover them on your own and develop your own style.

That being said, let's get down to business.

A Summary of What We're Going to Talk About

You Will Spend the Majority of Your Income on One of Two Things:

1. **Investments That Grow Your Wealth and Give You Freedom**
2. **Status Symbols that Put You in Debt and Limit Your Choices**

- You Must Grow Your Wealth and Avoid the Trap of Status.

- Abandon your need to appear successful and remove your emotional attachment to money.

- Give up on the idea of getting rich quick. Avoid any person, fad, scheme, hustle, "strategy," "opportunity," business or organization that promises wealth within a few months or a few years.

- You can become a millionaire. It's actually very simple, but it's not easy. It's like growing a forest from a bag of seeds.

- Financial independence is the result of small, consistent action taken over several years. There is no need to have a lot of money or take huge risks. Be the tortoise, not the hare.

- Put the maximum amount you can afford into a low-cost index mutual fund or ETF every single month for at least 20 years. Yes, it takes that long.

- Only use debt to buy things that get **more** valuable the longer you own it and avoid using debt to buy things that get **less** valuable the longer you own it.

- Invest in things that pay you money just for owning them. Yes, they exist. Check out the chapter on Dividends and Bonds.

- The Banking industry makes more from your **financial ignorance** than you can imagine.

- Pay off your credit cards every month. Never carry a balance month to month. If you don't have enough money to buy something with cash, don't buy it.

- Using debt means that you're agreeing to pay **more** for something tomorrow so you can have it **today**.

- Save your money for a purpose. Don't save money for the sake of saving.

- Don't be so focused on the monthly payment amount. Focus on the **interest rate**.

- Your Best Financial **Friends** are Compound Interest, Discipline, and Time.

- Your Worst Financial **Enemies** are Emotion, Impulse, and Impatience.

CHAPTER ONE
You Must Become Financially Independent

Ok. Here's the truth. I'm writing this book because I wish somebody told me this stuff when I was 25. I say that knowing good and well that I probably wouldn't have listened- because I was 25. I was relatively fresh out of college and I had a few years of working in the "real world." Frankly, I thought I knew everything I needed to know.

I didn't. Nowhere close in fact. What followed for roughly the next 10 years was me getting my financial butt handed to me repeatedly due to a combination of financial ignorance, misplaced ambition, and overconfidence in thinking that I was smart and already knew how to be successful.

Again- I didn't. I knew what my mother and my family taught me. I knew what school had taught me. And I mistakenly thought my success in school and my mother's claims of how smart I was guaranteed me success as an adult.

Yet again - it didn't. Are you starting to see a pattern here? Becoming financially independent has nothing to do with your grades in school or what your family thinks of you. Your innate talent and abilities could absolutely help you in your quest to earn a higher *income*, but wealth creation isn't necessarily about being talented. Quite frankly, it has **nothing** to do with being talented. It has very little to do with whatever job you choose. Being financially independent really means that you've learned the basic principles of money and you put those principles into practice *every month* over a long period of time. In short, it's the Tortoise vs the Hare.

You are the Tortoise. You are *not* the Hare. Stop trying to be the Hare. You know how that ends.

Financial independence is extremely satisfying and will give you peace of mind. However, it is not sexy, not fun, and definitely not short-term. It won't make you more attractive. It won't mean a life of sitting on a beach and drinking fancy drinks with umbrellas in them. It won't give you a staff of butlers with British accents. Anyone who tells you otherwise is trying to sell you something, gambling with their money, or lying to you. Financial independence comes as the result of being boring, repetitive, and unemotional over a long period of time. It's that simple.

Get this through your head *right now*: financial independence is NOT a measure of your abilities, your intelligence, your degree, your family, your luck, your faith, or any of that stuff that makes you who you are. It is simply math- algebra if you want to get technical. I can prove it. Everyone talks about the formula for success. Well, here it is:

$$FV = PV(1 + i)^n + [\,R(1 + i)^n - 1\,] \,/\, i$$

See? Easy Peasy.

Ok, so all terrible puns aside, my fellow nerds and finance people will instantly recognize this. For everyone else, it's the equation for the future value of money using compound interest and periodic contributions.

Plain English: invest money every month for a long time and eventually you'll have a ton of money. Trust me, it works. Here's what's in the formula if you're curious:

FV = Future Value: How much money you'll have in the future

PV = Present Value: How much money you have right now

i = Interest Rate: Sometimes you know in advance (i.e a bank savings account and/or bonds. Sometimes you make your best assumption based on historic performance and analytic projections (the stock market).

n= Number of years: How many years you plan to invest

R= A fixed amount you put in periodically (per month or per year)

Have I lost you yet? Well, here's the great part of investing:

You don't have to know any of this stuff for it to work. Just invest your money every month for a long time- ideally 20 years or more.

"20 Years? That's a long time!"

I knew you'd say that, but here's the irony: By the time you realize that it takes 20 years to realistically become financially independent, you'll be hovering around 40 years old. If you've never been taught financial intelligence, it takes around 20 years of financial screwups to finally figure out how to get it right. So instead of being financially independent at **45**, it will now be **65**. This is absolutely still a good age to enjoy life, but you won't have the energy or the mobility of a 45-year-old. The cruel truth of being human is that you don't realize how valuable time is until you're running out of it. So do your future self a favor and get started today.

As in **<u>RIGHT NOW.</u>**

Seriously- do **NOT** overthink this. It's like gravity. Sure, it can be expressed in a mathematic equation, but you don't need to know that to understand that to know that you'll die if you jump out of a plane. How do you know that? Because you've likely fallen off of something and it really, *really* hurt. Did you need to make good grades in school to understand the agony of a broken leg after falling off a skateboard? Did your ignorance of the law of gravity make you impervious to the pain and embarrassment of falling down a flight of stairs?

No. Your real-life *experience* with falling helped you understand gravity. *Reading* about falling and *actually* falling are two entirely different things. Humans learn the most when we have "skin in the game" and pain is the best teacher. Then we learn to avoid pain. Then we adapt our behavior and our environment to ensure that we minimize the chances of experiencing that pain again. Ultimately, we learn how to experience the fulfillment, the rush and the joy from skydiving. We learn to enjoy life even in the face of death.

Once you finish reading this book, you are going to invest a small amount. You will have gained knowledge, but nothing will prepare you for the agony of losing money. And trust me, you *will* lose money. Then you'll get scared. You'll doubt yourself. You'll swear to never do it again. Then you'll hear or read about someone *way* less talented than you that has become massively successful by investing. You'll attempt to be humble and have gratitude and stuff, but that person's success will piss you off immensely. Then you'll jump back in determined to be successful and not lose money. You'll make mistakes. You'll learn from those mistakes. Sometimes you'll get lucky. You'll start to figure it out. Then you'll begin to succeed more based on what you've learned through experience- just like you did with gravity. You'll never be invincible, but you'll eventually experience the fulfillment, the sense of purpose and joy that comes with financial success. That, my friends, is how you will become financially independent.

CHAPTER TWO
Jobs, School and Money Are Just Tools

Unless you come from a wealthy family, you probably *never* had anyone sit down with you and talk about wealth- much less how to actually become wealthy. You likely got the talk about the "birds and the bees", but probably not the talk about the "stocks and the bonds." Did you ever think that might be a problem if you want to be financially successful? What did you learn then?

> *Go to college, make good grades and get a good job.*
> *Then get a promotion or a higher paying job.*

That's it. That's all you learned. For some of you, maybe you were told to join the military and seek to get promoted there. But *who* told you that was the formula for success? Your parents? Your college professor? The Army recruiter that came to your high school? Would you assume that any of them were millionaires?

No, you wouldn't. Then why are you listening to them? It's because you **trust** them. Also, in their defense, they are giving you the best information they have based on their experience. They *believe* what they're telling you is *likely* to give you an above-average income. They *believe* that if you go to school, get a good job, and wait to have kids, there's a *good chance* that you'll end up being better off financially than they are now.

So...did that happen? Are you better off than your parents?

Statistically speaking, no. It didn't happen. If you are 21 in the year

2021, you are likely *living* with your parents. You can't afford to live anywhere else. In their defense, that advice statistically worked great around 1999 when *they* went to college. However, the dot-com crash of 2000 made jobs scarce for college graduates. Just when things started to improve, the housing crash of 2008 happened. Around 2010, America started a ten-year economic boom that unfortunately hit the brick wall of the 2020 COVID-19 pandemic. Since the time your parents graduated, there have been **three** major economic downturns that have eliminated millions of jobs and threatened the existence of entire industries. However, the old advice of "go to school and get a good job" has never changed. That advice obviously no longer works like it used to, but parents, teachers and loved ones still push it.

I graduated in 2002 with a Bachelor's degree from a respected school. I truly thought I was going to be successful within a few *months* after I graduated. Why *wouldn't* I? I made the dean's list and had a high GPA. I listened to all my high school guidance counselors, got into a good school, and followed all (ok-*most*) of the rules. According to everything I had ever heard up to that point, I was **destined** to be successful.

Long story short, none of that stuff mattered. I had **no** idea what I was in for. By the time I graduated, America was in the midst of the dot-com crash. It was so bad, my college advisor told me that I may have to be patient and work my way up from a salary of $23,000 a year. During our initial conversations four years earlier, he told me that I could expect to make $60,000. The earning potential of my degree dropped by **more than half**. Do you want to know the really sad part? In 2000, I made $24,000 selling appliances at my *part-time* job at Sears.

I've had the unfortunate opportunity to **start** my professional career during the first of those three crashes over the last twenty years. I was literally standing outside of Lehman Brothers in Manhattan the day it crashed in 2008. Let's just say I've gotten my butt kicked financially for 10 years straight. Here's what all those years taught me:

Most of what we've been taught about success and wealth is **wrong** and will keep us broke **FOREVER**.

Why? Because:

School is NOT designed to teach you financial independence.

-and-
People can't teach you what they don't know.

Think about it: Did your high school or college ever teach you how to invest? Did anyone ever teach you how and where to buy real estate? Will making a high salary automatically make you financially independent?

NO.

School only gives you a degree. A degree only gets you a job. A job only gives you income in exchange for your time. You're taught that everything else should just "work out" after that. You're sold on the idea that your career will automatically be placed in the fast lane in a self-driving car. But as anyone who's tried to take a picture with someone standing in front of a window knows- the automatic settings don't always produce the result *you* want. There are things happening behind the scenes that affect you even if you don't realize it.

Taxes are automatically taken out of your paycheck. You receive benefits like health insurance but are likely paying for these benefits out of your own salary. Paid vacation has to be *earned*. You get access to a 401K, which is great, but you have to manage your own investments. Again, *when* were you ever taught to manage an investment portfolio? You weren't. So either you make your best guess after watching a couple of YouTube videos or you don't participate at all.

It's possible that you never even thought to challenge what you learned about money. I remember hanging out with my friends and complaining about being broke, but I definitely couldn't tell you *specifically* why I struggled. I figured that I just needed *more money*. The obvious solution was to *work harder* or get more hours. But all I had to do was to find myself driving through a nice neighborhood to see that what I was doing would never be *enough*. I knew that somehow I didn't have all the information. I thought I was lacking something- that I somehow *didn't* have that special thing I needed to win. What I didn't realize at the time is that my problem wasn't that I was lacking something, it was viewing the things I *did* have the wrong way.

I didn't feel successful at 25 because of how I *felt* about those things. I had an emotional attachment to them because I viewed them as status symbols- or at the very least milestones that were supposed to prove my success and my progress to myself and others. Very few companies were hiring graduates with my degree. I ended up working retail to survive and constantly felt like my future was slipping away.

You see, it was important that I *felt* that I had a good job and that I *felt* I went to a good school and that I *felt* that I had "a lot of money." Those things were supposed to guarantee my success, so it was important that I acquired them. I never really sat down and specified what "a good job" was nor did I quantify what "a lot of money" even meant. Bottom line: I was caught up in my feelings and those feelings tended to rob me of the joy of my small victories, which truthfully I had plenty of. It took me a very long time to understand the **right** way to look at these things:

Jobs, School, and Money are Just Tools.

You use them to perform a specific function- just like a plumber uses a wrench. A plumber knows that there's no point in getting all emotional about a wrench or having strong feelings about a wrench. Because it's a wrench. Sure, the plumber might *like* a shiny new wrench or have a preference on the brand, but if it doesn't perform its basic job function, it's useless.

That's not to say that you can't use a wrench to do other stuff. Some people use a wrench to hammer something into place. After all, it's heavy and metal. It won't break if you use it that way. Some people use wrenches to knock people over the head. Is that wrong? Well, that depends on the situation. Honestly, if I'm being attacked, I'd feel a lot better with a wrench in my hands. My point is that some people use it in a way it *wasn't* meant to be used. If you really need to hammer something, use a hammer. And if you really want to defend yourself, there are far better options. In my case, I had a degree in Landscape Architecture. I didn't use it to work in my field of study, but I was able to use my degree as a basic qualification to work for the Department of Labor (long story).

But think about it. What if, as a child, you *only* saw your parents or the people you looked up to use a wrench as a hammer? Quite naturally, you would do the same as an adult. That's all you know. That's all *they* knew. But because you use a wrench, your nails go in crooked and your work never looks as good as you pictured it in your mind. Even if you become an expert at using a wrench as a hammer, an amateur with an actual hammer could produce work *faster* than you with similar (or better) results.

Worse yet, when you see some random, seemingly un-talented person brag about how successful they are at building stuff, you become jealous. "How did they do that?" "Why can't I do that?" It's infuriating, but they seem to know something you don't. So, you make it your mission to find out *what* that thing is. What happens when you find out that the answer is using a *hammer* to hammer things? Does it blow your mind? Does the light bulb *finally* go off? Or do you *resist* this new information? I mean, of course you've *heard* of a hammer (you're not an idiot), but something about it just feels *wrong*. It almost feels like *cheating*.

I mean, it takes *real skill* to hammer something with a wrench. You've got to *work hard*. You've got to *focus*. You've got to *study* and *put in the time and effort* to use a wrench to hammer things. Besides, everyone you know, love, and respect uses a wrench as a hammer. How would your family feel if you switched to using hammers all of a sudden? You decide that it's best to stick with the wrench. Maybe you'll even buy a hammer someday- just to say you have one.

I'm going to admit right here that I tend to take my analogies too far. So yes, I'm taking a very long time to illustrate to you that:

- o You're likely using jobs, school and money to do something they weren't designed to do.
- o You use these things in a similar way to those you know, love, and respect.
- o It's likely you feel an emotional obligation to do what your family expects you to do regarding jobs, school, and money and are afraid to go against it.
- o Your attempt to gain success by *incorrectly* using jobs, school and money will fall short as you watch people with far less talent and abilities surpass you while living the life that *you* want.

The biggest problem with jobs, school, and money is that you're told these things are the **solution**. It's either implied or told to you directly that once you attain these things, they will "solve" the problem of financial lack and failure- which will automatically provide "success."

By now, you should know that's not how capitalism works. In my case, my degree only qualified me to work in an industry that didn't want or need inexperienced workers in the midst of a financial crisis. My first "real" job paid me $23K a year. My Bachelor's degree cost me $30K. There *was* no automatic success. I didn't even make enough for automatic *rent*. I felt cheated by the system. I felt like a failure. If you learn nothing else from this chapter, learn these two things:

> You don't *GET* a job, a degree, and money to *GET* success.
> You **_USE_** a job, a degree, and money to **_BUILD_** wealth.

> Jobs, school, and money are **tools** to build wealth,
> **NOT** status symbols or a measure of success.

I'm not bashing employment or higher education. However, you've got to understand that the educational system is designed to produce employees, **not** business owners and entrepreneurs. Colleges spend a lot of money selling the idea that the key to success is an expensive four-year degree from a prestigious university. Affordable, two-year degrees that focus on skilled trades that are in high demand are ridiculed and frowned upon. Now add the constant barrage of advertising and consumerism and you create an environment where everyone spends all their money as soon as they get it. The result is that everyone, regardless of income or education level, lives check-to-check and struggles financially.

What I'm proposing is that you learn financial intelligence so that it doesn't matter what career choices you make or what school you attend. As long as you see jobs, school and money for the tools that they are, you can use those tools to build wealth.

CHAPTER THREE
Being Wealthy Isn't What You Think

Who comes to mind when you think of a rich person? What comes to mind when you hear the word millionaire? Bugattis? Champagne? A House in Beverly Hills? What kind of lifestyle do you think millionaires have?

Do you want to know the **number one** preferred vehicle of millionaires? It's a Ford F-150. That's right- a regular pickup truck. Can you guess why? It's because millionaires are most likely small business owners who use their trucks for their business. Purchasing a pickup truck also saves money on taxes, which helps them keep even more money in their pocket.

Do you know their favorite alcoholic beverage? It's beer. Why beer? Because if you drive a pickup truck, you're most likely performing a skilled trade like plumbing, HVAC repair, or pressure washing. In any case, it's likely a blue-collar type of work. Plumbers don't drink that much champagne, but they love a good, cheap beer.

Can you guess what kind of neighborhood they live in? It's probably a modest 3-bedroom, 2-bathroom single-family home in a decent neighborhood. It's most likely *not* a mansion and it probably isn't flashy.

Your average millionaire doesn't look like a millionaire, doesn't dress like a millionaire, and doesn't want you to know that he/she is a millionaire. Most millionaires are normal, average-looking people who started out performing a skilled trade and eventually turned it into a business. It's that simple.

Making you rich is not the goal of this book. I want you to achieve Financial Independence. Financial Independence is **not** being rich. They are two entirely different things. Once you understand financial independence and live by its principles, you will see "rich" for what it really is: a flashy way to waste money. *Rich* is what you see on TV. Financial independence is *Wealth*. That's why things like timeshares and VIP exist. They prey on regular people's need to *feel* rich- even if it's just for a limited time.

The problem is that the words *rich* and *millionaire* are associated with pure fantasy. You've been programmed to believe millionaires are rich people who fly around in private jets and take dumps in gold toilets. You've been taught to idolize and follow these people because the implication is that *you'll* never be rich. You're taught that they're somehow different from you and that you can never have their lifestyles. I don't blame you. Our minds have been pumped with this nonsense ever since we were kids. However, I promise you that you don't have to be some kind of extraordinary person to achieve financial independence and wealth.

I used to work at a bank. After working there for a couple of years, I noticed a definite pattern. The people wearing nice suits and designer clothes usually had less than $40,000 in all their accounts put together. They were always more than happy to tell me how much money they had with the bank anytime they bounced a check and complained about having to pay an overdraft fee. Two weeks later, they'd bounce another check and would be in my face again. I'd ultimately tell them that I wouldn't refund their fee and they would always threaten to close their accounts and take their *vast* amount of money somewhere else. However, a random, farmer-looking old guy wearing jean overalls had *$400,000*; and we were just *one* of several banks he had accounts with. As you might guess, he didn't bounce any checks. However, by some random chance he did, the bank would refund that fee so fast it'd make your head spin.

At that same bank, there was this priest who had an account with us. We knew he was a priest because would come in every once in a while wearing that priest collar shirt thing. All of his transactions were always low-dollar and unremarkable. Then one day we struck up a conversation and he told us that his son was famous: he was the spokesperson for a computer company and did all their TV commercials. We were shocked when we found out. We were even more shocked when we learned that the priest was there that day to withdraw money to help his son. Turns out the son got in some legal trouble and got dropped as the spokesperson by the computer company. The priest had us make an official check made payable to the son. That's when we realized that the priest had over half a million dollars in his savings account *alone*. He had more money than his famous son that had been all over TV for *at least* two years. I began wondering if I should go to seminary school.

Here's another story: I had a video production job inside the home of an NBA legend. His house was big, for sure. But his house wasn't the biggest in the neighborhood. *That* house belonged to a dentist. It blew my mind. The NBA player literally has a statue outside his team's arena. There have been documentaries featuring him. Sports analysts have praised his place in sports history. He is considered one of the top 50 players that ever played the game. By contrast, the dentist **might** have been mentioned in a magazine about dentistry. I can't tell you for sure because I don't know his name. You would likely not know who this dentist was even if I did know. And unless you're an avid fan of dentistry, you probably wouldn't care.

Now to be fair, it is very possible that the NBA player had several homes and/or didn't feel the need to get a huge house just for the sake of having one. I can tell you that he is involved in several profitable businesses and he's not short on cash by any means. I can only speak about how it made *me* feel. It surprised the hell out of me. It completely messed with my assumption of what success meant. Honestly, it confused me. It didn't seem *right*. It didn't seem *fair*. How could it even be possible that a dentist could be more successful than a legendary NBA player? The truth is that *I* was the one with misconceptions about wealth. Here's the takeaway:

Becoming financially independent is not hard. You don't have to be exceptional and you don't have to be famous. You might not ever be a legendary NBA player, but I bet you could be an above-average dentist if you really wanted to.

That Being Said, You Need to Be a Millionaire

That sounds dramatic, but the reason you need a million dollars is because....math. You're going to get sick of that word by the end of this book, but let me show you:

$$5\% \times \$1,000,000 = \$50,000$$

So, what are you looking at? It's saying that five percent of a million dollars is fifty thousand. Why do you care? It's because if you plan on retiring, let's say-*ever*, you're going to need a way to generate income without working. It means you need *at least* one million dollars and an interest rate of *at least* 5% to make the average income of fifty-thousand dollars per year. For my non-nerds:

Interest from a large amount of money gives you income you don't have to work for.

So, what would you even *do* with a million dollars?

Nothing.

I'm dead serious. Once you get it, don't go screwing around with it. Leave it alone. The better question is: "What can a million dollars do for *you*?" That answer is simple:

It allows you to spend your time however you want without worrying about income. It allows you to retire. And by retire, I *specifically* mean you can "retire" from the **obligation** of having to work at a job for money. Then you can focus on the important stuff you really care about. Let's say you want to:

- ✓ Travel the globe tasting food from all over the world.
- ✓ Become a professional bowler.
- ✓ Follow your dream of becoming a jazz flutist.
- ✓ Start your own goat yoga therapy business.
- ✓ Volunteer in your community.
- ✓ Find a low-paying but deeply satisfying occupation.
- ✓ Meditate under waterfalls because you saw it in an anime.
- ✓ Learn Japanese and travel to Japan just to see if you can run up all those temple steps.
- ✓ Travel first class by train from coast to coast just to experience the journey and appreciate the view.
- ✓ Become an activist that fights for the rights of turtles or some random animal.

You might laugh at some of these, but I guarantee some of those things are genuine life goals for someone out there. We're all different. I met a guy who dreamed of being a school bus driver. I admittedly was kind of shocked at this seemingly low bar of achievement, but he explained that it didn't pay enough to support him so he had to get "a real job." He was genuinely kind of sad when he talked about it. He really loved the idea of taking kids to school and his eyes lit up when he imagined seeing their smiling faces every day. What if *he* was the guy taking kids to school instead of the guy some of us had: some random, questionable dude that had no business working that job because he low-key hated kids?

Hopefully. now you're starting to see the real power of having the freedom of choosing your occupation. There are people who legitimately love flipping burgers and filling out excel spreadsheets. *They* are the ones that need to work those jobs, not some disgruntled miscreant that's having a shouting match with a customer in the drive-thru. You've all had a job you hated right? What if you only worked at jobs you enjoyed? How would your life be different? How would your interactions be with other people who worked at places they enjoyed? It would be pretty magical in my opinion.

The goal is to get enough money that pays you a decent income through interest. It doesn't matter if you achieve it by 45 or 70. This book isn't so much about retiring early just because you *can*, it's more about having the option to retire as early as 45 *should you choose to*. When you retire is entirely up to you. I'm just here to tell you that it will take most people 20 years. If you start at 20, you could retire in your 40s. If you start at 40 like I did, then you'll be able to retire in your 60s.

Is it possible to become a millionaire in less time? Absolutely. But there's a significant risk in chasing higher rates of returns. You might get lucky and invest in an Amazon, or you might start a successful business. However, you might get unlucky and invest in an Enron (Google it) or start a business that goes bankrupt. If you're hell-bent on going faster than 20 years, the good news is that you could potentially cut the time it takes to become a millionaire in half by making riskier investments. The bad news is that you could potentially double the time it takes to become a millionaire because you lost more than half your money making those risky investments.

If you're in your 50s or 60s, you don't really have a choice. You need to be more aggressive and take on riskier investments that pay a higher return so that you can (hopefully) retire by the time you're in your 70s. You *have* to take more risk because you won't have the benefit of time; unless you like the idea of strolling on the beach with a walker.

But you're not 40. You're not 50 or 60. You're 25 or maybe younger. That is why I am begging you: Please start now. As in *right now*. I'm dead serious. You have the benefit of **time**- something that we 40-year-olds *wish* we had more of when we **finally** figured out how this stuff works. I don't want you to have to do anything risky. You simply **don't have to do that** when you go slowly and consistently for 20 years.

You're the Tortoise, not the Hare. There's **No Need** to be the Hare.

My goal is to show you how to get to the point financially where you can choose to continue working or not. It doesn't matter if you had modest beginnings growing up on a farm, a poor neighborhood, the projects, or a trailer park. None of that matters. You need a million dollars no matter where you came from. Then use that money to live life as you see fit. Hopefully, you'll go back where you came from and help others do the same.

However, I do understand if you're feeling skeptical. I get it. You feel you'd be happy making enough money at a job you enjoy, right? You don't *need* a million dollars to be happy. It's not like you can just wake up and be Jeff Bezos or Mark Zuckerburg, right? You're absolutely right- because those two men are **billionaires**. The difference between 1 million and 1 billion is massive. It is literally one thousand times higher. Think about that for a second. Did you notice what you did? You likely associated the word *millionaire* with individuals that have a *net worth exceeding 1 billion dollars*. We already talked about this last chapter, but it's worth repeating: Being wealthy isn't what you think. Wealth is not a ***concept***, a status, or a feeling. It's an ***actual numerical figure.***

Of course you don't *need* a million dollars to be happy. Wealth has absolutely nothing to do with happiness. I've been happy hanging out with my broke friends eating ramen noodles and drinking cheap beer, but I **definitely** wasn't free to choose if I wanted to continue working. I didn't have a choice if I wanted to pay my rent. What I'm offering you is a choice. I'm here to tell you that becoming a millionaire is relatively easy to do. I promise you that **anyone** can do it given enough **time** and **consistent effort.**

I can also understand why you might resist the idea of becoming a millionaire. I mean, it *does* sound kind of excessive. I grew up in a very modest, religious family. The idea of seeking riches wasn't exactly seen as a good thing. Truthfully, it was somewhat presented as something wicked. The theme of "good, pure people are poor and bad, corrupt people are rich" was hammered into my head ever since elementary school. It was probably due to the fact that everyone my family knew and associated with was lower-middle-class at *best*. If you couldn't be wealthy, at least you could take comfort in knowing that you were a good person, right?

Morality has nothing to do with being a millionaire. It's not some reward you get for feeding the homeless or being a devout Christian. Becoming a millionaire just allows you the freedom to choose what you do with your life. It doesn't make you good or bad. It doesn't erase your family problems. It doesn't make you funnier, sexier, more creative, or interesting. It's not spiritual, religious, or any of that stuff.

It won't magically solve your problems.

One million dollars is just a numerical figure in a bank account. It's the end result of monthly contributions and compounding interest over time. It's math, people. Don't make it any more complicated than that.

CHAPTER FOUR
What is Financial Independence?

Financial Independence means that the things you own and invest in pay you **Passive Income** that equals or exceeds your monthly expenses. It means that you could stop working today and not have to worry about paying your bills or your rent. It also means that you can do whatever you want with your free time and your life. Let's break down the three parts of financial independence:

1. Things you own and invest in pay you
2. Passive income that equals or exceeds your
3. Monthly expenses

Got it? All three parts are important and they have to work **together**. Please don't be like me and countless other 40+ year-olds that thought they were clever and only did one or two of them at a time. **You must do all three. At. The. Same. Time.**

- **Not** when you're ready
- **Not** when you get a good-paying job
- **Not** when you finish school
- **Not** when you've achieved some random life goal
- **Not** when you've finished paying off a credit card, your car or some other random debt.

There Will **Never** Be a Perfect Time to Start.
Begin All Three **Wherever** You Are In Life **Right Now**.

Part 1: Things You Own and Invest In

Let's first talk about **investments**. First of all, they can't be called investments unless you own them and they pay you. This is crucial. The term *invest* gets thrown around a lot; usually by people who want to sell you something. Others may have good intentions, but don't know any better. Let's ask ourselves some qualifying questions:

1. Is a college degree an investment?
   - ✓ Do you own it?
     - **Yes**.
   - ✓ Does it pay you?
     - **No**. It helps you earn a higher income, but it does not pay you directly.
   - ✓ **Verdict: Not an investment**

2. Is a car an investment? -
   - ✓ Do you own it? -
     - If you have a car loan, **No**.
     - If not, **Yes**.
   - ✓ Does it pay you?
     - **No**. It does not pay you. Its value goes down over time.
   - ✓ **Verdict**: Only an investment if the car is vintage or a collector's item. Otherwise, it's **Not an investment.**

3. Is your house an investment?
   - ✓ Do you own it? -
     - Most likely, **No**. Most homeowners have 30-year mortgage loans to help them pay for the house with monthly payments. Your bank owns it until you pay off the loan.
   - ✓ Does it pay you? -
     - If the real estate value goes up and/or you rent all or a portion of it to someone else, then **Yes**.
     - If the home prices in your neighborhood are stagnant and you are not renting it out, then **No**.

✓   **Verdict: Potentially an investment**

4. Are clothes an investment?
- ✓   Do you own it?
  - -   **Yes**.
- ✓   Does it pay you?
  - -   **No**.
- ✓   Verdict: Again- unless you're dealing with collectibles, they're **Not an investment.**

I could go on, but hopefully you see my point: A lot of the things people say you should invest in are **not** investments. I'm sure you've heard someone you know say something like:

"You should really invest in a new laptop."

You could definitely *use* a new laptop if your current one is no longer capable of doing what you need it to do, but the word *invest* is wrong here. You don't *invest* in a laptop, you buy it. Here's another one you've probably heard:

"You should go back to school. It's always a good idea to invest in yourself."

Again, it *is* a good idea to strengthen your resume and sharpen your skills, but this is more like good advice versus actual financial strategy. Financial stuff can be confusing enough as it is, so let's talk about:

Assets vs Investments

Sure, a laptop and a degree may help increase your income down the line, but that makes them **assets**, not investments. Assets are things you buy to make money or make more money than you're making now. Assets can *potentially* be investments, but it depends on how you use them.

For example: If I'm a plumber and I need a toolbox that only *I* use, it's just an asset. It helps me do my job and may even increase my ability to earn more money *that I physically work for*. However, if I buy a really fancy toolbox that I use **and** rent out to other plumbers, that asset has now also become an investment because it earns me money *without me having to do any work.* Got it?

Unfortunately, a lot of smart people rack up a bunch of debt on credit cards or use up all their cash thinking they're investing when they're really just buying assets. Worse, if you use a loan or a credit card to buy assets, you end up *increasing* your monthly expenses, which makes achieving financial independence **way** more difficult. We'll talk more about expenses in a bit, but let's move on to the second part: Passive Income.

Part 2: Passive Income

So, what's Passive Income? It's "making money while you sleep." Or, more accurately, it's making money without you having to exchange your time for income. It's surprisingly easy to do. Here are just a few of the ways you could get it:

- ✓ Dividends and capital gains from stocks
- ✓ Interest you receive from savings accounts, bonds, CDs, etc.
- ✓ Renting property or equipment you own
- ✓ Royalties/Sales from books you wrote
- ✓ Sales from music you recorded
- ✓ Having a business that offers a subscription-based service
- ✓ Having employees or contractors that do work on your behalf
- ✓ YouTuber/Twitch Ad revenue
- ✓ Blogger/Podcast Revenue
- ✓ Certain types of insurance
- ✓ Basically, any money that you get automatically that you don't have to "go to work" for.

Still think it's complicated? One of the easiest ways to create passive income is to have a roommate. You've probably had a roommate at some point in your life, right? They gave you money every month to stay there, right? Well, let me ask you this: Did you work for the money they gave you? No? Then congratulations! You've *already* made passive income before.

Now you probably didn't think of it as passive income, but that's exactly what it was. Here's the trick though: You don't make any headway towards financial independence until you use passive income to *lower* your monthly expenses. So if you got a roommate in order to get an apartment that you normally couldn't afford *without* a roommate, it doesn't help you. In fact, it could wreck you financially if your roommate bails on you and leaves you to pay the full rent. However, if you could afford to live there by yourself and you rent out a spare room, the rent they pay you **lowers** your expenses and now you're on your way to financial independence.

For example, if your monthly expenses equal $1,500 and you rented out three rooms for $500 each, you would now be financially independent because your passive income equals your monthly expenses.

It's that simple.

Any money you got from your job would be icing on the cake, but you could quit if you really **wanted** to. That's all financial independence is: the freedom to do what you want with your time and your life.

But what if you don't have multiple rooms to rent out? What if you only have one bedroom? Don't worry. There are tons of ways to make passive income. Renting out a room is just something you've likely had experience with and I wanted to show you that it's easier than you may realize.

However, I don't want to mislead you. Growing your passive income to where it makes you thousands of dollars a month will take time. **A lot of time**. The goal is to have your passive income in place by the time you retire, **not now**. For now, your focus should be **growing** your money so that you can live off of interest and dividend income **20 years from now**. That's why I'm asking you to take action today so that you don't have to worry about it at 40. We'll go over some ways to make passive income later, I promise. For now, let's talk about the last part of financial independence: your expenses.

Part 3: Expenses

I'm not going to bore you with how to save $5 a day by not drinking Starbucks and canceling Netflix. You've probably already read a hundred *Top 10 Ways to Save Money* articles by now. Let's look at this another way:

Lower your monthly expense amount so that it's easier to invest in things that create passive income.

You're probably ahead of me in thinking that all you have to do is save money. That's not a bad idea; it's just an incomplete one. You're only tackling **half** of the problem. Let me show you what I mean.

Fixed vs Variable Expenses

I was hopelessly broke when I was 25, but my friends and I all thought we had the answer to getting ahead. We just needed to save money. "It's easy," we thought. All we had to do was-

- Make a budget
- Turn all the lights off when we're not using them
- Take shorter showers to keep the water bill down
- Live with a boyfriend or girlfriend and split the rent
- Get a fan and an electric heater and not use the thermostat
- Get roommates
- Skip Starbucks and buy coffee from the grocery store
- Eat ramen noodles for every meal
- Not eat out
- Not go on vacation
- Cancel cable and all our streaming services
- Get a cheaper phone plan
- Not get the new PlayStation
- And if none of that worked, we could always move back in with our parents.

Do these things save you money? Yes. Are they enough to get you financial independence? **No**. Why? Because these expenses are **variable**. You can lower or raise them based on *your* behavior and activities for any given month. You might spend $200 in February when you're saving for Spring Break and then spend $2000 in March when you fly down to Cancun.

Let's also be honest: All of these money-saving activities suck. While you may tolerate them for a couple of months, you're not going to do them for the next several years. And any of you who have already done these things before already know that they don't work- not for long anyway. It's likely that your financial struggles come from your **fixed** expenses: usually just three things:

1. Car Payments
2. Rent
3. Debt Payments (Credit Cards & Loans)

These three things are the biggest chunks of money that come out of your bank account. They will kick your butt the most because it doesn't matter if you adjust your personal behavior or not. You have to pay a fixed dollar amount every month and you don't have a choice. If you don't pay, you get evicted, get your car repossessed, get sued, and screw up your credit. Most times, you can't negotiate these payment amounts after the fact. After all, these three things involve contracts that spell out the terms of the payments. If you agreed to a $400 car payment, that's what you have to pay. Period.

Bottom line- It doesn't matter how many packs of ramen noodles you eat. You have to lower or eliminate your **fixed** expenses. Remember-

- **Variable Expenses** can **change** based on your behavior and activities.
- **Fixed Expenses** are payments that you are contractually obligated to make and **cannot change.**

Most of us feel out of control financially because we focus on the variable expenses and not the fixed ones. The fixed expenses are usually big-ticket items that speak to our quality of life: A nice car, nice furniture, a nice apartment, etc. It's far more difficult to scale back on fixed expenses because of how they make us feel about ourselves. Put another way, these fixed expenses are most likely tied to how we see ourselves and how we want *others* to see us- our image. But since we're focused on achieving financial independence, we have to cut down on our fixed expenses. This means you need to:

1. Get a cheap car that has a low monthly payment under $200 a month -OR- Pay cash for a car and have **no** payment.
2. Rent in an affordable part of town where the rent isn't so high **and** get roommates (but **not** girlfriends/boyfriends. **Trust** me

on this.)
3.   Avoid using credit cards or financing purchases at all costs or pay them off **ASAP.**

Don't get me wrong. Budgets are good. Not buying Starbucks every day is a good idea. Most money-saving tips are helpful, but they don't address the real problem of fixed expenses that take too much of your monthly income. That's why you could follow every tip and still feel like you're always broke. You have to knock down the big fish so that your financial sacrifices can make a noticeable impact. Lower or get rid of fixed expenses and I guarantee you will feel in control of your finances.

So now that we've hopefully cleared up some misconceptions, let's look at what financial independence means again:

Financial Independence =
1.   Things you own and invest in pay you
2.   Passive Income that equals or exceeds your
3.   Monthly expenses.

The goal is to reach financial independence in 20 years. Got it? Good. Now we're going to spend the rest of the book talking about how to get there.

CHAPTER FIVE
Don't Work for the Banks

1. You need to use banks. Trying to use other ways to manage your money is expensive.
2. Banks are for-profit companies that charge you for your ignorance.
3. Banks use the cash you give them to make money faster than you ever could (legally).

Here's the truth: You need banks. Everything I'm going to teach you involves interacting with a bank or financial institution in some way:

✓ Your bank account (obviously) comes from a bank.
✓ Your credit card comes from a bank.
✓ Your car loan will come from a bank.
✓ Your mortgage will come from a bank.
✓ Your brokerage account will come from a bank.
✓ Anything you finance or make payments on will use a bank.

If it involves money, a bank will be involved. You might be using an app or using some type of online service that doesn't involve going to your local Bank of America, but banks are still pulling the strings nonetheless. The banking system is the ultimate middleman that has placed itself right in the middle of anything money-related and it stands to profit from everything it touches.

Make no mistake- we all need the banking system in this country. It *is* possible to exist outside of it, but it's inconvenient. There are millions of "unbanked" people in America, but all the fees you have to pay for common transactions make it more expensive than having a regular bank account. There may come a time when we can use digital payments like Bitcoin, but as of this year (2021), it is very difficult to buy necessities like gas and groceries with cryptocurrency.

So, for now at least, you're stuck with the banking system. Since banks are for-profit businesses, they will seek to get a profit from everyone they do business with- and that includes you. That means they have a legally protected *right* to charge you money for the privilege of using their services.

✓ Your bank charges you:
- Monthly maintenance fees
- Overdraft protection fees
- Bounced check fees
- Stop payment fees
- Insufficient funds fees

✓ Your credit cards charges you:
- Monthly Interest fees AKA Finance charges
- Balance Transfer fees
- Late fees
- Over the limit fees
- Overdraft protection fees

✓ Your car loan charges you:
- Monthly Interest fees AKA Finance charges
- Late fees
- Dealership fees
- Optional Insurance fees

✓ Your Mortgage has fees you've probably never heard of:
- Finance charges
- Late fees
- Discount fees

- Loan origination fees
- Mortgage Insurance fees (aka PMI or MIP- more on this later)
- Application fees (yes, you have to pay to apply for a loan)
- Underwriting fees
- Credit report fees
- Flood certification fee
- Title insurance fee
- Escrow/signing fees
- Courier fees
- Appraisal fees
- Recording fees
- Homeowner's insurance premiums
- Property tax reserves

✓ Your Brokerage account has fees that reduce your return/profit:
- Management fees
- Fees per trade
- Account Management fees
- Fund expense fees

✓ And anything you finance will typically have:
- Finance charges
- Late fees
- High interest compared credit cards and banks

It's not important that you know what exactly these fees are right now. What is important is that you understand just *how many* ways banks can legally take your money in ways that might not seem obvious. Banks count fees as a source of revenue for their businesses. So yes, they *do* want you to pay a bunch of fees. Understand that it is in their **best** interest to make you pay as many fees as they legally can.

Sure, there are ways to avoid fees, but you'll need to remember a bunch of rules and jump through a lot of hoops. This is by design. The banks make all these rules knowing that you're likely to make a mistake or overlook the fine print.

"Oh, but I don't have fees. My account is free."

Actually, it's more complicated than that. You may not have a monthly charge associated with your account, but it can still *cost* you. Here's how it works: They'll give you a free account with the understanding that they won't give you any interest **at all;** as in you could have $1,000 in your account and you would **never** receive a penny in interest. They then use the money you gave them to loan out to other people in the form of loans and lines of credit.

That means they can now issue a $10,000 loan to someone else or even *back to you*. That was not a typo. Your $1,000 allows the bank to issue a loan for $10,000; **ten times** the amount you gave them. How is that possible, you ask? It's because of a little known, very legal thing called:

The Fractional Reserve Banking System

What it means is that banks are only required to have 10% of any amount they give out in loans to be backed up with actual cash. Let me say it a different way: For every dollar that banks loan out, they're only required to have just ten cents in a vault somewhere. When I learned about this while working for the bank, it honestly shocked me. I had always assumed that banks had enough money to back up any loan they gave out. I mean, how do you loan out money *you don't even have*?

Think about it. Let's say you have $0. Your friend gives you a dime for safekeeping. Your other friend asks to borrow a dollar. Can you give him a dollar? No. You physically do not have it. But banks can do it. They do it all the time. They can literally make up money out of thin air to make loans that aren't backed up by any real money whatsoever. On top of that, they can charge interest.

Let's go back to our earlier example. You have $1,000 in your free account. You make $0 in interest- forever. Let's say your car breaks down, so you decide to buy a used car because it's affordable. You heard that your bank offers car loans, so you go to a local branch or go online and apply. They tell you the loan will have a 10% interest rate on a 5-year loan. Your credit is decent, so you get approved. You're happy. You sign the loan documents.

The bank then takes your $1,000 and uses it as the fractional reserve required to issue you the $10,000 car loan. You take the check to the dealership and drive away with your used car. Fast forward 5 years. You kept the $1,000 in your account the whole time. You made $0 in interest. You just made your last payment. Because of the interest the bank charged you, you ended up paying $2,748 in addition to the $10,000 you borrowed for a total of $12,748. You're happy you paid off the car. You're also happy that you've had a free account all these years.

> The bank is happy because they made **$11,748**
> from the $1,000 *you* gave them.

That's right. In the five years you had that loan, they made over eleven thousand dollars and you made *nothing*. Let's say you put your $1,000 in the stock market instead of the bank account. Let's say that you managed to get an average 10% return every year for five years. You would now have **$1,464**. You got nearly five hundred dollars from your one-thousand-dollar investment five years ago. How do you feel? You *should* feel good. Historically, that's a pretty respectable return. But when you compare it to the nearly twelve thousand dollars the bank got over the same time period, it makes you feel not-so-good. It doesn't seem fair.

Your money was at risk the entire time. You could have *lost* money during that five years. Two of those years may have sucked. Maybe you only averaged 10% because of two decent years and one really good year. But the bank was **never** in danger of losing any money-unless you stopped paying for your car. And let's be honest; you weren't about to risk getting your car repossessed. The risk for the bank was essentially non-existent.

The fractional reserve system works with credit cards too. But instead of charging you 10% interest on a car loan, they can legally charge you as much as 36% interest (as of December 2020). Let's say you go back to your bank and get a credit card with a $10,000 limit and max it out in a few months. You're smart- you pay extra every month because you know better than to only pay the minimum payment. You still have that checking account. You've prided yourself on always keeping at least $1,000 for emergencies. You still don't make any interest, but that's ok because you still have a free account. You feel good. You've handled your responsibilities well. You pay off the credit card in five years. You're happy because you got rid of the credit card debt.

The bank is happy because they made **$20,679**
from the $1,000 *you* gave them.

This plays out with any loan you get from a bank. That includes mortgages, second mortgages, car loans, personal loans, lines of credit, credit cards, school loans, etc. It's a system that encourages them to lend out as much money as they physically can to whoever has halfway decent credit. Because a bank can lend out ten times the amount they physically have, they can charge interest on money that doesn't physically exist.

As an individual, you can't do that.

Not to add insult to injury, but the Federal Reserve (the central government bank) pays your bank interest on their fractional reserves. The bank gets to earn interest on your $1,000 while you **don't**.

Let's do the math. You paid off a car loan and a credit card over ten years. In that time,

- You paid the bank: **$34,427**
- The bank paid you: **$0**

Keep in mind, these are just two loans. Most likely, you have several credit card accounts, possibly two car loans, and a mortgage. You will likely pay your bank over six figures in interest *alone*. I'll say it again: You'll pay over **$100,000** of your hard-earned money just to have a basic car, a basic house, and a basic credit card. If you want a luxury version of any of these items, prepare to pay double or triple that interest amount.

However, the Fractional Reserve banking system does serve a purpose. It allows banks to do more with less. It's the same reason you use your credit card instead of your cash. You have wiggle room to spend money over time without spending all your cash at once and worrying about where the next dollar is coming from. Banks can lend that extra money to businesses that will hire people. Those people go out and buy stuff. Everybody pays taxes. The economy gets better. The private citizen, the business, the financial system and the government all benefit. Everybody wins. That is *good*.

Unfortunately, lobbyists for the financial industry spend millions of dollars persuading lawmakers to *reduce* protections for borrowers. That is *bad*. That means **higher** fees and **higher** interest rates. It's obvious why they want it. They make more money. But that money will come from you- the average citizen. The result is that you'll stay in debt longer and that debt will be more expensive. As more of your hard-earned money gets taken by high fees and interest, you'll have to work **harder** and **longer** to maintain your normal lifestyle. To put it another way, you'll have to make **more** money tomorrow to keep the **same** lifestyle you had yesterday.

Like I said at the beginning, you will need to use banks to get ahead. I just want you to have the correct mentality when you use them. They are here to serve you, not the other way around. And truthfully, banks can be very generous when they need something from you. Let's look at some ways that banks can actually help us.

CHAPTER SIX
Your Checking Account Has One Job

1. Keep 1 month's worth of expenses in your account at all times.
2. Use your bank's Bill Pay to pay all your bills in one place.
3. Avoid fees by knowing how banks set you up to make mistakes.

In my opinion, checking accounts serve one purpose:

To pay your monthly expenses.

It's a checking account- as in an account used to write checks (remember those?). Its whole reason to exist is to pay expenses. That sounds obvious, but be honest- Are you attempting to do other things with your checking account? Are you-

- Trying to get it to some psychologically important amount?
    - Like $500 or $1,000?
- Trying to have enough in it to buy something?
    - Like a new laptop or a vacation?
- Trying to have enough money in it so you feel better when you check your balance?
- Relieved and proud when you have money left after you pay all your bills?

If you're doing any of these things, you're not exactly wrong. I'm just not a fan of any of these habits. There's simply a better way. It's not the only way of course. Feel free to do whatever you want, but my method has given me peace of mind for years.

If you grew up in a family without a lot of money, chances are that you have a psychological attachment to money. What I mean is that you have really strong feelings about money- particularly the *lack* of money. While you obviously know what a checking account is, you're probably using it in a way you saw your parents doing it. Then as you grow older, you kind of just figure it out. I hate to tell you, but you're going to end up losing a lot of money. Forget what you know about checking accounts for now- just hear me out. I'll say it again: Your checking account has **one** job:

To pay your monthly expenses.

It goes without saying, but you need to know what your monthly expenses are. If you've purchased this book, you're probably the type that has a good idea of how much you spend each month. If you don't, add up all the money coming out of your account during a non-holiday month. **You need this number to continue.** Don't guess! Do the work. You'll be surprised how wrong your mental math can be.

Your checking account is NOT a savings account.

If you want to save money for something, open a savings account and keep your savings **separate** from the money you use to pay your bills. Consider viewing each of your bank accounts as having one *specific function or job*. That way, you'll know at a glance if your account is doing what it's supposed to do or if you need to make adjustments.

Think about your job. Can you do your job and someone else's job **at the same time?** What if you worked at McDonald's? Could you work the fries and mop at the same time? Even if you could, eventually you're going to make a mistake. Either the fries get burnt or someone is busting their behind on the floor. And it'll be your fault. That's why they *separate* those two jobs. Everything works better when everyone focuses on their specific job. Your finances work the same way.

The amount you keep in your checking account should NOT be tied to some personal feeling of accomplishment.

It might feel amazing to have $1,000 or even $10,000 in your checking account, but this amount has nothing to do with your expenses. Let's say your monthly expense budget is $2,000. Since your checking account's job is to pay your bills, it doesn't make sense to keep $4,000 in it. That's two month's worth of expenses. That's too much. If you have a regular job (or a gig that pays you consistently), you only need to keep **one** month's worth in your checking account. At the very least, have two weeks worth of expenses- which would be $1,000 in our example.

The amount you keep in your checking account should not be some random number that makes you feel "safe."

Feeling safe, stable, and secure is important- *especially* for someone that grew up broke or poor- but you've got to get out of that mindset. I used to think that if I had $500 in my checking account, I was really doing something. I'd feel good about myself. I'd stick my nose up in the air around my broke friends who only kept $30 in their accounts. But I **still** miscalculated and got overdraft fees. It didn't happen a lot, but it was enough to have me pay about $200 a year in fees. Folks, that's a LOT.

Again, let the checking account do its job. We already *know* what our expenses are: $2,000 a month. That's *exactly* what we need in the account. There's no point in keeping $500 in it- that isn't enough. If your rent gets paid a day before you thought it would, your payment will bounce and you get charged a fee.

But what if I don't have a whole month's worth of expenses lying around? What then?

You save a little every paycheck until it gets there.

Look, I understand. This isn't easy. But there's a good chance that you've never thought about keeping a month's worth of expenses in your checking account. You've probably never tried to do it. But trust me- anybody can do it. You just need a goal, some focus, and some discipline. Or a tax refund. It doesn't matter how you get there, just get there.

Your checking account should not be the source of anxiety or stress.

I spent a good portion of my childhood listening to family members and family friends talk about how they barely had enough in their accounts to pay all their bills. They were proud that they didn't get hit with any fees and they were relieved when they had anything left. I ended up saying and doing the same stuff when I grew up. That's a stressful way to live, and I hated it. Even after working at a bank, I still struggled to do it right.

The reason why you use one month's expense as your target balance is because it gives you peace of mind. You don't always have to check it when your bills are due. If you get caught up in some family drama or have to deal with life in some way, your checking account will have enough money to take care of everything without you having to do anything. When you finally get around to checking it, if you see you have too much, take the overage **out** and send it to your savings account or buy some stocks or something. If it gets lower than that, put money **in** until you reach your monthly expense amount.

Set it and forget it using Bill Pay.

Every bank has a service called Online Bill Pay. It's basically a screen that allows you to enter the information for all your bills (like account numbers and biller addresses) and then schedule them to be paid. There's a little calendar next to each bill. You click the date you want the bill to be paid, then you enter an amount. Then, on the day you picked, the bill is paid. When I was 25, this was a game-changer. Before Bill Pay, you had to mail your payments in OR give your billers the ability to Auto Draft your account.

Sidenote- Auto-draft/AutoPay is **bad**. It means that you give permission- in *advance*- to let a company come into your account and take their payment every month on a certain date. Some people think this is great. If the auto-draft comes out on the 5th of every month, that's one less thing to think about, right? Not exactly. If the 5th falls on a Sunday, then they take your money on Friday the 3rd- and they usually don't tell you. They do this because the bank doesn't do transactions on the weekend, so they have to use the closest business day *before* your due date so that you won't be late. But what if you had already planned for another bill to be paid Friday night? Well, now you end up paying *both* on Friday. You'll be in for a rude awakening Saturday morning when you have no money AND you have an overdraft fee.

This is why I don't sign up for any service that automatically takes money out of my account. I don't like it because it takes control away from you. What happens if your bill is wrong? You end up paying the wrong amount and you *still* have to try to get them to fix it *after* they have your money. And trust me, once they have your money, you have no power. You'll have to wait "two to three billing cycles" for a refund while you are out of money now.

There's only one benefit to Auto-Draft/AutoPay: Sometimes, billers will discount your monthly bill if you let them do it. That's cool, but if you want to take advantage of that, use your **credit card**. We'll talk more about that in the credit card chapter.

Online Bill Pay works far better than AutoPay in my opinion. Sure, you can set it up to automatically come out on a certain day, but if something comes up, you can change the payment date or cancel the payment. More importantly, with Bill Pay, you can **see** that your payment is coming out and **when** it's happening. All your bills that you set to be paid will show up in a list. You'll know at a glance who's getting paid and who isn't. You can even set up recurring payments to come out on the 5th of every month just like before. But- with Bill Pay, if the 5th falls on a Sunday, the service will send you an email **a month in advance** telling you that the system is temporarily switching your date to the 3rd.

Another good thing about Bill Pay is that you can send your bills directly to your bank. Here's what I mean: When you first start entering in your biller's information-say your electric bill from Georgia Power- Bill Pay might be a step ahead of you and will ask if you are trying to enter in a bill from Georgia Power. This is of course what you want, so Bill Pay stops you from entering in any more information and completes it for you. Why? Because Georgia Power already has a relationship with your bank. In the last step, your bank's Bill Pay might even ask if you want your bills delivered straight to your Bill Pay service instead of through the mail or email. It's up to you if you want to do that, but the benefit is that the bill amount and the due date show up when you sign in now. If you want to pay the bill, just click it and it'll be paid on time. Credit cards, mortgages, car payments and utilities can all be set up this way. You may not be able to have *all* your bills sent to your Bill Pay, but you're still free to manually enter the ones that don't have a relationship with your bank.

If you enter in all of your bills, you'll have **one** place where you can see **who** you're paying, **when** you're paying them, and **how much** is coming out of your account. It's like mission control for your expenses. Just to make this super clear: entering your bills, whether they have a relationship with your bank or not, does NOT mean they'll automatically get paid out of your account. You still have to choose a date, enter an amount, or at the very least confirm the payment. Unless you set up a recurring payment, **nothing** gets paid without you taking an extra step.

Don't Let the Bank Trick You into Paying a Bunch of Fees.

There's another benefit to keeping a month's worth of expenses in your checking account and using Bill Pay: It keeps you away from all the fees that banks like to charge you. I already know that you have common sense and you know how to manage your account, but banks have sneaky practices that will slowly needle you to death with fees. Here are some of the more common ones:

- Insufficient Funds (NSF) Fee: Up to $45 per transaction
- Account Maintenance fee: Up to $20 per month or $240 per year
- Overdraft Coverage fee (the bank chooses whether to pay the item) Up to $45 per transaction
- Overdraft Protection Transfer fee: Up to $10 per transfer
- Paper Statement Delivery fee: Up to $5 per month for mailing printed statements
- Non-bank ATM fee: Up to $5 per withdrawal to get cash from an ATM that doesn't belong to your bank or from getting cashback during checkout
- Foreign transaction fee: 3% fee on all transactions outside of the country
- Currency conversion fee: 1% on all transactions outside of the country
- Check cashing fee: A flat fee of up to $10 or up to 10% of the amount of the check
- Teller Transaction fee: Up to $7 a month for talking to a live

person inside of a bank

The fees are set up this way for a reason. If you go about living your life as a normal person, there will be times when you make a mistake, use another bank, need to get cashback during checkout or (*gasp!*) actually go inside a bank and do a transaction. Even if you're really responsible, you could easily pay nearly **$200** a year in fees.

Set up your account so that you don't have to think about it.

In addition to keeping a month's expenses worth in your account and using Bill Pay, here are some other things you should do:

1. Use Direct Deposit or make any deposits into your account before your bank's "cutoff" time (I'll explain in a moment).
2. Never allow your account to dip below its required monthly minimum balance- not even for an hour.
3. Turn off or opt-out of your bank's Overdraft Coverage.
4. Sign up for Overdraft Protection.
5. Sign up for Electronic Delivery for all of your statements and communications.
6. Don't use your debit card at an ATM that doesn't belong to your bank.
7. Don't use your debit card when you travel outside of the country.
8. Don't use your debit card for purchases. Use your credit card.
9. In general, don't cash checks. Just deposit them. If you have to cash them, do it at *your* bank.
10. Don't use banks that charge you to visit the tellers inside.

These solutions may sound overly basic, but everyone overlooks this stuff and pays more than they should. This book assumes you have common sense, so I will never intentionally insult your intelligence. Most people, given the right information, are smart. However, most people assume they already know how checking accounts work. Banks *know* that you *think* you know and take advantage of your assumptions. The result is that you get charged a ton of fees that you have no choice but to pay. Over time, these fees can *legally* take hundreds and even thousands of dollars away from you over time. I wish I was exaggerating, but unfortunately, I am not. I've worked at banks for years, and one thing I can tell you for certain is that:

Most people think they know how their checking account works based on what *they* think makes sense and what *they* think is fair.

I don't mean to be harsh, but whatever *you* think is fair doesn't matter. At all. Your bank has all kinds of tricks at its disposal to guarantee that they always win and you always lose- and no amount of yelling at customer service will change anything. Here are a few terms you need to understand:

- **Available balance** = The money you can spend or withdraw *right now*. It changes as you spend money, buy stuff, withdraw money, have direct/electronic deposits, or deposit cash.

- **Current (or Collected) balance** = The money that is left in your account after all withdrawals, deposits, and purchases have been processed. This is only updated once a day- usually around midnight and *only* on weekdays/business days.

- **Non-sufficient/Insufficient Funds (NSF)** = You wrote a check or used your card for an amount that exceeded your available balance.

- **Returned Item** = A transaction that was declined due to insufficient funds and your bank notifies whoever you were attempting to pay.

- **Minimum Daily Balance AKA Minimum Daily Collected Balance** = This is the lowest amount you can have in your account before you are charged monthly maintenance fees. If you drop below this amount, *even for one day*, you'll be charged a *maintenance fee* for that month.

- **Pending Transaction** = a transaction or deposit that you recently made. The amount of the transaction is immediately added to or taken out of your available balance. These are also known as "soft" posts. Pending transactions are sometimes the incorrect amount. If you've ever used your debit/bank card at a restaurant, you'll notice that the pending transaction amount didn't include the tip.

- **Hold** = When your bank freezes or temporarily debits an amount after you make a purchase. You've likely seen this when you buy gas. When you swipe your card, the gas station vendor will sometimes authorize a transaction for $1. This is to make sure that the card you're using is attached to a legitimate bank account (and that you at least have $1 in it). The $1 will show up as a pending transaction until it is settled.

- **Settle/Settled/Settlement** = the process to verify the amount of the transaction and debit or credit your account. In the case of eating out, the restaurant has to enter two amounts: the amount of the initial bill *without* the tip, and then later enter in the new amount that *includes* the tip. The initial amount shows up as a pending transaction, and the amount including your tip shows up in your completed transactions. Settlement always has two sides:

1. You swipe your card.
2. The vendor must submit their receipts to your bank as proof of the amount.

- **Transaction (aka Completed Transaction)** = Your debits and credits that have been settled- meaning that they have been verified by all the people involved in the transaction. These are also known as "hard posts." They are the official record and will show up online and on your bank statements.

- **Debit** = Any transaction that takes money *out of* your account (like your bills, ATM withdrawals, cashback transactions, purchases, etc.)

- **Credit** = Any transaction that puts money *into* your account (i.e your paycheck, Direct Deposit, cash, funds transfer, etc.)

- **Cutoff time** = The time of day when the banks are no longer accepting deposits for that business day. Most banks have a cutoff time of 9 pm. If you make a deposit after that time, your deposit will count towards the next business day *even if it's* *cash.* Let's say your $250 car payment is due to come out of your account Friday. You forget to make a deposit during the day. It's alright- you go to the ATM at 10 pm and deposit $300 in cash. You're saved, right? Wrong. The next morning, you see that your car payment came out, but now you have an NSF fee for $40. So now you have a balance of $10. What gives? Here's what happened: You missed the deadline for that business day and the bank charged you for the "convenience" of paying your car note when you *technically* didn't have the money in your account. I say technically because your $300 cash deposit is available immediately, but won't "hard post" into your account until Monday- the next business day. This brings us to:

Overdraft Coverage vs. Overdraft Protection

Overdraft Coverage = This is **not** the same as Overdraft Protection. This is something the bank does on their side **without** your permission unless you opt-out. It means that when an amount hits your account that's more than what you have in it, you give them the authority to pay it *or not.* For example: Let's say you have $200 in your account. Let's use our earlier example about your car payment coming out on the 5th. Because the 5th falls on a Sunday, your car payment of $250 comes out Friday night, the 3rd. With Overdraft Coverage, the bank could allow the transaction to go through. This means that you'll now have *negative* $50 in your account the next morning. On top of that, the bank will hit you with a roughly $40 overdraft (NSF) fee. So now you have *negative* $90 in your account on Saturday, which means you now **owe** the bank money.

This is where it can get *really* bad. If you were thinking that your car payment comes out on the 5th, you will continue using your debit card all day Saturday the 4th. After all, you think you have money until the 5th. You don't. Worse yet, because of Overdraft Coverage, the bank will allow every transaction you make that weekend to go through. It means that nobody's going to stop you from using your debit card and it will still work, even though your account is *negative* at this point.

So, on top of being $90 *negative* at the start of Saturday, you will get charged an NSF fee for **every single transaction** you made over the weekend. By the time you finally check your account Monday, you may have racked up over $200 in NSF fees **alone**.

It doesn't matter how big or how small the transaction is. I've personally seen an NSF fee of $39 for a $1.40 debit card purchase at a gas station. The customer came in the next day and was furious. The purchase was for a donut- a gas station donut. Unfortunately for that customer, it was a $40.40 gas station donut. I've seen customers in tears because they had over $300 in fees in **one** weekend. I'm telling you, it's bad. And the banks do not care. If it's just one NSF fee, they may let you off the hook…*once*. If it's multiple NSF fees, they may "cut you a deal" and give you a discount, but you'll still end up paying roughly half of the NSF charges.

Remember: Overdraft Coverage allows the *bank* to choose whether overdraft transactions can occur. If the bank chooses NOT to pay your car payment, the $250 won't go through, but the bank might hit you with a roughly $25 *returned item* fee- because they returned the charge back to your car payment company. (Your car payment company will likely charge you a fee for the returned item AND a late fee.)

Overdraft Coverage allows the bank to cherry-pick which items they pay and which ones they won't as well as **the order in which they pay them**. THIS IS VERY IMPORTANT. For example, let's say our $250 payment comes out on the 3ʳᵈ, like before. Remember, you weren't expecting it to come out until the 5ᵗʰ, but let's say this time, you had $300 in your account. You're safe right? Well, not really. Since you thought you had some time before the payment came out, you went to a bar with some friends and spent $50. On the way home, you got $10 worth of gas. Then you went into the gas station and got a Slurpee for $2. So, you spent $62 on Friday night.

What you didn't realize is that with your car payment, you actually spent $312 ($250 plus $62) Friday night. You check your account and you see that you overspent by $12. You're annoyed. You know you're going to get charged an NSF fee. But you're an adult. You're willing to take the hit because you realize that it was *your* mistake after all. However, Monday morning, you check your account and see **two** NSF charges. How is that possible? You only went over by $12!

I'll tell you how. You had $300. The bank *chose* to pay your $250 car payment **first**. Then it took out your $50 bar tab. That brings you to a balance of $0. But then your bank takes out the gas purchase: NSF fee number one. Then your bank takes out the $2 frozen drink purchase: NSF fee number two.

This begs the question: Why didn't the bank take out the smaller purchases first? They say it's to "help the customer," but it's really to help themselves. They will say that they always pay larger items first because those larger transactions are usually important payments. They claim to do this out of consideration for you, the customer. Um, No. They will most likely pick the order of what to pay based on what will generate the *maximum amount of fees*.

However, you now have the choice to **opt-out** of Overdraft Coverage. This means that if a bill comes through and you don't have enough in your account to cover it, the bill doesn't get paid- thereby avoiding all that craziness with negative account balances and all the charges that come with it.

Overdraft Protection = This is what most people are familiar with. This is when you choose another account, like a savings account or a credit card, to act as a backup just in case you overdraft your checking account. Now, when you overdraft your account, the bank will move money from your backup account to your checking account so that you don't get any NSF fees.

BUT! Some banks will still charge you a roughly $10 overdraft transfer fee. It's not as bad as an NSF fee, but it sucks when banks charge you to move *your* money.

There are other terms, but those are the most important. Now let's examine what happens when you swipe your card.

1. If you swiped or inserted your chip card, the purchase amount becomes a *pending transaction.*
2. The amount of the pending transaction is immediately taken out of your *available balance.*
3. Around midnight, your bank processes all your debits for that day **FIRST**, *then* processes your credits and deposits for that day.
4. Your pending transactions become completed transactions and your current balance is calculated.

This process happens every weekday. On the weekends and holidays, the banks are closed. Whatever you do after Friday night doesn't get processed until the following business day. In most cases, that's the following Monday. If Monday is a holiday, then all your transactions are processed Tuesday.

Most of this stuff happens in the background without you ever knowing. Generally speaking, if you keep one month's worth of expenses in your account, everything just kind of works out. As always, the devil is in the details.

CHAPTER SEVEN
Save Your Money Purposefully

1. Have at least two savings accounts: One for emergencies and one for personal spending.
2. Keep **at least** three months' worth of expenses in your Emergency Savings account, but **at most** six months' worth.
3. Outside of saving for emergencies, hoarding money in savings accounts is a waste of time and money.

Just like your checking account, your savings account has ONE job:

To save money for a specific purpose.

Notice that I didn't say, "to save money." Saving money without a purpose or target amount doesn't help you. After all, how much is enough? You need a *specific* number and a *specific* purpose. We've heard people say that a goal needs to be specific for it to be achievable. We need our savings account to have a target amount with a specific purpose in mind. I would recommend having at least two different savings accounts:

An Emergency savings account
A Personal Spending (Fun) savings account

We're going to focus on how you can use your savings accounts as a financial base that gives you peace of mind and helps you achieve your other financial goals. I won't talk much about trying to find banks that pay the highest interest because interest rates aren't very high right now. Most online banks are paying around 1% a year, while the banks you've heard of are likely paying less than half a percent. Online banks give you the highest interest, but it can be hard to get to your money. You'll have to do most (if not all) of your transactions online with a 2-3 business day waiting period. With your big bank, you can go into a branch, go to an ATM, or use an app on your phone. For what I'm suggesting in this chapter, **you need a savings account that you can access 24/7**. You won't get much interest at all, but at least you can go to an ATM at 3 am if you need to.

Emergency Savings Account

That being said, let's talk about your emergency savings account first. Your emergency savings account needs to have at least three months' worth of expenses in it at **all** times.

You may have heard this before. It's good financial advice because it gives you money for emergencies. If you lose your job or your car breaks down, you're not freaking out because you know you have enough cash to give you **time** to figure things out. This brings up an important part of this savings account's job:

The money in your Emergency savings account buys you *time*.

Does money actually buy you time? No, of course not. However, I'd like you to think about the money in your emergency account as a measurement of how much time it *gives* you. What I mean is that if your expenses are $2,000 a month, you'll need $6,000 in your account to have three months' worth of expenses. This means $2,000 equals one month, $4,000 equals two months, and $6,000 equals three months. If you lost your job tomorrow, you could glance at your emergency savings account and **immediately** know how much **time** you have before you run out of money.

Let me take a second to acknowledge that $6,000 is a lot of money. When I was 25, the only time I had that much money was from a settlement from a car accident. I don't want *you* to get hit by a truck (long story) to be able to afford six months' worth of expenses. At 25, I had about $300 extra every month after I paid all my bills. My expenses were about $2,000 a month, so I needed $6,000. At $300 a month, it would take me almost 2 years to build up my account. I know you don't want to hear that but you only have to do this **once**.

You'll have to do this slowly. You're the tortoise, not the hare. It's ok if you build this account up over several months or even a couple of years. Once you have at least three months' worth, you can switch your focus to other financial goals. I will spell it out for you so there's no room for interpretation:

Don't spend your extra money on ANYTHING ELSE until you have 3 months of Emergency Savings.

- Not Investments
- Not Cryptocurrency
- Not Debt Reduction
- Not Entertainment
- Not Vacations
- Not Relationships
- Not Business Opportunities
- Not Loaning People Money
- Not **ANYTHING ELSE!**

It's *really* important that you have emergency savings. As I write this, the US is currently in month thirteen of the COVID-19 pandemic. Every time you turn on the news, there are at least 5 stories of people running out of food or getting evicted through no fault of their own. The sad thing is that this isn't the first time the general public got screwed. Let's rewind to the housing crash of 2008. *I* was one of those people running out of food and facing foreclosure. I'm not exaggerating. I ate oatmeal and scrambled eggs every morning for breakfast and one double hamburger from McDonald's for dinner. I usually didn't eat lunch. I barely shopped for groceries. That was my life for about 6 months straight. I swore that if I ever got out of that financial black hole, I would never go through that @#$! again.

I'm telling you this because I don't want to just randomly tell you to put thousands of dollars in an account- as if you can just pull it out of your butt. I have been there. I have waited 2 hours to file unemployment just for them to turn me away. I have had banks screw me around for *months*- acting like they weren't aware of the financial relief that was passed by the government and was all over the f***ing news. It's incredibly humiliating and you end up waking up and going to bed mad as hell. For all this talk of the American Dream and self-determination, I was suffering because of someone else's stupid mistake. I ended up breaking off an engagement and I almost lost my house. *Everything* falls apart when you don't have any money.

Trust me when I tell you that America punishes you **daily** for being broke- and it *never* lets up. You need to arm yourself with the knowledge and the savings to fight back- or at the very least give yourself some **time** to come up with a plan B.

So yes, I recognize that I'm casually talking about thousands of dollars, but it's doable. I did it and so can you. When you finally achieve it, it makes everything soooooo much easier. Here's what I mean:

- Need new tires because your current ones are bald? Buy new ones. You can afford it. Now you can stop getting nervous when it rains.

- Need to do a tune-up or properly maintain your car so that it lasts longer? Do it. You can afford it. Now you don't have to panic when the service engine light comes on.

- Need to fix that leak in your roof? Pay for it. You can afford it. Now you can sleep at night knowing that your ceiling won't collapse over your bed. (This actually happened- another long story.)

- Want to buy that expensive ice cream you like? Buy it. You can afford it. No more random plastic tubs of Neapolitan.

What this savings account gives you is **peace of mind.** Worrying about money problems all the time puts a *huge* stress on your body, your mind and your health. You probably aren't even aware of it- until you finally get rid of it. Believe me, it's like someone lifting an invisible 50-pound rock off of your neck. Worse yet, stressing about money all the time is a full-time job. If you've been there, you know exactly what I mean. Whether you're at work, on a date, at church, or on the toilet, stressing about how you're going to pay all of your bills consumes every spare second you have. There is never any true rest when you're broke.

When you finally get that weight off your shoulders, it's like heaven. I don't mean to exaggerate, but suddenly you'll have all this free time on your hands. You won't actually have more time, but it'll feel like it because you can spend more of your spare time thinking about something else besides money. *Anything* else. Suddenly you'll start thinking about picking up the piano again or taking an acting class. You start to live again. You start to have fun again. Eventually, people will notice and then all of your broke friends and family members start asking for money. But that's another story.

Once we have 3 months' worth of Emergency savings, now it's time to build our account to six months' worth of expenses. I know it's asking a lot of you, but it's not that bad. Having three months' worth called for urgency. You can go much slower for the next three. If you were putting every spare dollar away to build your first three months' worth, now I'm only going to suggest putting away half of your leftover monthly income. So, if you have $300 leftover every month:

✓ **Step 1:** Use **all** $300 until you reach 3 months' worth of expenses.

✓ **Step 2:** Use **half** ($150) until you reach 6 months' worth. Use the other half to pay down high-interest debt (anything over 10%- usually credit cards, payday loans and title loans)

✓ **Step 3:** Once you reach 6 months' worth, **stop** saving. Use **all** $300 to pay down high-interest debt.

✓ **Step 4:** Once you pay off your high-interest debt, use **half** to pay down any non-mortgage debt (like your car loan). Use the other half to invest.

✓ **Step 5:** Once you pay off all non-mortgage debt, use **all** $300 to invest.

The reason you take steps is because you only have a limited amount of money, but you most likely have several financial goals. If you're interested in getting out of debt and becoming financially independent, it's really easy to get caught up in conflicting financial strategies. Think about it:

- How do you **invest** when you're using all your spare money to pay off debt?
- How do you **pay off debt** when you're trying to build up your savings?
- How do you **build your savings** AND invest AND pay off your debt?

The short answer is: **You don't**. If you only have a couple hundred dollars left at the end of the month, you can't save, invest **and** pay off debt at the same time. You need to prioritize based on where you are **right now**.

We'll talk more about credit cards and debt later, but the biggest takeaway from this five-step process is that you *stop* saving once you reach six months of expenses. Remember- This is an **emergency** savings account. Its job is to protect you against emergencies. Six months' worth of savings is likely to handle the majority of emergencies that could happen. Once you achieve this goal, STOP. Saving money for the sake of saving money is **hoarding**. Do you know any wealthy hoarders? I didn't think so.

Look, we're human. None of us are going to sacrifice indefinitely and commit to a life that sucks. We still need to enjoy life every once in a while. While you may agree that saving for emergencies is a smart thing to do, you most likely aren't happy about not being able to spend any of your money. I understand. That's why we're going to talk about your Personal Spending savings account.

Personal Spending Savings Account

Your Personal Spending savings account has its own job: to pay for the really important things that make life bearable. I recognize and agree that you should enjoy your life. I can't (and won't) ask you to become a hermit who never spends any money outside of the bare necessities. If you've ever tried to diet and exercise, you know how hard it is to stay consistent. That's why there are cheat days built into some of these diets. The reason is simple. You give yourself a break so that you don't give up on your overall health goal. Think of your Personal Spending account as your own financial cheat day.

This begs the question, **"How do you get money in this account?"** After all, if you're putting all of your spare money into your Emergency Savings account, there should be nothing left, right?

Yes and no. "Yes" in the sense that you are still using all of your spare money to focus on savings and your financial goals; "No" because we're going to now look at ways to find extra savings in how you already spend your money. It's like going to the grocery store: If a dozen eggs normally cost $2, but you're able to buy them for 50 cents because they're on sale, you've saved $1.50. Now you have $1.50 to spend on other stuff and still not exceed the normal cost for a dozen eggs.

You really *can* have it both ways. You just have to plan and make some decisions in advance. Finding money to put in your personal spending savings account is a combination of:

1. Saving money on the stuff you already buy and
2. Sacrificing the stuff that you don't really need or use.

However, You **must** know:
- Your monthly expense amount AND
- The amount of money you usually have left after paying your bills.

The secret to all this stuff is **basic math** and a **plan**. We've been using $300 as the money left over each month, but of course- life happens. Sometimes what's left over isn't as high and sometimes it's higher. I'm asking you to **commit to a definite amount every month** that you will use for your savings and your financial strategies. If you try to do this when you *think* you have the money to do it, NONE of the stuff I'm telling you will work. You need a plan.

Write. It. Down.

Your personal spending savings account keeps you on track with your financial goals by removing FOMO- Fear Of Missing Out. Once you have money in it, you can spend it on the important stuff that you really enjoy. I can't tell you what's important to you, but I can tell you that when you can feel confident about spending money *without* feeling guilty, it's a great feeling- and *that's* what's important.

Here's the deal: with a personal spending savings account, you need to choose your sacrifice *in advance*. What I mean is that you figure out that thing you *absolutely* must have to feel like your life doesn't suck, then **sacrifice** the rest. Everyone loves to talk about sacrificing a daily $5 cup of coffee to save $150 a month, right? I personally am not willing to spend $150 a month on coffee, but for some people, it's not about the actual coffee, but the *experience* of an enjoyable routine. Coffee shops tend to have a small community of people who seem to be really chill. Everyone is smiling, studying, or hanging out with friends. It's like a bar you can go to in the morning and not be judged. Cutting out that expense would also mean cutting out the experience that goes along with it. If that experience isn't a big a deal to you, sacrifice it and buy Starbucks from the grocery store. If it is a big deal to you, keep it and sacrifice something else. Then, put the money you save from the thing you sacrificed into your personal savings account.

Conversely, all that stuff that you think is good to have, but you **never** use, has to go- **now**. Like I said, everyone is different. I think that all of us feel good about spending money on things like community and experiences. But if we're honest, we don't really care about some of the things we pay for. For example:

- Are you really using your gym membership? Be honest. You're not. Scrap it.
  - **Money saved = $25/mo.**

- There aren't enough hours in the day to watch Disney Plus, Netflix, Hulu, HBO, AppleTV, Peacock, **and** YouTube. Use a free month promotion to watch the show you want and then cancel it. Pick one or two services. Scrap the rest.
  - **Money saved — $30/mo.**

- You don't need to pay extra to store anything in the cloud. Unless you're a professional that needs to send files to people, stop paying for that stuff.
  - **Money saved = $15/mo.**

- Check your phone plans. Stop paying for data plans, add-ons, and features you don't use. Only pay for what you need.

- - Money saved = $10/mo.

- In fact, check *all* of your subscriptions. I guarantee you're still paying for Pandora or some random prep meal service because you forgot to cancel after the trial period.
  - - Money saved = $20/mo.

- Be honest. You've known for a while that Amazon Prime takes longer than 2 days. Scrap that too.
  - - Money saved =$13/mo

I could go on, but there are a million articles out there that talk about saving money. I just wanted to show you that you are likely spending around **$100 a month** on services that don't make your life any better or solve any real problem. They're just fluff that you'll barely use. Worse yet, you always have to give them a credit card. There's a chance that you're not even aware that you're still paying for them. At least with the daily coffee, you'll drink the whole cup and you get an actual experience. There's no waste.

Whatever money you save by canceling subscriptions and memberships, take that amount and stick it in your personal spending savings account every month. I'm asking you to do this so that you don't leave it in your checking account. If you leave the money in there, it's hard to know if you're saving it or not because it's all mixed up with the money you use to pay your bills. After a few months, you should have a couple hundred dollars. In a year, you'll have around a thousand. If you were able to cut out $100 a month, that's **$1,200 yearly.**

Do you know what you could do with $1,200? You could buy that laptop you've been looking at. You can take your family on a well-deserved vacation. You could buy a new grill. It doesn't matter what you use it for. Buy whatever you want. The most important part is that now you can stay on track with your financial goals without sacrificing your happiness. Better yet, you won't have to use a credit card, a line of credit or a loan- which keeps you out of debt.

CHAPTER EIGHT
Things You Can Do With Certificates of Deposit

1. CD's offer the highest interest rates a bank can offer.
2. CD's offer a risk-free way to save. You cannot lose money- it's protected by the FDIC.
3. You can use a CD as collateral for a bank loan with lower interest.

Certificates of Deposit (CDs) are pretty basic. This is how they work:

1. You stick money in a CD account at a bank.
2. You agree to leave it in there for a fixed amount of time (i.e. 6 months, 1 year, 2 years, but usually not longer than 5 years).
3. The longer the time you agree not to withdraw, the higher the interest rate they'll pay you.
4. At the end of the time period (**maturity**), you can take your money with interest or start a new time period and begin earning more interest.
5. If you take your money out before it matures, you have to pay a penalty; usually in the form of losing some or all of the interest you accrued.

As of this writing, this is how much you can expect to earn:

6 months = 0.5% (as in a *half* of 1 percent)
1 year = 0.65%
2 year = 0.80%
5 year = 1%

So basically, they're like checking accounts that hold money you can't use, penalize you for taking money out, and pay you next to nothing for your sacrifice. If you had $500 in the highest paying option, the **most** you could make is $5 a year if you agreed to a 5-year term. That would earn you a whopping $25 after half a decade. Ready to sign up yet?

In this day and age, CDs are a bit out of touch and irrelevant. The interest rates they payout are based on several factors, but the bottom line is that they want to be competitive, but not too generous. They also have to take the economy into account. Right now, we're in a pandemic. The Federal Reserve (the central banking system for the US) says the federal funds rate is 0.25%. That's the interest rate that banks can earn on *their* extra money. If they're only making a quarter of a percent, you can't really expect that they'll pay you much more than that.

They used to be a big deal though. When I was in college, people would take **all** of their money out of one bank and stick in the bank with the best interest rate- which was around 6%. Back then, 6% was so normal no one really cared about it. Today, that would be insanely high. If a bank offered 6% now, you'd have to get on a waiting list to open an account. Why? Because of one thing:

FDIC Insurance.

That probably didn't have the dramatic impact I wanted, but it's a big deal. It means that any money you put in a deposit account is **guaranteed** against loss. You cannot, under any circumstance, *lose* any money in a bank deposit account (i.e. a checking, CD, money market or savings account). The government provides this insurance to banks and citizens to instill confidence in the banking system. If your bank goes out of business, it doesn't matter- you still can't lose your money. FDIC insurance is why people *used* to use banks to grow their money. Believe it or not, you used to be able to make a good amount of interest income from CDs. If you were older and/or had $100,000 lying around, you could stick it in a CD and make a cool $6,000 a year doing **nothing**. The best part was that you were guaranteed that rate and there was absolutely no risk.

These days, even if you had $100,000, the most you could make (with a bank that you've heard of) is about $750 a year. Folks, that's terrible. The result is that older people and people close to retirement have no choice but to put their money in higher-risk assets like stocks and corporate bonds that are definitely not guaranteed from loss. You get higher interest, but you could lose 100% of your investment. If you choose not to put your hard-earned money at risk, then you'll have to get a job to make ends meet. That means working at Walmart, McDonald's or wherever they take pity on senior citizens. It sounds like I'm being mean, but it's the truth. Unfortunately, in the coming years, you're going to see more even more seniors working at jobs meant for students. I just don't want **you** to become one of them.

I often talk about the fact that I wasn't taught about stocks and investing when I was growing up, but here's the truth: CD rates *used* to be high enough to be an investment strategy. You could have completely avoided the stock market and investments with inherent risk and unknown performance in favor of CDs that had **no** risk and a **guaranteed** return. This is one of the reasons why parents from the '70s and '80s always told their kids to save their money in a bank account. At one point, that was sound financial advice. Unfortunately, the dot-com bust of 2000 ended that party- and it's never been the same since. Worse still, those kids are now adults who still believe what their parents told them 20 years ago. Now they're broke, living at home with those same parents, and wondering why they're not successful.

And just in case you're wondering, yes- there is a limit to how much money FDIC insurance covers. It's currently $250,000. That means anything up to that amount is covered. But what happens if you have $500,000? Don't worry. Just go to another bank and open an account there. Now you're covered for the rest. You can do that for as much money as you have. If you exceed your limit at one bank, just go to another one.

And that's just for accounts owned by individuals. Once you start getting into joint accounts and accounts under different types of ownership, you can actually have more than $250,000 at the same bank and still be protected. When I worked at the bank, I knew several customers who would keep up to the exact amount of FDIC protection in their accounts. When they exceeded it with the interest from a CD, they would wait until the CD matured and then withdraw the excess to deposit into some other bank.

So, do I recommend CDs for the average 21-year-old? **Absolutely not.** Unless CD interest rates get higher than 3%, there are **far** better ways to grow your money. I can only think of *one* reason to have a CD:

CD Secured Loans

CD Secured loans aren't well known. The only reason I know about them is because I worked at a bank. Here's how they work:

1. You need to borrow money.
2. You already have money in a CD- let's say for $3,000.
3. You ask the bank to use the money in your CD as collateral for the loan.
4. The bank agrees- giving you a loan of up to $3,000- the amount in the CD.

Basically, by using the money in your CD as a guarantee (or **collateral**), you take the risk out of the bank giving you a loan. If you don't pay the loan back, the bank just takes the money out of your CD. It's pretty simple, but there are a few things to keep in mind.

Pros:

✓ Interest rates for CD Secured loans are usually way lower than unsecured loans- which makes the cost to borrow much cheaper. Unsecured loans and lines of credit (like credit cards) have no collateral and the interest rate you get is based on your credit score. Unsecured loans- even for people with excellent credit scores-usually have interest rates around 15%, while CD secured loans for "credit challenged" people could be as low as 5%. You save money.

✓ It's easy to get approved for a CD secured loan. If your credit score is shaky, or if you want to build your credit without using credit cards, CD secured loans might be a good option because the bank has nothing to lose by giving you one. After all, you're guaranteeing the loan with your own money.

✓ It's a way to loan yourself money. Let's say you had a car repair for $3,000. If you cash out your CD, you lose all the interest you gained and you'll have a $0 balance- forcing you to close the CD account. If you get a CD Secured loan, you keep the original $3,000 in the account and you continue accruing interest. The loan would give you a *separate* $3,000 that you would pay off over time by making monthly payments. When you're finished paying the loan, you have access to the $3,000 in your CD again.

Cons:

✓ Obviously, once you get approved for the loan, you can't withdraw the money in the CD. Typically, that's not a problem. Normally, you wouldn't withdraw your money until your CD matures anyway. In general, if you need the ability to withdraw money, use your checking or savings accounts. If you haven't been listening to me and you have all your cash tied up in CDs for whatever reason, don't use CD secured loans. It will cut off access to your cash.

✓ Some banks charge you a fee for this type of loan. Try to avoid this and find a bank or credit union that won't charge you. High fees make low-interest rates kind of pointless. Ultimately, it'll still be expensive. For example, 5% on a $3,000 loan is $150 per year. That's not bad, but if the bank charges a $150 fee on top of the 5% interest rate, then your total cost per year is $300, which is **10%**. That's too expensive to borrow your own money.

✓ If you have a really good credit score, the interest rates you can get for an unsecured loan may not be all that different from a CD-secured loan. If that's the case, there's really no point in having the bank restrict your access to the money in your CD. Of course, you should always shop for the best rate, but sometimes it's better just to get a regular loan.

I'll tell you the one time a CD-secured loan helped me: I went on a road trip to Tennessee with some friends and my car died the moment we pulled into our destination. After getting my car towed to a repair shop, the mechanic told me it would be $1,700 to fix. Obviously, if I'm vacationing in Tennessee, I didn't have $1,700 lying around. On top of that, my two credit cards were basically maxed out, so I was screwed. Suddenly, I remembered that I had a CD at my bank. There was a branch down the street and I was able to get approved for a loan. So, there are cases when CD-secured loans can be useful. That vacation sucked, by the way.

Think of CDs as that weirdly specific tool in your toolbox that you hardly ever use and keep forgetting about. It has its uses, but more often than not, you'll reach for something more useful.

CHAPTER NINE
Get Out of Debt and Stay Out

1.   You will lose thousands of dollars to debt if you operate like everyone else.
2.   Debt prevents you from getting loans and credit when you actually need it.
3.   Financial institutions lure you with gimmicks to trap you into carrying large amounts of debt and then penalize you for having that debt.
4.   Lower-income people pay far more fees and interest than wealthy people.

This may seem obvious, but you can't be financially independent if you have a bunch of debt. It's already hard enough to keep your head above water financially: Debt is the rock that you have to carry while you swim. Get rid of it so you can move around freely.

Debt is the devil. It sounds like I'm exaggerating, but I don't think I am. Debt in the United States is the closest thing to Satan I feel there is. Not in the sense of satanic worship with blood and mutilation and all that horrific stuff- more like how the serpent persuades Eve to eat the fruit from the forbidden tree. It's far more subtle; far more rational; far more *enticing*. Debt strokes your ego, flatters your intelligence and seduces you into thinking your life will be better once you use it. And then before you know it, you're kicked out of the garden with its simple, easy lifestyle and forced to mindlessly labor for the rest of your days in the unforgiving wilderness. Debt is the weapon formed against you so that you shall **not** prosper.

Folks, it's that serious. Debt can ruin your life for *decades*. If there were adequate consumer protections in this country, debt would allow you a way to afford large expenses in a way that is fair and easy to pay back. Unfortunately, that's not how it works here.

Let's play a fun little game. Go to your mailbox. There's probably a credit card offer in your mail right now. Look at the return address. It's probably from Delaware. Now open the letter. Ignore the intro APR, the blank checks or whatever gimmick they're using to get you to sign up and go to the Terms and Conditions. Don't attempt to read all of that crap. Go straight to the section that's probably labeled "Late Payments and Penalty APR." This is the **most important** part. This explains what'll happen if you're ever late on a payment. It'll probably say that you'll have a late fee of around $40 and that the Penalty APR of 29.99% will kick in if you're ever late- *once*.

Read that *again*. It doesn't matter what your credit score is or what the special introductory interest rate is. If you are ever- and I mean *ever*- late one *single* f&@*ing time, your interest rate is now **thirty percent**. This interest rate is life-changing in a very, *very* bad way. Let's say you used one of those blank checks to do a balance transfer of $5,000 from a higher interest card you already own. You're pretty smart: you figure you can save money by taking advantage of some low introductory interest rate for 6 months or a year or whatever. Three months later, you forget that your payment falls on a holiday and you end up making your payment one day late. You pay the late fee and think nothing of it...until you get your statement and notice that your interest charges are ridiculously high.

Your late payment triggered the penalty APR, so now your plan to save money blows up in your face. Your $5,000 balance transfer will now cost you **$1,500** every year that you have it and unless you have $5,000 lying around, you have no choice but to pay all that interest. On top of that, you were *so* excited to take advantage of their low-interest rate gimmick that you overlooked the 5% transfer fee- which cost you $250. Worse still, now this card has the highest interest rate out of all your cards- which completely defeats the purpose of having transferred the balance in the first place.

You might think it's somewhat understandable that you pay a penalty for being late, but let's go back to Delaware for a second. The reason why credit card companies are based in Delaware (specifically Wilmington, Delaware) is because that state allows credit card companies to charge whatever interest rate they want. You see, individual states control how much companies can charge for interest. Some states allow higher rates than others. Some states aren't very profitable for lenders because the maximum interest rate they can charge is lower than other states. A decent number of states feel that interest rates shouldn't be crazy high and have imposed interest rate limits.

Companies generally don't like being told what to do, but they have no choice but to charge under the limit if they are based in that state. Yet some states, depending on the type of loan, don't have any limits **at all**. Years ago, some government random in Delaware got the bright idea to let companies charge whatever they want in exchange for bringing business to the state. It was done in the name of progress and community investment and jobs and blah blah blah. Over half of the financial institutions that offered credit cards and lines of credit got the heck out of whatever state they were based in and hightailed it to Delaware. The state, happy to get all this investment from these huge banks, allowed these credit card companies to basically write their own rules. Consumer protections were thrown out and these companies even gained protections from lawsuits and hostile takeovers. Seemingly overnight, Delaware became a safe haven for pirates. And whatever financial scheme they cooked up was entirely legal and blessed by the state.

I pick on Delaware, but what I'm getting at is that, when it comes to the debt and financial services that are marketed to you, the companies behind them find legal loopholes to make sure that they can charge you interest rates that help *them* and hurt **you**. Your best move is to only take on debt for things that increase in value (a house) or things that are absolutely necessary to make a living (a car). Even then, you have to be careful. These institutions are NOT your friends- no matter how friendly the person at the bank is to you. They are pirates. And what do pirates want? Booty. Specifically, *your* booty. Don't give them your booty. Protect it at all costs or they will take it.

Think about it. I gave you an example for **one** credit card. Most likely, you have multiple credit cards, a car (or two), a house, student loans and maybe a second mortgage. How much do you think you're paying in interest per year? For most Americans, it's around $8,000 a year.

Let that sink in.

Now think about paying that debt for five years. Now ten years. Now twenty. Want me to spell it out for you?

5 years at $8,000 a year = **$40,000**
10 years at $8,000 a year = **$80,000**
20 years at $8,000 a year = **$160,000**

You might think that you don't even *have* that kind of money to pay somebody, but you do. It just doesn't *feel* that way because you're focused on the payments that you *think* are affordable. All that interest is in those payments. You know that. You just haven't realized how expensive it is. Statistically, you've been paying it since you bought a house and started paying your student loans. Everyone is doing it, really. Does that make it okay?

Uh, No.

If you are a regular, average adult in America, you're getting **bodied** by debt every year and told that it's normal. Folks, it's **NOT** normal. It's a lie told to you by banks and reinforced by school and maybe even your family. You only *think* it's normal because everyone around you is doing it. It's like your house being on fire and you don't escape because you look around and every else seems to be cool with it. That burning sensation isn't some figment of your imagination: It's fire.

I can clearly remember hearing my grandparents, parents, uncles and aunts all saying, "You're always gonna have debt." I've heard this several times throughout my life from people I respect. After a while, I started believing it too. In fact, I didn't stop hearing it until I started working at a bank for high-net-worth clients. The conversations were *completely* different. They were far more focused on the interest rates and getting them as low as possible for their loans and lines of credit. They were only marginally interested in the payment amount. I could go on and on, but the most important part is this:

Being around people with money eventually taught me *how* to get money.

This is really important. If you're hanging around people who use their credit cards and loans like their own personal Santa Claus, you will eventually make similar mistakes. Even if you think you're pretty smart, the smartest person in a group of ignorant people is still ignorant. Your goal is to get away from that mindset and those people and get around financially intelligent people. Listening to podcasts and watching YouTube isn't enough. The people around you must reinforce good financial habits by applauding your good decisions and calling you out on your bad ones. Once you get the hang of it, see if you can bring some of your old financially ignorant buddies around. But manage your expectations. You'll likely convert one or two, but the rest of them won't listen. Some of them may even reject you. It's happened to me on more than one occasion.

Let's go back to that letter you got from the credit card company. The reason they're contacting you is because they want to offer *you* the opportunity to make *them* money. Don't see a credit card offer? That means you've already maxed out your current credit cards and they've cut you off like the drunk guy at last call for alcohol. Unfortunately for you, that's when you could desperately use a 0% interest promotion to get back on your feet.

This is the cruel catch 22 of debt. When you are financially secure and don't need it, you get all kinds of offers for credit cards and loans. When you desperately need it, no one will give you any money or even talk to you. In nerd talk, credit offers are inversely related to need. So what happens if you need money for an unforeseen repair or medical expense? If you're like most Americans, you pull out your credit card or get a loan. But what if you've already maxed out your credit cards and already have several loans? You're screwed. When you try to apply for a new credit card or a loan, you get rejected. Banks figure you won't make payments on additional cards or loans, so they deny you because now there's a risk for them. They lose money when you don't make your payments. To add insult to injury, they'll send you rejection letters saying that you're denied because you already have too many credit card and loan accounts.

Imagine going to a bar where they give away free drinks. You don't believe it, so you only have one drink to make sure it's legit. When you see everyone else getting free drinks, you drop your guard and get plastered drinking into the wee hours of the morning. Then, when you finally attempt to go home, the bartender takes your keys. You don't mind- you'll just order another free drink to pass the time. Nope. You're cut off. You can't order any more because the bartender has determined that you've already had enough. You ask for a cup of water to help you sober up. The bartender says that will cost you $40. You're furious, so you decline. But you're feeling sick. You weren't paying attention to the bartender using bottom-shelf liquor in your drinks. You *really* need that water so you pay the $40. The water helps, but you still feel nauseous. You make your way to the bathroom. It's locked. You'll need to pay another $40 to use it. This is ridiculous! You consider walking home, but it's way too far and you can barely walk in a straight line. So you pay it and hug the toilet for a while. You feel better, but now you need some more water. That'll cost you another $40. At this point, you check your bank account. You had only planned on spending around 30 bucks, not $120. You demand to speak to a manager to complain about these deceptive (and in your view-*illegal*) practices. The manager points out that it was **you** that had too much to drink. You could have stopped drinking at any time, left with your car, and gone home to drink water and use the bathroom as much as you wanted. As much as you hate to admit it, she's right. You look around and notice several other people in the same situation. Earlier, you wondered how a bar could make money giving away free drinks. Now, you finally understand. The drinks weren't the money maker. **You** were.

This is how debt works in America. You are not the customer. You are the product. You generate more income for financial institutions than you could ever legally generate for yourself. **You** are the goose that lays the golden egg. And once you've maxed out the debt you can carry and outlived your usefulness, you are discarded and abandoned. Then the vultures come and pick your bones. You're probably familiar with them. They're the:

Payday Loan companies
Rent-to-Own stores
Title Pawn Businesses

Also known as Predatory lenders. They're the only people who will deal with you once the banks start ignoring you. Their interest rates are far worse. You think 30% is bad? Try *300%*. I'm serious. Your typical Payday loan has an Annual Percentage Rate (or APR) of nearly **400%**. You wouldn't think of it that way because they advertise a fixed dollar fee for every $100 that you borrow. However, if you calculated the interest rate like a regular credit card, the yearly interest rate would exceed 300%. Even if you paid off the loan by your next payday, it's still a rip-off. Here's an example:

1. You want to borrow $500 until your next payday.
2. The fee is $15 for every $100 borrowed. You borrowed $500, so your fee is $75.
3. The total loan is now $575. It's due in two weeks.
4. If you pay on time, your interest rate for **TWO WEEKS** is **15%**
5. If you can't pay the loan in full, so you have to get an extension or "roll over."
6. It's still $15 per $100, but now you're borrowing $575- the total you owe *now*.
7. You get charged an additional $86.25 fee for a new total of $661.25. It's due in two weeks.
8. If you pay on time, your interest rate for **ONE MONTH** is **32%**

Do you see how this can get out of control? This is how lower-income people pay **MORE** than higher-income people. A person with decent credit will pay an interest rate of 30% a year *max*. A lower-income person using these predatory lending services could pay around **400%**, and it could be *higher* in some states. That's why so many of these predatory businesses are on the poorer side of town: It's **extremely** lucrative. Wealthier communities wouldn't tolerate these businesses being in their neighborhoods. They know it's a rip-off and, quite frankly, they think the people who use those businesses are eyesores. In fact, let's talk about some of the other businesses that are usually in the same shopping center as these predatory lenders:

- Pawn Shops
- Blood Donation Centers
- Liquor stores

You're smart, so you tell me: What's the common theme here? It's your zip code. If you're in a low-income neighborhood, you're literally surrounded by businesses that profit the **most** when you make bad decisions. Eventually, it can cost you your car, your paycheck, and even the furniture in your house. And when you can't pay, you'll have no choice but to sell all your stuff before eventually selling your own blood. Think about that for a second. Imagine selling your own damn blood to pay your bills. Some of you don't have to imagine. Thousands of people do it every week. That's how out of control America is. I hope I'm not pointing out the obvious, but you need your blood to survive and stuff. At least there's a liquor store around to make you feel better.

Debt is like salt. A little doesn't hurt, a moderate amount will give you health problems and too much will put you in the hospital. It's hard to be responsible because these businesses advertise debt as something that will make your life awesome. You can fly on planes and go on your dream vacation and have a great lifestyle. That's not how debt should be marketed. However, there aren't many protections for the average consumer because American capitalism believes that the consumer should be able to enter into any financial arrangement they choose- regardless of how terrible and deceptive it is. That means that the responsibility to take care of yourself falls squarely on **you**. Please understand that financial institutions spend **millions** lobbying lawmakers to charge you higher and higher interest rates and remove consumer protections that limit their profits.

Your goal is to seek the debt that best serves you and helps you to reach **your** financial goals. Being financially intelligent means no longer responding to random offers. So the next time you get a credit card offer in the mail, do yourself a favor and throw it in the nearest fire.

CHAPTER TEN
How to Make Your Credit Score Work for You

1. Your Credit Report is like a financial report card and your Credit Score is like your overall GPA. 850 is an A+ and a 300 is an F-. You'll need at least a 650 (a B), to get decent rates when you get a car, a house, or apply for a credit card.
2. High score = **SAVE** a ton of money in interest. Low score = **PAY** a ton of money in interest.
3. Your score is graded by at least 5 **different** companies/bureaus. You could have *different* scores based on who graded you.
4. The most common score used by the banks is the FICO score. Know your FICO score first.

Your credit score, at some point or another, is going to be a source of anxiety for you- mostly because of what "everybody" says about it. Ignore them and let's get right to the point. There's only **one** reason your credit score exists:

Banks and lenders use your credit score to decide if you can be trusted with a loan or credit.

That's it. It's no more complicated than that. Scores range from 300 to 850:

- A score of 670 or above is considered **high**- meaning you have *good* credit.
- A score of 579 or below is considered **low**- meaning you have

bad credit.

- Anything between 580 and 669 means you have *fair* credit -not bad, but not great either.

A **high** credit score makes you attractive to banks and companies that are in the business of loaning money. It means you're a **low-risk** borrower and you're not likely to bail on your loans and your credit cards. You're considered a **prime** borrower. You likely:

1. Have a job that pays significantly more than your monthly expenses,
2. Keep your overall debt level low relative to your income, and
3. Pay all of your bills on time.

Lenders give borrowers with high credit scores low-interest rates and other favorable terms like 0% financing, "90 days same as cash" offers, no down payments, low fees, etc. because they think you're *safe*.

A **fair** credit score makes you unattractive to the best lenders, but attractive to lenders with a higher risk tolerance. It means you're a **medium-risk** borrower that's likely to miss a payment or two, but you probably won't bail entirely- you'll *eventually* pay it off. You *may* be considered a **sub-prime** borrower. You likely:

1. Have a job that pays a little bit more than your monthly expenses,
2. Keep your overall debt expenses at or just under your income, and
3. Are occasionally late on paying your bills or miss payments.

With a fair credit score, lenders will think twice before letting you borrow money. Some lenders may disqualify you immediately, while others will give you **unfavorable** terms like high interest, random application fees, high upfront costs, high down payments, etc. because they want to make their money back **early in the loan** just in case you bail out early. If you stick around and pay until the end, their profit is huge. It's risk vs reward. You're the risk.

A **low** credit score makes you unattractive to everybody because you're a **high-risk** borrower who is likely to bail on their loans and stop making payments. You are *definitely* a **sub-prime** borrower. You likely:

1. Have a job that barely pays your monthly expenses,
2. Max out every credit card you have, and
3. Are frequently late on paying your bills and have several bills in collections.

The only lenders that will loan you money at this level are title pawn and payday loan companies. With a low credit score, you're not getting a loan or a credit card unless you can give them collateral: things that you own that they can take if you don't pay back your loan. Even then, since you're such a high risk, you get the worst of everything: super-high interest rates, short-term loans, high penalty fees, upfront cash costs, and the possibility of having someone come and take your stuff. This definitely isn't where you want to be. The terms and rates for low credit borrowers hover between unethical and criminal. This is where you hear the term "predatory lender" get thrown around a lot. It's because they use your low credit scores as justification to **mistreat** you- all the while telling lawmakers that they're the only ones that will help you when you need money- which by their logic makes them a *benefit* to your community. It's disgusting.

This is probably a good time to remind you that your credit score- good or bad, high or low- has **nothing** to do with your character or your personal value. At some point, credit scores became personal badges of honor or shame. It doesn't really matter how or why this happened. Just know that it's bad to mix financial stuff with your sense of identity or your emotions. Credit scores don't judge you personally. They were designed as a way to statistically predict your likelihood of paying back your debt. Truth be told, they are fairly accurate. However, these scores aren't a measure of whether or not you're successful. It's ok to have a personal sense of pride for achieving a high score, but a credit score is not meant to be a status symbol. Unfortunately, it *is* to some people, but I'm going to recommend that you avoid those people and avoid becoming that person. Please don't go around telling people your credit score on your dating profile. All you're saying is that you're a good candidate to profit from (AKA a sugar daddy or sugar mama).

On the other hand, a low credit score isn't a death sentence. It doesn't mean you're a bad person or doomed to fail. Trust me, I worked at a bank. One of the worst credit scores I've ever seen belonged to a multi-millionaire who was and still is very famous. It primarily impacts your ability to get a loan. However, some employers, apartment complexes, and rental businesses use it to qualify applicants. It's not important to be perfect, but it is important to know what your score is and what things might be affecting it. Most importantly, you need to know that your credit score is **not** permanent. You can always improve your score over time. Just because it's low now doesn't mean it will always be low. Conversely, a high score is not guaranteed to stay high. It all depends on your payment history.

Credit Report vs Credit Score

As an individual with a Social Security number, you have a credit **report** and a credit **score.** They are NOT the same, but they are related. You can get your credit report for free, while you usually have to pay for your credit score. Your credit report is a list of all the loans and credit cards you've ever had. If you've ever had a bill sent to collections, that will be on your report as well. Your credit score is based on what's in your credit report, so it's super important that your credit report is accurate. Put another way, your credit score is like your GPA and your credit report is like your report card.

Who Creates Your Credit Report and Your Credit Score?

Three credit bureaus and at least two credit scoring agencies create everything related to your credit. Each credit bureau has its own credit report and its own score. You've probably heard their names:

TransUnion
Equifax
Experian

Why are there three? Because each one of them services a different part of the country. I'm in Atlanta, which is serviced primarily by Equifax. Although all three credit bureaus have information about my credit history, Equifax is most likely the one that will be contacted anytime I apply for a loan or a credit card. But here's the most important thing to take away:

You have **THREE** credit reports and **FIVE** credit scores, but only **ONE** score really matters.

Wait, what? Why? And where did those two *other* credit scores come from? They came from:

FICO
VantageScore

You've probably heard of your FICO score. VantageScore is newer, but it serves the same purpose: to give companies a **single** place to go to check an applicant's credit history. FICO is a paid service by a company called the **Fair Isaac Corporation** (FICO, get it?). FICO is a company whose clients are banks, car dealers, credit card issuers, or whoever is looking to get info on a potential borrower. You are not their customer. You are their *product*. Specifically, your credit history is their product. Does that make you feel kind of creeped out? It should, but that's a discussion for another day.

Basically, lenders pay FICO for access to their information about **you**. They do the work of going through all your credit information from all three bureaus and make a single score that they make available to lenders. That way, lenders don't have to analyze three different credit reports and come up with their own score for every single person that applies for money. It's a convenient service. And since it is *your* information after all, FICO will share all your personal credit history with you as well…for a fee.

FICO has been around for decades and everybody trusts it, but it's kind of a monopoly so another service called VantageScore popped up around 2006. What had happened was- the three credit bureaus were missing out on a bunch of money because FICO was using the bureaus' information to make a FICO score. FICO was getting paid by everybody simply by doing the work of going through the 3 credit bureaus' information. Imagine getting paid by making the cliff notes on other people's books. Cliff notes? Is that still a thing? I'm old. Ok, so imagine someone else posting your content on their channel and it goes viral while you're hovering around 200 views. Is that better?

Anyway, so the three bureaus finally got together and made their own score off their own information. They called it VantageScore and it is a competitor to the Fair Isaac Corporation (FICO) score. Let me tell you something you may not know about financial institutions. They hate change and they hate spending money. So, although the VantageScore comes directly from the three bureaus, everybody still checks FICO. Ok?

The most important credit score is your FICO score.

Got it? It gets confusing because you're probably getting all kinds of offers and promotions saying that you can check your credit score for free. That's *partially* true. Remember that VantageScore is the new(er) kid on the block and wants to compete against FICO. So anytime you see an offer for a free score, it's most likely your VantageScore and NOT your FICO score. It may even be just one score from one of the credit bureaus. Don't be confused. The only one that really matters is your FICO score, which you'll either have to pay for or have some type of bank or credit card account that allows you to check your FICO score for free. For example, Bank of America will let you check it for free if you have a credit card with them.

Again, if you're shopping around for a house or a car, know your FICO score before you apply. That's the score the banks have historically trusted the most. All the other scores may be higher or lower and could potentially give you a false sense of confidence. The other scores just give you an *idea* of where you are. Your FICO score is *precisely* where you are- at least in terms of how lenders view your creditworthiness.

How to Manage Your Credit

Here's the deal. Managing your credit is super easy. You can do it in three steps:

Step 1: Pay your bills on time.
Step 2: Don't carry balances on your credit cards.
Step 3: Only apply for loans and credit cards if and when you *need* them.

Ta-da! That's it. Aren't you glad you bought this book? What's that? Not helpful, you say? Honestly, it really is that simple. Do those three things and you'll automatically improve your credit score over time- no matter what your score is now. Here's why this works:

- Paying your bills on time,
- Having older accounts, and
- Keeping your debt level low

These are considered **positive items** and will make your credit score go **up**.

What if you've already maxed out your credit cards? What if you've had some identity theft? What if you have collections harassing you and your family members? Those situations will hurt your credit score. Here's why:

- Using more than 30% of your credit card's limit
- Paying your bills 30, 60, or 90 days late (the later it is, the more it hurts)
- Having too many credit cards and credit lines open at the same time
- Having a lender on your report that is known to make sub-prime loans
- Applying for credit too many times (like more than once every 3 months)
- Having a bill sent to collections because you refused to pay it

These are considered **negative items** and will make your credit score go **down**.

If your score is above 670, keep managing your credit and you'll be fine. If your score is already jacked up, don't worry- none of us are perfect.

How to Fix Your Credit

STEP 1: Download Your Credit Report From All Three Agencies

1. Equifax
2. TransUnion
3. Experian

Don't pay for these reports. By law, you get a **free** one from each credit bureau once per year. You'll just have to create an account and you're good to go.

STEP 2: Make Sure That EVERYTHING in Your Credit Reports Is **Accurate**

- If you closed an account, it should clearly say so.
- If you paid off a balance, it should say that it's paid off.
- If you have a credit card or a loan and you're making payments on it, it should say *paid as agreed* or something to let you know everything is cool.
- If something that went to collections got paid off, it should say that it's paid.
- If a report says you were late, you should agree with *when* it said you were.

BUT!

- If you *don't* recognize an account on any of your reports,
- If a report says that you were late on a payment and you know that's **wrong,**
- If an account says it was "closed by lender" when you know *you* closed it,
- If you see something that went to collections that shouldn't be there,
- or If you see anything wrong or suspicious AT ALL...

STEP 3: Dispute Items on Your Credit Reports

You have a right to **dispute** anything you don't agree with. If you have proof that something on any one of your credit reports is wrong, then you need to get that negative item off your report ASAP. Seriously, a few points can save you **thousands** of dollars- especially when you start making big purchases like cars and houses.

Each credit bureau will give you instructions on how to dispute an item. Just follow the directions and be patient. It's tedious and a pain in the butt, but it's worth it if it can help your credit score.

STEP 4: Pay Down Your Credit Cards and Stop Applying for New Ones

Credit cards are where people usually get in the most trouble with their credit score. As a general rule, don't carry balances on your cards from month to month and you won't have to worry about staying under 30% or trying to remember debt-to-income ratios. But if you have high balances on your cards, focus on paying off one card at a time (after you've built your emergency savings account). Then,

STOP USING THAT CARD.

Seriously. Please don't be like me. Don't pay off a card, pat yourself on the back, and then find some reason to max it out *again*. Once you pay off one card, then go to the next one, then the next one. Mathematically, you save more money by paying off your highest-interest debt first. However, psychologically, it's important to feel like you're making progress. I liked paying the smaller balances first because it made me feel like I was getting somewhere. This might take months- or *years*. It's fine. Going slow is absolutely necessary sometimes. In fact, get used to going slow when it comes to your finances.

Lastly, don't- I repeat- **DON'T** apply for a new card to pay off an existing one. It doesn't help. It doesn't matter if you get some gimmicky promotion for 0%- because if your credit is bad, you won't qualify for 0% anyway. What'll end up happening is that you'll either:

Transfer a balance and get charged a fee (meaning it won't be free)
OR
Get denied when you apply for a new credit card.

Applying for new cards brings your credit score down. Moving balances around doesn't solve the problem anyway. Suck it up and just pay down your existing cards. Sure, there are methods and strategies to help you do it but use trusted methods like the debt snowball. If you're not familiar with it, here's the quick version:

Debt Snowball Debt Reduction Strategy (smallest debt first)

    ✓   Decide an amount (like $100) that you will pay extra every month.

✓ **Add** that extra payment to the monthly payment of your lowest balance card or loan. For example, if your smallest balance is on a credit card that has a $150 monthly payment, you will pay an extra $100 a month. Your total monthly payment will be $250 for that card until you pay it off.

✓ With the $150 payment gone, you have $250 a month available as an extra payment to pay down debt. **Add** it to the monthly payment of the *next* lowest balance card or loan. If you have another card with a $200 a month payment, pay a total of $450 per month until you pay it off.

✓ Repeat the process by "snowballing" all your extra payments until all your debt is gone.

Get it? A little snowball (your initial amount) becomes a big one (your initial payment plus all the freed-up monthly payment amounts) as it rolls down a hill of snow. This is probably the most popular debt reduction method around. With this strategy, the only extra money you need is the initial amount you committed to at the beginning. All the other money comes from paying off debt.

If you're looking for other ideas, there are several finance professionals on social media that have great information as well. However, **avoid** listening to unqualified people on YouTube and TikTok. Their advice tends to be "life hacks" for finances and they constantly give out incorrect (or half-correct) information. Stick to trusted financial sites, read books like this one, or talk to a debt counselor over the phone or in person. Debt counselors frequently work with non-profit organizations that provide their services free of charge. So don't pay any money for this.

STEP 5: Pay Off Loans from Subprime (aka Bootleg) Lenders

Not all lenders are created equal. Some purposely go after people who struggle with their credit. These lenders aren't very respected in the financial community, so if other lenders see that you have a loan with a bootleg lender, they'll think *you're* bootleg. Like birds of a feather, you'll be considered subprime even if *your* credit score is decent. This happened to me. A bank closed my credit line account when they found out I had a loan with a subprime housing loan company. It really pissed me off because I didn't do anything wrong. I became bootleg by association.

STEP 6: Pay That Bill in Collections Already

I'm a fairly rebellious person. If I don't believe that something is fair, I certainly won't cooperate. However, this has caused some issues with my credit. Mostly because there was a dentist or doctor's office visit that wasn't covered by my insurance and I felt that it should have been so I refused to pay on *principle*. I have to admit, ignoring all those notices felt pretty good, but then I started getting all the phone calls from the collection agencies. Their phone calls pissed me off even more and it made me even more determined *not* to pay.

Folks, please don't do this. I was being stubborn and dumb. If you really want to cuss someone out, do it *before* the bill goes to collections. Complain to the insurance company, complain to the doctor's office and demand to speak to a manager. Trust me, if you call enough people, they'll get tired of you harassing them and they'll work something out with you. Don't let your emotions mess up your credit. It only hurts *you*.

If something does end up in collections, swallow your pride and pay it off. Make sure to ask for written confirmation that the bill was paid. It's very likely that you'll need this proof if you have to dispute this item on your credit report later. And you will want to dispute it- or at least update it- so that the credit bureaus know that it has been paid. Don't rely on the collection agencies to update your reports. They're not being paid to do that. That being said….

If you are absolutely opposed to paying a bill in collections, wait 7 years and it will go away.

You heard that right. Negative items on your credit will fall off your credit report after 7 years. It's a long time to wait, but it can be worth it- especially if the bill is in the thousands of dollars. Just be smart about this. Don't suddenly decide to start making payments on a bill that's 6 years old. You'll re-open the account and your 7-year period

starts over again if you don't fully pay it off.

I'll say it again: If your strategy is to let a bill fall off your credit report after seven years, don't contact the collections agency or the original biller regarding the bill. Don't discuss the bill with anybody who calls you. As a matter of fact, don't even pick up the phone if you know it's the collection agency. You'll start the 7-year period all over again and it can stay on your credit report way longer than intended.

STEP 7: Don't Pay Anybody Anything to Fix Your Credit or Help You with Debt

The sad part of being in a hole financially is that there's an entire industry of jerks who want to profit off of you and put you in an even deeper hole. So I'm going to say this again:

Do. Not. Pay. For. Credit. Repair. Or. Debt. Help. Period.

There are plenty of services that will help you **for free.** These organizations are usually non-profit services that are making a difference. The ones that charge you are preying on the fact that you are desperate and don't know who to turn to so they will smile and make you believe you have a friend that's looking out for you. They are **not** your friends. They are your financial enemies.

The best way out of a financial hole is good information, hard work, consistency, and determination. I can give you the good information, but you'll have to sacrifice and go without some of your comforts and luxuries so that you can get out of this hole yourself. If you try to cheat; if you try to speed up the process; if you try to pay someone to make it go away, it will come back to bite you in the butt when you least expect it. There's a reason why you see credit repair services advertised on construction paper stapled to a telephone pole. It's **bootleg.** Would you seriously trust a telephone pole ad with your Social Security number? The answer is no, by the way. **Never** give bootleg people your financial information. There's no telling what these people are doing with your credit information. **Do it yourself.**

In fact, beware of ANYONE that offers to help you manage your finances for a fee. We'll come back to this statement again, but "helpers" will end up costing you thousands and thousands of dollars.

They're like mosquitos- you won't even feel them sucking the life out of you. Worse, you'll have to deal with the irritating aftermath of their sting...for *years*.

STEP 8: Don't Use Consolidation Loans Unless You Close Existing Accounts

Consolidation loans are a way to transfer multiple credit cards or loans into one **big** loan. If you have multiple debt accounts with high monthly payments, this may be a good option. With a consolidation loan, you'll use the loan money to pay off all the debt you want to transfer, leaving you with a smaller monthly payment. However, don't be like me. Don't do some consolidation loan to get a lower payment and then continue using the credit cards. You'll only dig yourself into a deeper hole that's now **harder** to get out of. If you know you don't have the discipline to not use your paid-off cards, **close them**. You can always open new accounts later.

STEP 9: Freeze Your Credit

Freezing your credit means contacting all three credit bureaus and telling them to "freeze" your credit file. This will block any attempt to inquire about your credit score and history and **no one** will be able to open any credit or loan account- not even **you**. However, that's the point. You can always unfreeze it whenever you feel like it. The primary reason you'd do this is to avoid identity theft and fraud. Scammers and criminals won't be able to open accounts in your name even if they have your private information. Freezing your credit has no negative effect on your scores and you can have it done for less than $5 or for free.

Dealing with identity theft is a nightmare that will consume your life for several months- maybe even *years*. Thieves and scammers are getting really good at tricking people into handing over their private information through legitimate-looking emails and websites. It's only going to get worse as society moves from cash to digital transactions, so consider being proactive and freezing your credit so you have one less thing to worry about.

Another benefit of freezing your credit is that you won't get as many credit card offers. Also, you won't be so quick to apply for more credit because you'll have the additional inconvenience of having to unfreeze your credit every time you apply.

STEP 10: Get to the Root of the Problem

Lastly, figure out your psychological reasons for running up your debt. **This is the most important step.** Your relationship with money goes all the way back to when you were a child. Regardless of whether money was scarce or abundant during your childhood, you have emotional attachments to money that may be affecting your financial well-being. If you grew up poor, you may attempt to escape the negative feelings of poverty by surrounding yourself with lavish material items. If you grew up with abundance, you may spend money with the assumption that it will always be replenished and that you'll be bailed out if you ever run into a problem.

I'm not here to judge you. It doesn't matter to me whether you grew up with scarcity or abundance. All I'm saying is that for most people, money (or the lack of it) makes them **feel** a certain way. If you grew up poor, it *feels* good to own a luxury car because you can drive it to *escape* from poverty. If you grew up with abundance, it *feels* good to put everything on your credit card without thinking too much about it because you can *escape* financial accountability.

Most people have an emotional attachment to money that dictates how they spend it- and it has nothing to do with how smart or talented you are. If you've never really thought about it, you are likely on **autopilot** regarding your finances; and your **parents** are the ones who set your course. You must **remove** your emotional attachment to money and **separate** your emotions from your spending if you ever hope to get your financial house in order.

CHAPTER ELEVEN
Don't Pay Interest on Your Credit Cards

1. Credit Cards are not free money. If you don't have the cash to pay off the balance **every** month, **don't** use them.
2. Unless you have a 0% promotion on the card, **never** carry a balance month to month.
3. Credit Cards have the highest interest rates outside of predatory loans. If you have balances, focus on paying off your credit cards **first**.

Credit cards are like alcohol. If you have a drink a day, you'll be fine. If you have 5 or 6 a day, you *won't* be fine. All sorts of negative things happen: You become an addict, you'll likely destroy any relationships you have, you'll likely lose your job and you'll eventually destroy your liver. Is this an extreme analogy? Obviously, your liver has nothing to do with credit cards, but all the other stuff could happen.

Credit cards, in my opinion, are the worst offender when it comes to preying on people's emotions and insecurities. Everybody wants the "Platinum" this or the "Black Card" that. Credit cards are a status symbol. When you slap down some extra-thick, shiny credit card at a fancy restaurant, people take notice. You *know* they do. Payday loans are obviously not status symbols, so no one brags about having one. It's like admitting that you still suck your thumb as an adult. You know it's bad, so even if you do it, you're not going around telling everyone.

So what happens when you mix the promise of an awesome lifestyle with a piece of plastic that you can swipe to your heart's content?

Problems, man. **Problems**. Credit cards aren't free money. That new PlayStation that you swiped your card to get has to be paid back, with **interest**.

Unless you do it the *right* way. Then you pay no interest *at all*.

That's right. There's a way to use your credit card and not have to pay a single penny in interest ever. All you have to do is.......wait for it...

Always pay your balance in full every month.

By now, you probably hate me. I get it; no one likes Captain Obvious. Everybody knows that you don't have to pay any interest as long as you pay off your credit card in full every month. This is nothing new and you want a refund. But give me a chance. It gets better and there are some benefits you probably aren't considering or aren't aware of:

1. You never have to worry about credit utilization or keeping balances below 30% of your credit limit- because it will always be 0%.
2. Having a credit utilization of 0% means that your credit score goes up.
3. Your credit score going up means you automatically get your limit increased.
4. Your limit increase means that you utilize 0% of even **more** available credit.
5. Having even more credit raises your score even more.
6. An even higher credit score means credit card companies start sending you 0% promo offers. Ignore them.
7. Ignoring those offers means that you don't have credit inquiries.
8. Not having credit inquiries means your credit score goes up even more.

Do you see what's happening? When you pay off your balance every month, you create a situation that spirals UP- completely to your benefit. Let's call this the **"Good Credit Spiral."**

The opposite of this, of course, is the "**Bad Credit Spiral**." That's what can happen when you carry balances on your card from month to month. That's when you run into all kinds of issues:

1. You're always worried about credit utilization -because it will always be higher than 30%.
2. Having a utilization higher than 30% means that your credit score goes down.
3. Your credit score going down means you automatically get your limit decreased.
4. Your limit decrease means that you utilize even more of your available credit.
5. Having even less credit lowers your score even more.
6. An even lower credit score means credit card companies start raising your interest rates for your existing cards or closing your accounts altogether.
7. Having your accounts closed means that you make credit inquiries to get new cards.
8. Having credit inquiries means your credit score goes down even more.

Oh and by the way, you'll be paying interest the whole time- a **lot** of it. And the more interest you pay and the higher interest rate they assign you, the harder it will be to pay it off. I've been here before and I hated it. Nothing is worse than seeing half your payment get sucked up by interest charges all while your principal balance barely goes down. It's depressing. But I got out of it and you can too.

You obviously want the Good Credit Spiral. But you have to pay off your credit cards first (after you build up your emergency savings). It really doesn't matter how you pay them off. Financial advisors will tell you to focus on the ones with the highest interest rate. For me, if I have one card with a balance of $500 and another with a balance of $5,000, I'm knocking out the small one first. But that's just me. It gave me a sense of accomplishment and it was easier to focus. If you want an actual strategy, check out the "Debt Snowball" section from the previous chapter.

Let's say you've finally paid off your cards. Congratulations! Pat yourself on the back. Now let's get to work. We're going to get you some free stuff on top of your Good Credit Spiral.

Get Free Stuff and Better Credit

The process is simple:

1. Put small purchases and small bills on your credit card
2. Pay big purchases and big bills through your bank's Online Bill Pay

Here's how you do it:

Step 1. From here on out, you're only going to use ONE card. Put the other ones (that you've paid off) in a sock drawer somewhere. Choose the card that has the perk that is most important to you. If you travel a lot, use the free miles card. If it's cashback, then use that one. It doesn't matter. You just want free stuff.

NOTE: One card means ONE card, but sometimes you may need to get cash. **Don't use credit cards to withdraw cash or to get cashback.** You probably have a debit card attached to your bank account. Use that one for cash withdrawals, but NOT for purchases. Stuff it in the back of your wallet in that super hard-to-reach pocket that requires you to pull everything out to get to it. For this strategy to work, you can't have money coming out of too many places.

Step 2. Set up your credit card billing for automatic payments (AutoPay). Set your preference to pay off the entire balance every month and link it to your checking account. This is the ONE time I will suggest using automatic payments. You do this to make sure that you are never, ever late. But you have to keep money in your bank's checking account. If you followed my suggestion from the chapter on checking accounts, you should have a full month's worth of expenses in your checking account. If you do this, you'll never have to worry about the AutoPay transaction because you'll always have enough to cover it.

If you don't feel comfortable doing this or don't yet have the discipline to only spend what you can afford, **STOP**! It took me a while to act right with credit, so there's no judgment from me.

Step 3. Put all your regular purchases on that one credit card. And I mean *regular* as in gas, food, dining, groceries, entertainment, clothes, cell phone bills, etc.

<u>NOT</u> Your rent/mortgage, your car payment, or other big-dollar loans or bills.

Once you get used to using your credit card and paying it off every month, you're free to put the bigger stuff on your card. But for me, I don't like the sticker shock of seeing a huge bill show up on my statement. I like for my bill to be a few hundred dollars. It makes me feel like I could pay it off easily.

Step 4. At the end of the month, you'll get a notice that you've automatically paid your balance in full. You'll have no interest charges. You'll also get a notice saying how many points or miles you earned- for free.

Over time, those points or miles can pay for a free vacation. I use my cashback points to put cash directly back into my bank account. I actually **make** money from my credit cards. Ta-da! Free stuff with **no** interest charges. The beautiful thing about this method is that it really doesn't matter what your interest rate is. Since you never keep a balance on that one card longer than 30 days, you never get an interest charge.

That's how it should work, folks. These cards should be *helping* us, not wrecking our lives. I was never taught to pay off balances every month, so I used to carry balances month-to-month all the time. I got charged at least $1,000 a year in interest because I only paid the minimum payment for **years**.

Why Using Your Credit Card is Better than Using Your Bank (aka Debit Credit) Card

Using a credit card has perks you probably don't even know about. More importantly, these perks could save you thousands of dollars if you ever have fraud, theft, a broken gadget, or an accident in a rental car. Let's look at a few situations:

What If Someone Steals Your Credit Card or Your Identity?

Credit Card:
   ✓   Whether you're aware of the theft or not, the credit card
       company usually calls or texts **YOU** to tell you they've noticed

strange activity or your account. They verify your identity ask you to confirm the transactions. If you don't recognize them, they freeze your credit card, close the account, and send you a new card. You are not responsible for the charges.

✓ If you know your card was stolen, you call the credit company and report the theft. They will ask you about your most recent transactions. If you don't recognize them, they will freeze your card, close the account, and send you a new card. You are not responsible for the charges.

✓ **Summary**: Being a victim of fraud sucks, but the credit card company handles it.

Bank Card:

✓ You might get a phone call or text. Maybe. Sometimes, they'll just freeze your card without telling you and any purchase you attempt to make will get declined. This will make your dinner date super awkward.

✓ If you know your card was stolen, call your bank and report the theft. They will ask you about your recent transactions. If you don't recognize them, they will freeze your card, **BUT**...now they will open a fraud investigation and your account stays **open**. It stays open because you most likely have bills that still need to be paid. During that investigation, whatever money was taken out does NOT get returned. Ultimately, you are not responsible for the charges, **but you don't get your money back until the end of the investigation.** If the thief emptied your account, you are now getting insufficient funds penalties because your bills are hitting an account with no money in it. The bank will waive these penalties during the investigation, but you'll *still* have to find a way to magically pay your bills without any money. So now you'll have to call everybody that you owe money to and tell them you were a victim of fraud and that you need an extension to pay your bills. Some billers will be helpful and some won't. You'll have to deal with late fees and it may even hurt your credit.

✓ **Summary**: You're screwed. You're a victim of theft AND you've got no money.

What Happens When I Have an Accident in a Rental Car?

If you've ever rented a car, you know that at some point the person at the counter is going to offer you insurance on that car. Here's the thing: that car already has insurance. Insurance on cars is required by law. No rental company is crazy enough to let you drive off in an uninsured car. Of **course** they have insurance on it. What they're really offering is a way for you to waive *your* responsibility for any damages that may occur.

If you pay for rental insurance:

The rental car's insurance company pays all the deductibles, fees, and costs for repairs. You may still have to deal with getting a ticket if you're at fault, but as far as any costs regarding *that* rented vehicle, you're off the hook.

If you don't pay for rental insurance:

You choose NOT to waive your responsibility- which means that the rental car company's insurance has a right to come after you to pay for damages. You have car insurance on your personal vehicle, so you file a claim with *your* insurance company. Unless your auto insurance is complete crap, the rental car you drove is probably covered under your policy. BUT- you'll have to pay any deductibles and your premium may go up because this will count as an accident. Accidents make your insurance costs go up.

If you don't pay for rental insurance, but put the rental on your credit card:

You will still file a claim through your insurance, but your credit card may reimburse you for that deductible you had to pay. Considering that most people have deductibles that range from $500 to $1000, this could save you a good chunk of money. This is considered Secondary Insurance. That means it kicks in *second* after your insurance processes the claim.

Some cards offer even better protection: Primary Insurance. Primary Insurance is exactly the same as what you have on your car. It's the *first* insurance that kicks in when there's an accident. Primary

Insurance from your credit card means that you DON'T file a claim with your personal insurance. You file a claim with your credit card instead. Better still, there may not be a deductible with primary insurance from a credit card. It's almost like having two separate policies, but only having to pay one. The benefit is that since you're not using your personal policy, you don't have to worry about your insurance costs going up because you never involved them.

What Happens if I Have a Broken (or Stolen) Gadget?

FREE Extended Warranty: Some credit cards give you a free extended warranty that extends the original manufacturer's warranty by 1 year (or more). Pretty cool, right? Now you can finally say no to all those random offers to buy extended warranties when you shop for electronics and appliances.

Insurance on New Purchases: some credit cards offer some form of purchase protection that will cover your new purchases for 3 months or more. The credit card will pay to replace, repair, or reimburse you for any damages or loss of the covered item. Of course, there are limits to this. Your credit card will let you know what's covered and what isn't, but it's a handy thing to have- provided that you actually *know* you have it.

This brings up a good point about credit cards: You have to know about the benefits you already have before you start buying additional benefits from other people.

I'll spare you the life lesson contained in that sentence. Actually, no- I won't:

Know what you have before seeking to add something new.

You're going to see this time and time again when it comes to your personal finances. Companies make **billions** of dollars selling you stuff you don't even need **and already have**. Credit card companies offer you a bunch of free stuff to get you to use them instead of a competitor, but you're not even aware that you have it.

Annual Fees:

Lastly, let's talk about annual fees. Some cards have them, some don't. In general, the more attractive the card's main perk is, the more likely there is an annual fee to help the credit card company offset that cost of that perk. For example:

- Credit card A has 1% cashback on purchases.
- Credit card B has 5% cashback on certain items, and 2% on regular purchases.

Which is more likely to have an annual fee? Obviously, it's credit card B. Five percent cashback is pretty high, so they'll use an annual fee to help get some of their money back.

That being said, don't pay annual fees unless you've done the math and determined that the benefit you get is **more** than the annual fee you're paying. Another example:

- Credit card A has 1% cashback.
  1. You spend $2,000 that year.
  2. You get $20.

- Credit card B has 5% cashback with a $99 annual fee.
  1. You spend $2,000 that year.
  2. You get $100.
  3. You spend $99 on the annual fee, so...
  4. ...You end up getting $1. ($100 cashback *minus* $99 annual fee)

Credit card A, for this particular situation, makes more sense. You didn't lose any money with credit card B, but you can see that the credit card company ultimately won't offer something that they plan to lose money on. In fact, you'd have to spend $2,380 to end up getting $20. That's $380 *more* that you have to spend to get the same amount as the card with no annual fee.

Credit cards get a bad reputation and they deserve it. A credit card is like if Santa Claus was a vampire. He'll come to your door bearing gifts, but he will always ask your permission to come in. Accept the gifts he brings, but don't be an idiot and invite him in. He'll devour you and your entire family. Having a healthy fear and keeping him at arm's length means you get all the benefits with none of the dangers.

Used correctly, credit cards are an amazing tool to build your credit, and protect your cash, and get a bunch of free stuff. If all these fraud events, damages and insurance claims are likely to happen to you at some point anyway, why not use your credit card and let *them* deal with it? Likewise, if you're going to spend the money anyway, why not get cashback or points or some other perk for free?

Once you develop the good habit of paying your credit card in full every month, you can actually **make** money just from having it. Credit cards don't have to be the bane of your existence. **Change the way you use them**. Make them work for you.

CHAPTER TWELVE
How to Get the Best Terms on a Car Loan

1. Don't go to a dealership to get financing. Go to your bank or a credit union.
2. Don't let the dealership add a bunch of unnecessary stuff to your loan.
3. Get a low monthly payment, but **also** get a low-interest rate. You want **both**.

Most of us have the same experience with getting a car:

1. We go to a dealership.
2. A salesperson approaches us. We tell him or her what we want.
3. We go to the salesperson's desk. They say words.
4. We attempt to negotiate. The salesperson seems to take us seriously.
5. We go to another person's desk. Let's call him "Paperwork Guy."
6. Paperwork Guy explains that we're getting the absolute best deal. We agree(?)
7. We get a bunch of paperwork. They talk really fast. We sign all of it because we're hungry.
8. We walk out with the keys. We have a vague idea of what just happened, but hey- new car!

Unless you have a salesperson that wants to do the right thing and save you from yourself, you're going to get ripped off doing it this way. The reason is that you unknowingly entered a surgically methodical sales process that the dealership has mastered to perfection. You are led around the dealership the entire time and you have no real input on the process. You think your objections are meaningful negotiations. They're not. They get around those types of objections every single day, 365 days a year. In contrast, you may buy 8 cars in your *lifetime*. You are woefully underprepared to swim with these sharks. It's like jumping in a river and letting the current take you wherever it wants. The problem is that you're likely to get smashed against the rocks. You already have enough common sense to know that you don't jump into a river and try to swim. You know you need a boat and a way to steer.

So that's what we're going to do in this chapter. I'm going to give you the knowledge to serve as your boat and paddle so that you can *use* the river to go where **you** want.

Step One: Decide If You're Going to Get a New or Used Car

Yes, it matters. Interest rates are **higher** for used cars. Since the interest rate is higher, the monthly payment will be higher than a new car loan for the same amount. However, if you're buying a used car, you're probably financing a lower amount because you're trying to save money. Don't stress it; just be aware that you will get *different* quotes on new vs used car loans.

Step Two: Look Up Auto Loan Rates Using Your Credit Score

You need to know what your loan interest rate and monthly payments are going to be **BEFORE** you start applying for loans. It's easier to plan when you know what you can afford to pay in **advance**. Hop on over to a site like bankrate.com and check the auto loan rates. You'll probably see a page where they break down what the average interest rate is likely to be with your credit score. Keep in mind that this interest rate is not a quote. It's just an average to help you figure things out. You won't know the exact interest rate you'll get until you actually apply for the loan.

Step Three: Figure Out Your Monthly Payment

Now that you know the average interest rate that goes with your credit score, head back over to bankrate.com or just do a search for "car loan calculator." Type in the interest rate, the cost of the car you want, and how long you plan to make payments. Most car loans are 5-year loans, but now 6 and 7-year loans are becoming more popular. Either way, you'll need to type these in as months. So, 5 years will be 60 months. After you type those three things in, you should see two figures:

1. The monthly payment amount
2. The total cost of the car loan

Ta-da! Now you know how much you can expect to pay per month. The benefit of doing this at home is that you aren't relying on some salesperson or paperwork guy to tell you the truth at the dealership. And since you have this handy loan calculator, you can play around with the numbers to see how much car you can afford. You may want a $25,000 car, but you may not want a $500 monthly car payment. If you want to get a lower payment, you're going to have to buy a cheaper car or get a better interest rate.

This brings me to my next point: I know you're focused on the monthly payment. *Everyone* is focused on the monthly payment. However, I encourage you to play around with changing the **interest rate** as well. Watch what happens to the second figure we talked about: The total cost of the car loan. This number is important too. It lets you know how much you'll have to pay to get the loan. Let me give you an example:

- You want to buy a car for $25,000. It's new.
- The average interest rate for your credit score is 5%.
- Your loan is for 60 months (5 years).
- Your monthly payment is $472.
- The total cost of the loan is $28,307.
- By the end of the loan, you will have paid $3,307 in interest.

See how that works? Most people focus on the payment and not the interest. Most people don't even care about the total cost of the loan. They **should**. Imagine if I told you that you had to pay **$3,307** upfront just to get a loan? You'd probably report me to the police. But you're still going to pay that amount- because it's included in your monthly payment of $472. It doesn't feel like you're paying thousands of dollars because you're slowly paying that amount over 5 years.

Think about it like a mosquito bite. It feels so painless that you lose the significance of what's really happening. You're losing blood, but no one thinks of it that way. That's the genius of the mosquito. You don't see them as a threat because they take so little blood at a time. You'll swat at a mosquito, but you'll never run away from one. Because why would you do that? They're not dangerous. They're just *irritating*. Unless you consider the massive amounts of death they've caused over the years with malaria and other diseases. Turns out mosquitos aren't so harmless after all. What I'm trying to say is that these loans can be parasites. The bigger the interest rate, the bigger the mosquito. The bigger the mosquito, the more they suck the life out of you. If you have no choice and you *must* get bitten, at least choose the smallest mosquito.

Step Four: Find the Lowest Interest Rate

Now you need to find someone who's going to give you a loan. Notice that you still haven't gone into a dealership. This is a good thing. You're still building your boat. I'm going to cut to the chase and tell you who has the best interest rates; starting with the best and ending with the worst:

#1. Online Banks/Lenders
#2. Credit Unions
#3. Community Banks
#4. Regional or National Banks
#5. Car Dealerships

1. Online banks are the cheapest because they don't have to pay a lot of expenses to take your application. You'll probably do everything online or through your phone. This cuts out talking on the phone to customer service reps, walking into a building, and printing out a whole bunch of paperwork. All those things cost the banks money. Since online banks don't do that, they're the cheapest.

2. Credit Unions are non-profit organizations that exist for the benefit of their members. That's why you get better rates from them. If you have an account with them, you're not a customer, you're a **member**. This is really important. It means that if you want to get a loan, they're going to give you what you need without trying to make a ton of profit

off of you. If they do make any profit, they share it with their members in the form of lower interest rates and dividends. They're very friendly and they usually give free cookies and stuff.

3. Community Banks are for-profit companies, so they definitely want to make a profit from you. However, they know that nobody knows who they are. They have no name recognition because they don't have commercials. Worse, there's probably only one or two in the entire city. They know they're at a disadvantage, so they'll give you better rates than bigger banks. Their rates are lower than big banks because of **competition**. Remember, competition is good when you're looking to borrow money.

4. Regional and National Banks are for-profit companies that have no need to compete to get your business. They're like the cheerleading captain or the varsity quarterback: Everybody wants to date them, so they don't even have to *attempt* to win you over. Their rates will not be competitive. However, there is no denying that they are **popular**. It's more likely that they'll have branches all over the state. They may have 24-hour ATMs and 7 days a week customer service. They'll have apps for your phone that will send you notifications. They're undeniably **convenient**. That is their biggest advantage.

5. That's right- car dealerships are dead last. Remember- your biggest advantage when you're looking for loans is that several people have to compete for your money. If you go straight to the dealership, **there is no competition**. Your only choice is what they give you. That's bad.

Step Five: Pick the Car You Want to Buy in Advance

You want to pick the car in advance so that you don't show up to the dealership with an open mind. You **never** want an open mind when you're negotiating. You need to know **exactly** what you want and the terms you want before you even show up. Got it? Cool.

Once you've picked out your car and you know how much it costs, do a search for "total car cost calculator." A good calculator will have the following fields:

- Car Price
- Loan Term (in months)

- Interest Rate
- Down Payment
- Trade-In Value
- Your State
- Sales Tax
- Title, Registration, and Other Fees

You know the first three things, but we haven't talked about the other stuff. These other things are just as important because they will help you figure out the total cost of the loan. The last thing you want to do is to get a loan for the wrong amount. Then you won't have enough money to pay for the car when you go to the dealership.

Down Payments & Trade-In Values
Unless you have excellent credit, you're going to have to either put some cash towards the purchase of the car OR trade in your old car. Which one you do is entirely up to you. I've had times where I traded in my car and I've had a time where I put as much as $1,200 as a down payment. Where did I get that $1,200, you ask? It was what the insurance company gave me when my old car got wrecked by some random teenager in a Burger King parking lot. It's a long story.

That being said, I don't want to get too bogged down into details here. My point is that you probably won't do both a trade-in **and** a down payment. Your trade-in *is* your down payment. If you don't have a trade-in, you'll need to use your own cash. Where you get the cash from is your business.

Just understand that if you are trading in a car, you're not going to get the best price for it. Since the dealership will be buying it, they're going to want a price that's cheaper than it's actually worth. At the very least, you should visit a site like bluebook.com to see what you can expect your car to sell for. That way you'll know if someone's offer is fair or insulting. You can always sell your car to a regular person for more money, but only if the car is paid off and you follow your state's guidelines. You can't sell a car that you're still making payments on. You'd have to go to a dealership to trade it in.

State and Sales Tax
Put in your state and the sales tax for your state. If you don't know,

look it up.

Title, Registration, and Other Fees
You probably don't know what these amounts are off the top of your head. That's ok. Just do a search for your state's average costs for these things. It'll probably be in the low hundreds, but make sure you put it in there.

Lastly, make sure that there's an option that lets you include all the fees in the loan calculation. Now you have your total loan amount and you won't have to worry about not having enough money to buy the car.

Step Six: Apply for a Pre-approved Loan

Pre-approved? Huh? All that means is that you're applying for a loan without knowing the exact dollar amount. You won't know what the *exact* loan amount is going to be until you actually **buy** the car at the dealership. We've only been making estimates up to this point. What you're doing in this step is trying to get approved *up to* a certain dollar amount. So if you've estimated that your car is going to cost $18,376, you'd want to get pre-approved for *up to* $20,000. Let's say your estimate was pretty close and the car ended up costing you $19,012. Your loan amount would $19,012. And since you were pre-approved for $20,000, you had some wiggle room.

At this point, you should still be in your underwear. We're not going to the dealership yet and all the banks have an online application process. Pick the lenders that give the lowest interest rate and a decent customer service experience. If the lender looks bootleg, trust your gut. If you've never heard of them, look them up and see if you can read some reviews. In any case, this is when you start filling out some loan applications.

Get Ready to Have Your Credit Checked…. Hard.

That sounded nasty, but it's accurate. You're going to have to enter your social security number and other info as part of the application process. They will ask permission to check your credit. You don't have a choice, so say yes. This will count as a "Hard Credit Check." It sounds bad, but it's only *kind of* bad. Let me explain:

Hard credit checks, hard pulls, and hard hits all refer to a lender checking your credit to give you a serious offer. Whatever they offer at this point is what will be included in the sales contract. Anytime a lender does a hard credit check, it can affect your credit score- so you only want to allow this to happen when you're serious about getting a loan. Don't go nuts applying for loans and credit. If you're just shopping around, use estimates.

But since you *are* serious about getting a loan at this point, it's ok. Credit bureaus **don't** penalize you for multiple hard credit pulls as long as you're:

> Applying for the same type of loan (in this case, it's an auto loan)
> -AND-
> Applying within a short period of time (within a month or so)

Credit bureaus understand that you're shopping for the best rate and will give you a break. Just in case you were curious, **soft** credit checks exist as well. Soft credit checks don't impact your credit score at all. It's like someone dating you vs proposing to you. They're just checking you out, so they don't need to know your entire history. If you ever get credit card or loan offers in the mail, it's because they did a soft credit pull on you. You didn't ask for it but remember, credit bureaus provide your information to lenders so that those lenders can find potential customers. With credit bureaus, you are not the customer. You are the product.

After a couple of days, you'll get a response from all the lenders. They'll send you a letter, a PDF, or an email telling you:

- How much money you qualify for,
- Your interest rate (the **APR**), and
- How long the loan is for (the **term**).

In that letter, they'll tell you how long their offer is good for. It's usually for 30 days from the date on the letter. All you have to do now is pick the best offer and print it.

Step Seven: Get a Couple of Auto Insurance Quotes

We'll talk more about insurance later, but if this is your first car, you'll have to have insurance before you can drive your new car (or *used* car that's new to you) off the lot. Since you already know the make and model, get quotes for auto insurance off the internet. Once you find the price and coverage you like, start the application for insurance online. You may not be able to finish it because you'll need specific information about the vehicle that the dealership will provide. That's ok. Just save your application's process. You can always come back and finish it later.

If you already have car insurance on the car you're trading in, then you'll just add the new car to your existing policy. You should still get a quote in advance because you don't want any nasty surprises. Some cars cost more to insure because of safety issues, high theft rates, or other reasons you may not be aware of.

Step Eight: *Now* **Go the Dealership**

Armed with your pre-approval letter, you are finally ready to navigate the river. You've got your boat and your paddle. You can finally get dressed and go to the dealership. Don't be in a rush. Be prepared to go to multiple dealerships. Remember, the sales staff at these places are not your friends. They want to make money. That pre-approval letter in your hand will **limit** the amount of money they can make off you and they won't like it. Therefore- and this is *very* important:

Do NOT tell them that you've been pre-approved.

Seriously. Shut up. You want them to believe that you are the typical customer that randomly goes car shopping and is completely open to whatever nonsense they tell you. They know that most people focus on the price and the monthly payments, so play along. You've already done your research on the car price and you're already pre-approved, so this is when you need to use your best poker face.

Your initial goal should be to get the **price** as low as you can get it. The salesperson may actually lower the price- saying that they're running some promotion or whatever. Again, it doesn't matter what they tell you. Don't believe them. As long as the price goes down, that's all you should care about. They're only offering to lower the price because they know they'll get their money back once they give you financing.

The reason is that dealerships make additional profits by working with banks to offer you financing. The banks are happy to get loan business from dealerships. So, they'll offer to mark up the interest rate by 1-2% and give that markup to the dealership. If the dealership tells you the interest rate for your financing is 7%, the odds are that the bank is getting 5% and the dealership is getting 2%. This 2% markup is called a **brokerage fee**. It means the dealership wants to be compensated for sending business to the banks. A TON of businesses work this way behind the scenes and most people don't even realize this kind of thing exists. If you own stocks, you've heard of the term *brokerage* before. It's the company you use to buy stocks. Put simply:

- ✓ **Broker** = The Middleman who connects a Buyer and Seller
- ✓ **Brokerage** = The Middleman's Business
- ✓ **Brokerage Fee** = The Middleman's fee for connecting a Buyer and Seller

Have you ever heard the phrase "The House Always Wins"? Sure you have. That's what they say about casinos. But this phrase also applies to dealerships. Even if they lower the price of the car, they can always raise the total purchase price by adding fees or manipulating the financing terms. This is also why you keep quiet about your pre-approval letter. If they know upfront that you are pre-approved, they won't negotiate on the price of the car and may even charge you a fee for using outside financing.

Now test drive the car. Act disappointed at some random feature that's impossible to change. You want the salesperson to sweeten the deal to make you want to buy the car. When you get back to his or her desk, tell them your "concerns." They'll make you a formal offer. If it's not what you want, suggest a lower price. Tell them you can get a lower price on the internet. Ask them to match that price. They probably will. However, if they don't want to work with you or they refuse to play ball, **leave**. Seriously, get out of there. Don't waste your time haggling with someone that's overcharging you. Go somewhere else and start over.

When you've finally gotten the price that you want (or the price that you expected), allow the salesperson to talk to you about the financing.

They'll need to do another hard pull on your credit. It's ok. Remember that it doesn't count against you if you're doing repeated credit pulls for the same type of loan. They'll come back with a quote for the interest rate and the term of the loan.

It's pretty much a guarantee that their offer won't be as good as your pre-approved loan offer. Tell the salesperson that you'd like a better interest rate. This is usually when you go see the Paperwork Guy. The salesman will disappear for about five minutes and then escort you to the Paperwork Guy's office. The salesman may stay or he or she may leave. It doesn't really matter.

This is when the Paperwork Guy, who is actually called a **Finance Manager**, tells you that because of negative issues with your credit, the interest rate and price they quoted you is the best they can do. Ignore them. This is also when they'll try to sell you things like gap insurance and extended warranties. I'll explain those in the chapter on insurance. For right now though, you don't want any of that stuff. Again-**anything** they suggest you buy at this point just adds to their profit. Some of the things they're suggesting aren't bad ideas, but I guarantee you can get them cheaper if you shop around.

At this point, they'll act all disappointed and treat you like you're making a mistake. You aren't. They'll eventually give up and give you a sheet that has your total cost for the car. It will include all the various charges, sales tax, fees, etc. Just make sure there are no random additional fees. I had one dealership try to charge me for a waxing treatment they put on all their cars. I didn't ask for that, so I refused to pay for it. They took it off. They weren't happy.

After you're satisfied with the price of the car and confirmed the absence of random crap you didn't ask for and don't need....

Now tell them you are pre-approved.

The look on their faces will be priceless. Trust me, they don't normally deal with people who know the process. Be prepared for their tone to completely change. They'll stop smiling and they'll suddenly get very serious. They may even be short with you. Don't let it get to you. You're there to do business, not make friends.

This is the moment of truth. They've revealed their hands and given you a sheet with the total costs. They can't exactly take it back and scribble additional fees on it, so they're going to do one of three things:

1. Thank you for your business AKA Tell you to leave.
2. Say they can't accept financing from outside lenders because of a conflict of interest, some special agreement between the dealership and their lending partners, or some other reason that has nothing to do with you.
3. Begrudgingly move forward with your pre-approved loan.

If it's #1 or #2, go somewhere else. **Never** believe #2. If you had cash, they would take it. Why? Because it's money. The last time I checked, money was an acceptable form of payment for a car. **Be careful!** They're really good at twisting your arm. They may even try to convince you that your pre-approved loan isn't a guarantee and that you might lose the chance to get the car. **Don't waiver.** These are all just sales tactics.

If it's #3, Tell the finance manager the information from your pre-approved offer letter and finish your saved insurance application. The finance manager will most likely call the bank from your letter while you're there. That way, the bank can verify that it's you and the finance manager can give the bank all the information they need. After the phone call, they'll send the loan paperwork to you and/or the finance manager via email or fax. Depending on whether you used an online lender, a credit union, or a bank, this part may be a little different. Some lenders will give you a check or some other paperwork other than just a letter. Just ask them to explain their process beforehand so you're not trying to figure it out at the dealership.

Step Nine: Read Over the Paperwork and Sign It

Alright. So they've sent you a bunch of paperwork that you need to review. Look over it. Make sure that the interest rate and the monthly payment were what you were expecting. Double-check to make sure the loan amount is the same price the finance manager told you earlier. Most importantly, look at your "**Truth-In-Lending**" disclosure. I'll spare you the details of why it's called that and what government law brought it into existence. Just know that it looks like this:

Truth-In-Lending Disclosure

Annual Percentage Rate	Finance Charge	Amount Financed	Total of Payments	Total Sale Price
The cost of your credit as a yearly rate.	The dollar amount the credit will cost you	The amount of credit provided to you or on your behalf	The amount you will have paid when you have made all scheduled payments	The total cost of your purchase on credit, including your down payment of $ 2,000.00
23 %	$ 5,292.44	$ 9,829.00	$ 15,121.44	$ 17,121.44

Payment Schedule. Your payment schedule is

No. of Payments	Amount of Payments	When Payments are Due
48	$ 315.03	Monthly beginning 7/3/2013.
0	$ 0.00	NOT APPLICABLE
0	$ 0.00	NOT APPLICABLE

Security. You are giving us a security interest in the Property purchased.

Late Charge. If all or any portion of a payment is not paid within 10 days of its due date, you will be charged a late charge of 5% of the unpaid amount of the payment due

Prepayment. If you pay off this Contract early, you will not have to pay a penalty.

Contract Provisions. You can see the terms of this Contract for any additional information about nonpayment, default, any required repayment before the scheduled date, and prepayment refunds and penalties.

By the way, you should recognize this example is a horrible, *horrible* deal. This poor soul is about to pay **HALF** the amount of the car in interest *alone*. The interest rate is **insanely** high for a car loan, but it's what you could expect from a "Buy Here, Pay Here" kind of dealership. This is exactly why I wrote this book. If you didn't know any better, you might overlook this disclosure or have some salesperson tell you that these numbers are perfectly normal. They're NOT. Don't believe them. If you ever see a disclosure like this, **immediately** cuss out the person who sent it to you.

This disclosure is the most important page because it tells you what this loan is about in **plain English.** Years ago, when I worked at the bank, lenders didn't have to put this disclosure in their paperwork. That meant that they could bury the important numbers throughout the document. They knew you wouldn't read it- especially not at a sales counter in a dealership. Trust me, bad actors **hate** this required disclosure and will try to gloss over it as fast as they possibly can so that you won't look at it too hard. Let's break it down:

Annual Percentage Rate: Your interest rate. It should be close to what you expected.

Finance Charge: All the interest that you'll pay. It will be a lot, but you already knew that.

Amount Financed: This is how much you're borrowing. It will be the cost of the car, plus taxes.

Total of Payments: The total cost of the loan. This is what you'll pay after all your payments.

Total Sale Price: This is the final price of the car. In this example, the person put a $2,000 down payment, so they're only borrowing $15,121.44.

Number of Payments: How many individual payments you'll make. This example is 48 months or 4 years.

Amount of Payments: How much your monthly payments will be. You should already have an idea of how much this should be.

When Payments Are Due: This is your payment due date. This will be good to know. Some lenders will ask you your preference for the due date. That might be a good option if you have a whole bunch of other bills due on the 1ˢᵗ and you'd like your car payment to be due on the 15ᵗʰ to give you some breathing room.

If everything checks out, sign the paperwork and you're done!

Congratulations! You just scored a car that you want at the price, interest rate, and monthly payment that **YOU** wanted. It's a big accomplishment- one I hope you'll repeat for anything you buy in the future. Now take the keys and go to IHOP. You deserve pancakes.

CHAPTER THIRTEEN
Get an Affordable House That's Also an Investment

1. Shop for the best rates before you apply for a loan.
2. Get pre-approved for a loan before you talk to real estate agents.
3. Take advantage of government programs to save money on down payments and interest.

Buying a house is a lot like buying a car. You'll still get a loan and you'll still have to sign a bunch of documents. It's just that now you'll be on the hook for 15 or 30 years instead of 4-7 years. And since it's a *much* more expensive purchase, you'll probably want to take more time researching. This research is called **due diligence**. (Get used to this term. It basically means "let me do my homework so that I don't get ripped off.")

Buying a house is a pretty straightforward process…if you have a ton of cash lying around. Here's how it would work for the wealthier among us:

"Traditional" Home Buying
1. Find a house you want.
2. Put 20% in cash as a down payment on the house.
3. Finance the other 80% with a traditional bank loan.

What's that you say? You don't have the $25,000+ for the down payment? That's ok. It just means that you're like most normal people. This is how it works for the 99%:

Realistic Home Buying
1. Figure out how much money a bank will qualify you for.
2. Put 5% in cash as a down payment OR
3. Use some government program to **not** have to make a down payment at all.
4. Finance up to 105% with a government-approved lender.

Step One: Check Out Housing Prices

Housing prices can be all over the place- even within the same zip code. It's probably a good idea to shop around on the internet to give you an idea of how much a house is going to cost you. More than likely, you're going to buy a house from someone who wants to sell theirs, but there are a few occasions where you'll see a brand-new house for sale in a newly-built community. You can also have a house built from scratch.

My point is that you have options. However, you still need to know how much these options will cost. Try not to make any assumptions about pricing based on your current level of understanding or what you've heard from friends and family. Look it up yourself. Here are some good resources.

- Zillow.com
- Opendoor.com
- Orchard.com
- Redfin.com
- Trulia.com

All of these sites do the same thing: You type in an address and it'll tell how much that house costs. If you don't have an address, you can just open a map of the area you're interested in and you can zoom in and out on what you want. You may be pleasantly surprised that a nice area you like isn't that expensive. Conversely, you may be shocked to find that an area known for gunshots and drag racing is *insanely* expensive. Here are a few things that can affect home prices:

1. **Neighborhood comps**: If you ever say, "comps," people will assume you're a real estate agent. It's not a term regular people use. Here's what it means:

✓   **Comps** = sale prices of comparable homes in that neighborhood that have recently sold.

It's not an exact science. It goes something like this:

- I want to sell my 3-bedroom, 2-bathroom house with a garage.
- Some guy in the neighborhood just sold his 3-bedroom, 2-bathroom house with a garage for $150,000.
- Therefore, *my* house is worth $150,000.

Does it mean your house will actually sell for $150,000? No. It just means that you could expect to sell it for *roughly* the same price. If your neighbor spent a lot of money updating the kitchens and bathrooms and you haven't updated anything, the chances are that you won't get as much as he did.

2. **Location, location, location:** this is WAY more important than I realized when I bought my first house. The closer your house is to desirable things, the more expensive your house is likely to be. Those desirable things are:

- High-quality schools
- Good-paying employment opportunities
- Shopping, entertainment, parks and other fun stuff

None of these things may be important to you right now, but don't be shortsighted. When you attempt to sell your home in the future, these things **will** be important to the people who are looking to buy. If you're already in a good location, buyers will have to compete to bid on your house. Remember- anytime people compete to get your business, you win.

3. **Age, Condition, and Upgrades**: newer houses typically cost more than old houses. Why? Because old houses need work- a lot of work. If you buy an old house, you are buying all the problems and issues that the house has. Trust me, there **will** be issues and you need to have the home professionally inspected before you buy it. Don't worry- a **home inspection report** is usually part of the home buying process, so it'll likely get done regardless. Just be sure to read it and take it seriously.

Please don't be like me. I got a home inspection done and didn't bother to read it all. Years later, I had all kinds of problems with my house- ALL of which were mentioned on the home inspection report. I got so excited about my house that I didn't do my due diligence. I got ripped off. Royally. This brings up an important thing to keep in mind when buying a home that used to belong to someone else: Every homeowner is different.

Some homeowners continually improve the property- which will make their house look better than all the other homes in the area. This house won't need much work at all (if any). Other homeowners don't improve it at all and just "stay" in the house- hoping to save their money to buy a better house. That means that it's going to cost you to do some maintenance that's slightly overdue. You'll likely need to repair the roof, get some new carpet, and get a fresh coat of paint. These aren't deal-breakers, but you'll need to keep these costs in mind when you look at prices.

Lastly, some homeowners completely neglect the care and maintenance of their homes. Maintenance will be seriously overdue and the house likely has serious issues including water damage, foundation issues, mold, and leaking. More than likely, the home will need to have the roof and siding completely replaced. Each of these things costs thousands of dollars. These types of houses are often called "fixer-uppers." Also, if you're ever looking online and it says that a house needs "TLC" (Tender Loving Care), **be careful**. That's a nice way of saying that the house is a dump that will need major renovation just to be *livable*.

It'll be fairly obvious what type of homeowner you're dealing with once you start visiting prospective homes, but keep this in mind:

- Updated homes will likely cost **more** than the comps.
- Homes **without** updates will be in line with the comps.
- Neglected Homes will likely cost **less** than the comps.

Step Two: Look Up Mortgage Rates Using Your Credit Score

Just like with an auto loan, we're going to go online and check out rates. You could even do a search for "current mortgage rates." Again,

I like using bankrate.com anytime I research loan stuff. At this point, you should already know your credit score, so use Bankrate or Google to see what interest rate you can expect to pay with your score. Get in the habit of knowing your credit score and looking up rates before you start applying for loans. It'll save you a lot of time.

Step Three: Figure Out Your Monthly Payment

Now that you have a pretty good idea of what interest rate range you're looking at, do a search for "mortgage loan calculator." You know the drill. Type in the interest rate and the cost of the house you want. The difference with a mortgage loan is that you only have 2 choices:

1. A 30-year loan, and
2. A 15-year loan.

Thirty-year loans will have lower monthly payments because you have more time to pay the loan. However, the interest rate will be higher and 30 years is a LOT of time for you to rack up interest charges. Conversely, A 15-year loan will save you thousands of dollars in interest because you're paying a lower interest rate over a shorter period of time. However, the monthly payment amount might be a little too high for comfort. People who choose 15-year loans typically have a large amount of cash on hand, so they're not too concerned with the high payment. If you're on a budget, the 30-year loan might be the better plan. You could always pay off the 30-year loan early by making additional payments.

The calculator is where you can see just how much house you can really afford. Right now in March 2021, the interest rate is hovering around 3%. That's the lowest it's been in years, but house prices are now super high as well. As you can see by playing with the numbers in the calculator, lowering the interest rate makes your payment *lower*. However, increasing the price of the home makes your payment *higher*. This can create a situation where a high-interest, low-priced home could have the **same** monthly payment as a low-interest, high-priced home.

This can get tricky. At some point, you may want (or need) to sell your home. Even if you got a low interest rate, you may not want to commit to paying a really high price because housing prices can go down. If you owe more on your house than the market says it's worth, your house is considered **upside-down** or **underwater**. This is what happened during the housing crash of 2008. I got caught up in this myself. I bought a home for $110,000. At the height of the crash, my home was only worth $27,000. I still owed over **$90,000**. I was beyond depressed, mad and frustrated. The values eventually got better, but it took **ten years** and I basically broke even when I sold it. I don't want this to happen to you.

CAUTION: There is another loan option called an Adjustable Rate Mortgage (**ARM**). These allow you to have a really low fixed interest for the first couple of years, but then it *adjusts* to some higher amount after a specified time period- like 3 years. It means your interest rates will start changing **all the time** after your time period ends. It will be variable- just like your credit card. For most people, this is **BAD**. Just like with any non-traditional financial product, there's a time and place for this kind of strategy. For example, if you had planned on paying off the house during that fixed period, it's a great strategy. You'd save money. It would also mean that you have a ton of cash lying around. Most people can't pay off a whole house in 3 years. What makes these bad is that sketchy lenders (and even some big banks) marketed these loans to people who had no intention of paying off their houses early. Worse, these lenders pushed people to borrow more than they should have. When I was looking for my first home, one lender approved me for $175,000. I made $27,000 a year working at a bank inside of a grocery store. There's no way I could have afforded the monthly payment on that amount with the interest rate I qualified for. "It's ok," they said. "Just do an ARM loan and refinance once the fixed period is over. That way you can afford the payment."

This right here is why so many people lost their homes in the housing crash. Hell, this is *why* the housing crash happened. Folks, there's **no guarantee** that you can refinance when your fixed period ends. Even if you could, you'd have to pay closing costs **again**- costing you thousands of dollars. Do your own homework and **don't trust anyone who gets paid by selling stuff to you.**

Step Four: Find the Lowest Interest Rate

Remember: Online Banks and Credit Unions give you the best interest rates for mortgage loans. Check out the chapter on auto loans to see why.

Step Five: See If Your State Offers Any Home Buying Incentives

It is **very** likely that your state offers **multiple** programs designed to help first-time homeowners purchase a home. These programs are designed to help get around the typical requirements of buying a home, like:

- A 5% required down payment for conventional loans
- A 3.5% minimum down payment for government-backed (FHA) loans
- Closing costs
- Mortgage insurance (PMI)

If you're buying your first house in 2021, chances are that your house is going to cost at least $150,000. If you were required to pay 5% as a down payment, you would need to magically produce $7,500 in cold, hard cash. If you had to pay 3.5% down, that would still be $5,250. Now I don't know about you, but I had **nowhere near** that around lying around when I bought my first house. I think I had $500(?). The point is: I was broke, but I still got a house! On top of that, I didn't have to pay a down payment at all. Here's why:

First-Time Homebuyers Programs: The great thing about buying a house for the first time is that there are all kinds of programs designed to help you. Most of these programs and loans are offered by your state, but a few are offered by the federal government as well. Can you say *yes* to any of these questions?

- **FHA loan (Federal Housing Authority):** Are you wealth-challenged?

- **USDA loan (Yes, the steak agency):** Do you live in the middle of nowhere?

- **VA loan (Veterans Affairs):** Are you a veteran?

- **Native American Direct Loans:** Are you a veteran AND a

Native American?

- **Good Neighbor Next Door:** Are you a cop, a teacher, or some other public servant that is willing to live in a sketchy neighborhood to get a 50% discount?

- **Fannie Mae & Freddie Mac:** Are you wealth-challenged AND open to the idea that your mortgage will be packaged into some weird financial product that can potentially bring down the entire economy just like in 2008? Ok, so I'm still bitter.

- **Fannie Mae's HomePath Ready Buyer Program:** Are you willing to take an online education course to get 3% in closing cost assistance on foreclosed "HomePath" properties owned by Fannie Mae that may or may not be available?

- **State & Local First Time Homebuyer Programs:** Do you live in a state?

If you said yes to any of these programs, **Congratulations!** You can be broke and *still* get a house. I was broke and I got a house, so I know this works.

Why and How the Government Gets Involved in Mortgages

The important thing to understand here is that **banks want to minimize the risk of lending to you**. They want somebody to pay their money back in case something goes wrong. They don't care *who* pays it back- just that it's paid back. The government wants to make sure that its citizens have access to affordable housing that doesn't discriminate against income levels, so they work with the banks to minimize that lending risk. This is why government-backed loans typically don't have things like Private Mortgage Insurance (PMI) and down payments: the federal or state government is guaranteeing the loan. This means that the government agrees to buy the mortgage from the bank in case you bail.

This effectively means that the **government owns the house**. This is why you hear terms like "HUD homes" and "Government-owned properties." When you hear that, it means that the original bank lender is off the hook and you would buy your house *directly* from the government. Since the government owns these houses now, they'll try to sell them at a discount to people who may struggle with getting a traditional mortgage and need assistance buying a home.

Technically, they'll sell them to *anybody*, but they'd prefer that you're someone that's actually wanting to live in the home and improve it. If you're interested in buying a HUD (Department of Housing and Urban Development) home, then it's likely going to be a fixer-upper. These properties have been abandoned, after all. People don't tend to abandon beautiful homes.

Let's define a few terms real quick because they're going to keep coming up:

Closing Costs

Closing costs are all the random fees and expenses you didn't even *think* about when you decided it would be exciting to buy a house. Warning: this list is long, so I'm going to make it as un-boring as possible by explaining it my way. Explaining each of these things properly would take another book. Feel free to Google this stuff if you want a "serious" explanation.

Attorney Fees: lawyers found a brilliant way to make money by making people sign real estate documents in their offices.

Title Service Costs: lawyers team up with businesses called Title Insurance companies to make sure that the house you're buying (and the land that it sits on) doesn't actually belong to some dead person or their descendants. Just imagine if you bought a house and then some random person said it was theirs? It would suck, but it can happen.

Recording Costs: the fee for changing the name on the property from the seller's name to your name. It's the government. What can I say?

Taxes. Forgot about the tax, didn't you? And you thought buying a house would be awesome.

Survey Fee. If it hasn't already been done, someone's got to go out there and physically measure the property to make sure that the measurements and the boundaries of the property are correct and aren't owned by anybody else. The *last* thing you want is to find out that there's a 20-foot wide lane of state property going through the middle of your house. Yes, it can happen.

Brokerage Commission: this is the money that goes to all the real estate agents and real estate agencies involved. Remember the previous chapter when I said that the **Brokerage Fee** was the middleman's fee for connecting a Buyer and Seller? Well, this time the **real estate agents** are the middlemen/women. They connected the seller of the house and the buyer of the house (aka YOU), so they get to collect a fee. It's one of the biggest (if not *the* biggest) closing costs for home sales. However, it's totally possible to buy a house without real estate agents being involved. Usually, that happens when an investor uses cash to buy a "fixer-upper" or the buyer and seller know each other (like family members).

Mortgage Application Fees. Yes, you have to pay to apply for a mortgage at your bank or credit union. The lender charges you to check your credit and do all their due diligence on **you** to make sure you're not likely to abandon the house and rip out all the copper in the walls.

Points. Here's another insider term. If you say, "points" when you're shopping around for loans, people will suddenly respect you more. They'll be like: "Ooh, he said *points*, let's pull out the *real* application." It means you're paying for a discount. Paying points means you pay money upfront to reduce the interest rate on that loan. It sounds like a down payment, but it isn't. I'll explain. Let's say that the interest rate that you qualify for is 4.125%, but you are firm on wanting an interest rate of 4% because you spent way too much time on that loan calculator and you know 0.125% will still end up costing you thousands of dollars long-term. The bank might offer to lower your rate to 4% if you agree to pay 1% of the loan upfront. If the loan you're approved for is $100,000, 1 point would cost you $1,000. 2 points would cost you $2,000, and so on and so on. But be aware- while a point usually costs 1% of the loan, the amount of the interest rate discount **is up to the lender.** Don't go around telling people that I told you that 1 point equals a discount of 0.125%.

Appraisal Fees. This is where someone drives by your house, (maybe) gets out, and walks around the house for sale while rubbing their chin and frowning. A lot of times, they'll take pictures- which makes nosy neighbors want to "introduce" themselves to find out what the heck is going on. This **appraiser** better have some business cards and a good explanation or there might be some drama. The appraiser's job is to let the lending bank know how much the house is actually worth. It's not an exact science, but the banks trust them completely for whatever reason. If you're black and you're wanting to sell your home, have one of your white friends act like the homeowner when the appraiser arrives and your home's value will miraculously increase 23%. I wish this were a joke.

Inspection Fees. It's a good idea to have the house inspected for roaches, rats and termites and stuff. This a good, good fee. You don't want to buy a home that you later find out has a giant killer beehive in the crawl space. I'm serious. That kind of thing happens more than you think. This is also when a **Home Inspector** comes and inspects the home for sale for general maintenance and structural issues. They'll report any problems with the roof, the foundation, the siding, the HVAC (Heating, Ventilation, & Air Conditioning) and the plumbing. They'll also give general recommendations for what things need to be repaired now vs later. It is *super* important to read this report. I glossed over mine when I bought my first home. It cost me over **$20,000** in completely avoidable repairs. I'm still mad about it. Also, if your real estate agent tells you *not* to worry about something in that report, **find another agent**. Ok- I'm done. I promise. Maybe.

Home Warranties. Whoever invented this racket is a genius. It's like an extended warranty for your whole house. It's supposed to give you "peace of mind" when you're buying a house full of uncertainties and potential disasters. It usually covers all the "major household systems" for up to a year or two after buying a house. Fridge not working? Call the Home Warranty Company! Garbage disposal on the fritz? Call the Home Warranty Company! However, be prepared to wait for weeks to get things *actually* repaired. You'll usually get someone to look at the problem within a day or two but ordering parts could take a while. Can you go for weeks without a fridge? Just sayin'.

CAUTION: real estate agents love to say, "just buy a home warranty" when something like the A/C unit is ancient and clearly broken. **Do not believe them**. It has to be working when you move in. Home Warranty companies aren't idiots and they know people try to game the system. They won't fix stuff that was already broken before you moved in. Then you'll have to end up buying something new anyway-which can cost you thousands. Me? I had to end up buying an entirely new furnace AND an air conditioner. It cost me $9,000. See how easily this can get out of hand?

Private Mortgage Insurance (PMI). Another good insider term. However, *never* ask "Does this loan have private mortgage insurance?" You'll *instantly* lose respect. It's like asking someone you're dating if you can touch their genitals. Of course you can't. Because **no one** says it that way. They'll tell you that they're busy and that you should make an appointment for February 31ˢᵗ. Say it this way: "What's the PMI on this?" Not only will you get the real application, but they'll also fetch you a bottle of water as well. After all, you must be important.

PMI is what banks make you get if your down payment is less than 20%. Banks see your 20% down payment as your "skin in the game." They figure that if you don't have any skin in the game, you're way more likely to abandon your obligation to pay the loan. To fix this, banks came up with a solution- mortgage insurance. This is **NOT** home insurance. Home insurance protects you- the homeowner. Mortgage insurance protects the banks *against* you - or rather- what you *might* do. This insurance would reimburse the bank if you ever bailed on the loan. Insurance costs money, so they're passing the cost to you. It will have a monthly cost that usually gets included in your mortgage payment, but the bank may require that you pay an entire year upfront as part of the closing costs. They may require that you pay this every year until you've got 20% equity in the home. Once you've reached that amount, they'll drop the requirement and your mortgage payment becomes a little cheaper. Real quick:

o   **Equity** = The Appraised Value of the Home *minus* Mortgage Loan Balance

Remember: Government programs offer down payment assistance while also guaranteeing mortgage loans. You may not have to pay PMI on government-backed loans.

Pre-Paid Homeowner's Insurance:
Just like insurance on your car, you have to get Homeowner's insurance. It's not really an option. However, you can price shop from

different providers like GEICO and Allstate. Pretty much anyone who sells car insurance will also sell home insurance. As far as closing costs go, the buyer (**you**) might be required to have a year's worth of insurance paid upfront. The idea is that you don't want your policy lapsing because you're so focused on moving and settling in your new home. Trust me, settling in takes longer than you think. I never did have a housewarming for my first home. I kept putting it off. I had stuff that stayed in boxes until I sold the house.

Here's something important that you should know though: Most home insurance policies **DON'T** cover flooding. This is a big deal. If you live on the coast or right next to a river or a lake, you're **required** to get it. If you live in the mountains, there's nearly a 0% chance that you'll experience a flood, so it's **optional**. The problem is everywhere in between; places that don't normally flood but *can* every once in a while. Those places don't require flood insurance, but you should definitely consider buying it. It will cost more, but you will avoid the complete financial devastation of a flood. Floods can literally wash away everything you own **overnight**. Most people don't realize that they don't have flood insurance until it's too late.

Pro-rata Property Taxes. This sounds complicated, but it's not. It just means that the yearly property taxes need to be paid fairly between the buyer and the seller. For example, if you bought the house on January 1ˢᵗ, you would owe all the property tax for the year. The seller already paid their property taxes for the previous year, so they wouldn't owe anything. However, the odds are that you and the seller haven't coordinated this transaction to consider a tax strategy. So if you buy the house in October, the property taxes for the year have likely already been paid by the seller. Well, since you're moving on October 1st, it's not fair for the seller to pay property taxes on a house they no longer live in. You'll need to pay 3 months' worth (Oct, Nov, & Dec) of property taxes for that year for it to be fair.

By the way, you have to pay property tax if you own a house. I probably should have mentioned that first. This "house" thing just gets better and better, doesn't it? You don't have any control over the amount. You just get a bill and you have to pay. The more your property value increases, the higher the tax. If you ever hear people talking about **gentrification**, this is the reason why. As the area you live in becomes more popular, your property taxes could double or triple. This is inconvenient, but you're not exactly mad because that also means that you're getting more and more **equity**. It's just that you have to pay property taxes **now** and you won't *fully* benefit from higher property values until you sell the house **later**. Sometimes, the property tax is included in your mortgage payment and you don't have to think about it. However, that could mean that your mortgage payment amount **increases** over time.

Pro-rata Homeowner's Association Dues. This works the same way. Any dues are split between the buyer and seller to make sure everything is fair. What's a Homeowner's Association? That's a whole other book. It's basically like the Jedi council of your subdivision or your neighborhood. They get to decide what is "proper" for the exterior of your home and your yard. If you cross them or disobey their commandments, you will receive a passive-aggressive letter reminding you of the "community guidelines." If you ignore them, they'll penalize you with a fine for **every day you don't fix the problem**. Don't even *think* of putting that anime-inspired wooden practice dummy in your backyard. Association dues are usually billed to you monthly for things like landscaping and neighborhood amenities like playgrounds, pools and gazebos. They serve an important function but are typically run by lunatics who have Obsessive Compulsive Disorder with a hint of Napoleon Complex. Don't say I didn't warn you.

Whew! That's it for the closing costs. So back to what we were talking about.

Step Six: Apply for a Pre-approved Loan

Now that you know *way* more than you asked for, you can make sure that the banks you're looking at are government-approved lenders that will help you get the right type of government-backed loan. Most likely, you'll be applying for an **FHA loan**. If there are any requirements for points, PMI, down payments or any of that other stuff, the bank will let you know before you even start applying. Pick the one that works best for your situation. Just remember that this will count as a hard credit pull, so only apply when you're actually ready to move.

Just like with the car loan, you'll get a response from all the lenders.

They'll let you know the amount you qualify for and your interest rate (the APR). Again- the lenders will tell you how long their offer is good for. It's usually for 30 days from the date on the letter. But unlike with car shopping, there's no need to print it. We're not going to use this letter as a negotiating tool this time. Mortgages are more regulated, so it's harder for bad actors to screw you over. It's not impossible, but it is less likely. We just need an amount that we can keep in our head and communicate to the real estate agent- should you choose to use one.

Step Seven: Go See Some Houses

Now that you've done all the legwork, it's time to start visiting some of the houses listed for sale on the sites I mentioned at the beginning of the chapter a million pages ago. You have a few options.

1. Contact the real estate agent/agency from the listing online. This is the **listing agent**- the one that represents the seller(s) of the house.
2. Contact that friend or family member that does real estate on the side. You know who they are. This will be the **buyer's agent**- the one that represents the buyer of the house (that's you).
3. Drive by the house all creeper-like unannounced (sketchy, but educational)

Obviously, if you want to go inside and actually see the interior of the home, you'll need to schedule an appointment with the listing agent OR tell your (buyer's) agent that you're interested in seeing a **listing** (a house *listed* on whatever website you used). Either way, you shouldn't be talking directly to the existing homeowners unless you know them personally. The listing agent will agree to show you and your agent around or leave a way for you and your agent to get into the house to look at it yourselves.

Truthfully, you'll know if the house is right for you pretty quickly. Houses have "vibes." That sounds weird but trust me. The second you step into a home with a vibe that doesn't fit you, you'll want to leave immediately. As soon as you step into the "right" house, you just *know*. However, don't fall in love just yet. You should still get the house inspected and check out the neighborhood. Drive by at night and during rush hour traffic to make sure that it works for you. Most house visits are on the weekend during the daytime. You most likely won't have any traffic at all then. But if you move there, you'll be dealing with potential bad traffic 5 days out of 7. Also, visiting at night helps you know if it's safe to walk around after dark. Please don't be like me and realize after buying my house that the neighborhood had no street lights or sidewalks. After sundown, if people didn't have their porch lights on, it was pitch black. It was pretty sketchy.

If you like the house you'll tell your agent that you want to buy it and he or she will tell the listing agent. If you and the seller agree on the price, the house becomes **under contract**. That's not just a fancy term. It's an actual contract that you and the seller sign. It doesn't mean you've bought it yet. It just means you've reserved it until you've completed all the paperwork, financing, and filing required for the legal purchase of a house. After that, the listing is updated as being under contract and no more potential buyers can make offers.

This is the point where you get inspections and stuff done. You want to make sure nothing is wrong with the house. There might also be some cosmetic things you want to be fixed or replaced. You may even decide to lower your offer based on what you find out or ask that certain maintenance be completed before you agree to purchase the home. The seller may agree, or they may tell you to kick rocks. Either way, if the two of you agree, the deal moves on. If not, the deal falls apart and the house is no longer under contract. Just keep this in mind: once you put a house under contract, the buyer (you) may be asked or required to put up "good faith" money. This could be $500 or it could be $2,000. If you come up with some lame excuse and decide not to buy the house, you could lose that money as a penalty for wasting the seller's time. If there is a serious issue that was found during the inspection that was never disclosed, that's another story. However, if you do buy the house, that good faith money would go towards the purchase of the home. You wouldn't lose it.

Step Seven: Get a Couple of Home Insurance Quotes

Just like with a car, you'll have to have insurance before you get the keys to the house. It'll be easy to get quotes online because you'll have the address and all the details of the house already. If you already have a car, get a quote from your car's insurance company as well. Sometimes they'll give discounts if you insure multiple things with the same insurance company.

Step Eight: Close on the House

Alright, you've visited the house, put it under contract, and the seller agreed to replace all the old carpet but didn't agree to replace the kitchen countertops. That's ok. You win some, you lose some. In any case, you and the owner agree to move forward and all the inspection and legal stuff check out. Now you're going to close on the house. It just means you're closing the deal and finalizing the sale.

The buyer's agent(your agent) and/or the listing agent will get with a law firm they trust and set a date for both you and the seller to come into the law firm's offices and sign the paperwork. Typically, you're not there at the same time. The seller has their appointed time and so do you. The law firm will sit you down in some little room with a bunch of pens and some bottled water. Your agent may be there with you, but it really doesn't matter at this point. The lawyer kind of works like a neutral third party that only enters the process to make sure everyone gets paid fairly and that all the documents are written properly and signed appropriately. They're kind of like quality control. This is also when your agent gets paid, so there's a good chance they'll ghost you like a one-night stand once this is over.

Congratulations! You own a house! Now you get to yell at your neighbor for the next ten years about keeping his leaves/kids/dogs/guests/drunk kids/drunk guests out of your yard. It'll be awesome.

CHAPTER FOURTEEN
Insurance Stuff You Need to Know

At some point, you're going to need and/or want insurance. In fact, sometimes you're legally required to have it. Any time you have to choose a plan from your job or if you are looking for insurance on your own, use this chapter as a reference. Here's the insurance you're **required** to have:

- Auto insurance
- Home insurance

Here are the **optional** types of insurance:

- Life insurance
- Dental insurance
- Health insurance
- Vision insurance
- Renter's insurance

Each type of insurance could realistically have its own chapter or its own *book*. As far as coverage needs, strategies, and all that stuff; it's probably best to do additional research on your own. My goal is to quickly explain some of the terms you're going to see over and over again.

Policy Period: the time frame when your insurance policy is effective. It's usually a year for most insurance but can be longer based on the type of insurance you're buying.

Premium: what you pay to have insurance. It can usually be paid monthly, once every six months, once a year, or all at once for a specified period of time. Your premium will be the total of all the various features and benefits of your insurance coverage. The more benefits your plan is, the more it will cost. Low premium plans are attractive for your budget but may not include the benefit you need for adequate coverage.

Home & Auto Insurance

Deductible: the money you have to pay out of your own pocket **before** the insurance company pays anything. For example, if a rock hits your car on the highway and your insurance has a $1,000 deductible, you have to pay $1,000 before the insurance company pays anything. If the repair only costs $800, there's no point in calling your insurance company because you'll have to pay out of your pocket regardless. On the other hand, if your car gets **totaled** (completely wrecked or deemed not worth repairing), then paying $1,000 suddenly isn't such a bad deal. You'll get the cash value of your car and money for injuries if you have any.

Plans with high deductibles cost less because the insurance company knows you won't call about small damages like a rock hitting your windshield. Plans with low deductibles cost more because you're more likely to file a claim for minor repairs and damages. Be careful though: the more claims you make, the more expensive your policy will be when it comes time to renew.

Liability. If anyone gets hurt on your property or if you hurt someone while driving in your vehicle, you are **liable** for that person's costs for receiving medical attention, replacing lost wages, getting a new car, etc. Your liability protection will be a fixed dollar amount. Every state has a minimum amount you must have, but you can always choose to buy a higher dollar amount of liability coverage. This will increase your premium, but it may be worth it if the accident is really bad. If the damages you cause are higher than your liability coverage amount, you are responsible for the balance. That could bankrupt you or cause you to have your wages garnished.

Gap Insurance: insurance you buy to act as protection against

depreciation. When you buy a car, it begins to lose value the minute you drive it off the lot. That's depreciation. You've probably heard this term before. It basically means that the more you use it, the less "new" it becomes. Since it's no longer new, you can't charge the "new" price for a used car. I think everyone understands that part.

However, there's a second part to a car's value that isn't so obvious: the reliability and expected lifetime of a car. For example, Hondas last longer than Kias. On average, they also require less maintenance over the life of the car. That means that a Honda will **retain** its value and depreciate **slower** over time. A Kia is a good car, but the lower life span and increased maintenance must be considered when figuring out the value of a car. Consequently, if a Honda and a Kia were the exact same price brand new, the Kia would be worth *less* than the Honda a year later.

This becomes a **big deal** if you ever get in an accident while you're still making payments on your car loan. Why? If the accident is bad enough to where your auto insurance company **totals** the car, the insurance company is only obligated to pay you what the car is worth, NOT how much you owe on your car loan. This means that there could be a **gap** in the amount that you owe and the value of the car. For a Honda, the gap may not be that large because Hondas retain their value. For a Kia, the gap may be big- like more than a thousand dollars big.

You would assume that your insurance company would pay off your loan. **They don't**. They only write you a check for the value of the car. That means that you could *still* owe money to the bank for a car **you don't even have anymore.** With gap insurance, you pay around $20-$40 a month so that can't happen to you. If your auto insurance company totals your car, the gap insurance will pay any leftover balance.

Anytime you buy a car, the dealership will always offer gap insurance. However, just like you can get a loan outside of a dealership, you can get gap insurance outside of the dealership. Just call your auto insurance company to get a quote. I'm willing to bet it'll be cheaper than whatever the dealership is offering.

Extended Warranties. In general, extended warranties are not the best use of your money and they are largely unnecessary. Every car maker provides a manufacturer (or factory) warranty that covers most of the internal components of the car. Best of all, it's **free.** It's included with the purchase of the car. However, it can get a little confusing because there is no such thing as a *standard* car warranty.

Every car manufacturer offers different warranties based on the reputation of the vehicle and the brand.

Car manufacturers know what the "word on the street" is for their brand and the cars they make, so they attempt to reassure consumers with manufacturer warranties that address consumer opinions. For example, in the mid-'90s, Hyundai had a horrible reputation for making cars that had early transmission failures. I drove a Hyundai. My transmission failed. The reputation was justified. Back then, I would have never recommended a Hyundai.

So what did Hyundai do? Around 2000, Hyundai promised an unheard of (at the time) 100,000-mile transmission warranty. The common belief was that cars tended to be problem-free until 100,000 miles, so the warranty addressed the reputation regarding their transmissions while also showing that Hyundai was willing to stand behind their product. This new warranty was **not** an extended warranty. It was the regular manufacturer warranty that came with the car. If you were my friend and you wanted to buy a Hyundai *before* they announced this new warranty, I would tell you not to UNLESS you got an extended warranty that would cover transmission failure. Are you starting to see what I'm getting at?

Extended warranties are good if you want to protect yourself against the **increased likelihood of failures of lower-quality products**. Under normal operation and routine maintenance, a quality-made car won't randomly break down. There's no need to buy extended warranties on cars with a great reputation. They earned that reputation **for a reason.** However, cars with great reputations cost more. So if you're on a budget, but you still want something that looks nice and has the features you want, you may have to roll the dice with a budget brand that has a reputation for being *less* dependable. An extended warranty may be good in that situation. If you buy one, you **recognize** that the quality of the item you're buying is suspect.

Some extended warranties offer protection against freak accidents and damages as well. You'll see this a lot for things like car batteries and new tires. It doesn't matter how well a tire was made; if you run over a nail, it's going to go flat. An extended warranty that covers **damages** would protect you in that situation. In any case, you can buy extended warranties from almost anybody within a certain time after buying the item. You don't have to buy them from dealerships.

Health, Dental, & Vision Insurance

You can get health, dental and vision insurance through your job **or** you can buy it *yourself* for you and your family.

- If you get it through your job, it's considered a **group** plan.
- If you get in on your own, it's considered an **individual** plan.

Group plans just mean you're buying it as a person that's part of a bigger group, like "Coca-Cola employees." It's usually cheaper than individual insurance because insuring a group is less risky than insuring one individual.

Regardless of whether it's a group or individual plan, health insurance has a lot of things that make it hard to figure out the expenses you are responsible for vs. what your insurance company is responsible for, so let's take a little more time to look at what's involved.

Deductible. It's the same as auto and home insurance. It's the money you have to pay out of your own pocket before the insurance company pays anything. Once you pay the amount of your deductible, your deductible has been "met." *Now* all the benefits and coverages you paid for kick in.

Also, your deductible resets every year. If your deductible is $5,000 and you paid $4,999.99 out of your pocket by Dec 31, you have to start over at $0 the very next day. If you had knee surgery on Jan 1, you'd have to pay another $5,000 before the insurance company pays anything. Keep track of your deductible and try to plan your known medical expenses beforehand so that this doesn't happen.

Co-pay: the amount **you** pay every time you visit the doctor, dentist, or eye doctor. It's usually in the $30-$50 range and you pay upfront before you're seen. If your plan has a co-pay, you pay it **regardless** of what your deductible is. In fact, co-pays typically don't count towards your yearly deductible. The **benefit** is that you don't have to worry about meeting a deductible just to go see your doctor.

Co-insurance: the percentage **you** must pay any time you see your benefit coverage expressed as a percentage. For example, your plan could be an 80/20 plan. That means the costs are split 80/20. If the coinsurance is 20%, then you know the 20 "side" is what **you** are responsible for. **You** must pay 20% of all the costs *after* you meet your deductible. In this same example, if the coinsurance was 80%, then you'd want to keep shopping. That would mean you're responsible for 80% after meeting the deductible. That would be really, really bad.

In-Network. Every insurance company has a list of doctors and hospitals that have agreed to accept their insurance coverage. In order for you to receive all the benefits and services that are presented to you when you signed up for your policy, you'll need to go to an In-Network provider. If you don't know, **ask**. **Never (ever!)** assume that a doctor or hospital is In-Network. I know it's ridiculous to ask you to plan for random accidents. However, try your best to know which hospitals in your area are in-network and choose a plan that is accepted by the closest one to your home in case you have an emergency.

Out-of-Network. Insurance companies have to allow for the fact that you may not be near an in-network provider when you need services or have a health emergency. If you are in another state or out of the country, you are still covered. However, since you are now **out of network**, the costs will be significantly higher. Like **way** higher. The closest hospital may be out-of-network; meaning you'll have to have the ambulance drive you past a perfectly good hospital just so you don't go bankrupt because of an emergency.

HMOs vs PPOs:

Typically, when you have to choose a health insurance plan, you'll have a choice between HMO and PPO.

- HMO = more limitations and restrictions at a cheaper cost.
- PPO = more freedom to do whatever you want at a higher cost.

HMO (Health Maintenance Organization)

There are more rules you'll need to follow in order to save money. With HMOs, there may be **no** Out-of-Network coverage. You'll have to choose from a list of participating providers. Also, you'll have to choose a primary doctor who has to refer you to see someone else before you can see a specialist. Let's say you break your leg. After you get discharged from the emergency room in a temporary cast or splint, you'll have to see your primary doctor *first*; **then** he or she will refer you to the bone doctor that will fix your broken bone. When you aren't sure why you're feeling bad, an HMO is a good system; there's a fact-finding process that eventually gets you to the right specialist. However, when it's obvious what the problem is, it would be nice to go straight to the specialist without needing a recommendation.

PPO (Preferred Provider Organization)

This plan lets you go straight to a specialist without referrals. If you have a broken leg, go see an orthopedic doctor right away. PPOs have In-Network providers you can choose from, but they have some Out-of-Network options just in case you need it. If you had a random emergency that obviously wasn't planned in advance, having a PPO could provide a better chance that you have at least *some* insurance working on your behalf. If you're unconscious or bleeding out, it's not like you're going to have a conversation with the ambulance driver about which hospitals are in-network for your particular plan.

Life Insurance

The purpose of life insurance is to leave money behind to loved ones if you die. That sounds really grim, but death is something that we all face and it would be good to leave money behind for the people that depend on us financially. I'm married with a kid. If something were to happen to me, my family loses the income that I would have brought every year. Life insurance makes sure that my family has the money they need to thrive in my absence.

That being said, if you're young with no kids, you don't really *need* life insurance. There *are* some tax advantages and strategies that you can use as a young person with no kids, but those are advanced concepts that are beyond the scope of this book. Let's just stick to the basics for now.

Beneficiary. This is who gets the money when you die. It could be one person or it could be split between multiple people. If you're splitting it, you'll need to assign a percentage to each person so that it's clear how much each person gets. As the purchaser of the policy, this is entirely your decision and you can change beneficiaries at any time.

Death Benefit. This is the amount of money that goes directly to your beneficiary or beneficiaries when you die. This is also known as the **Face Amount** of the policy. When you buy a life insurance policy, you will know the dollar amount of coverage upfront (i.e a $10,000 policy). The dollar amount of the policy is the face amount or death benefit.

Term Life Insurance. A basic insurance policy that has a "term" that lasts anywhere from 5 to 30 years. During this term, you'll pay a fixed premium amount that does not change. When the term ends, you will have to purchase another term. Because you will be older (and therefore closer to death), the premium will be more expensive. The older you are when you **start** a term, the more expensive term insurance will be. **This insurance only has a death benefit;** there are no other features or benefits. It's beneficial for most because of its lower cost. Like we discussed before, the fewer benefits an insurance policy has, the lower the cost. Just as a heads up, you generally want to get a longer-term policy before you turn 35. After that age, the price skyrockets.

Whole Life Insurance. A life insurance policy that is active for your entire life and has a cash portion that automatically increases in value the longer you pay your premiums. You can use that cash at any time for any reason and can get loans against it at low interest rates. Have I confused you yet?

Here's another way to put it. A whole life insurance plan is like a forced savings account. You pay a fixed premium amount that never ever changes and you pay it until you die. "Whole life" means you literally pay your premium your whole life. If you die, your beneficiaries still get the death benefit. However, while **you** are still alive, you can dip into the cash balance **within** the insurance policy should you ever need it. So yes; your whole life insurance policy is like a savings account and a life insurance policy **combined** into one product. Furthermore, the cash value in your policy can have a guaranteed rate of return; meaning your money will grow with compound interest as long as you have the policy.

However, this doesn't come cheap. Whole life insurance policies cost 6-10 times more than term life policies. You're paying for all those extra benefits and features. Sure, that cash can help when you need it, but you must always make your premium payments on time. If you ever miss payments, your premiums will come out of your built-up cash value. Once that is gone, your policy will be canceled if you continue to miss payments. The insurance company will make every attempt to notify you so that you can reinstate your policy, but after a certain time, your policy will be permanently canceled.

There are entire books on this type of insurance. It can get complicated. Whole life insurance is almost like a 401K or an IRA. It can contain both investments and cash balances in a tax-advantaged account. Therefore, it's more of an **investment vehicle** vs. a simple product like term life insurance. Most people who get whole life insurance typically understand the pros and cons, but some others buy it because of some random insurance salesperson or because of a recommendation by a trusted person. You need to know exactly **why** you're getting it. Don't just get it because someone tells you it's awesome. It needs to fit your overall financial goals.

If you've ever heard of people talking about **Infinite Banking** or **Self Banking,** they're talking about using whole life insurance as a way to get the cash or loans you need without having to go through a bank. Also, the fixed returns that whole life insurance policies offer are higher than banks while avoiding the investment risk of the stock market. Your cash value cannot go down in a traditional whole life insurance policy; making this one of the safest investments you can make.

Don't get too excited though. The guaranteed rate is still in the low single digits. However, there are other whole life policies that have exposure to the stock market in hopes of getting a higher return. In those products, your cash value can go down, but you will still never lose your death benefit; even if the market crashes.

CHAPTER FIFTEEN
You Can't Save Your Way to Wealth

1. Saving will never make you wealthy.
2. You must use your money to make more money. If you don't, someone else will use your money to make **themselves** money.
3. Save your money to give you peace of mind today. Invest to have peace of mind in the future.

If you grew up like me, your momma knew how to make a dollar out of fifteen cents. My momma would stretch every penny we had and somehow could get ten pieces out of a chicken instead of eight. She would "borrow from Peter to pay Paul" and it would always work out. I admired her ability to always have enough to get by. She seemed like she always had a plan. When I became an adult, I did everything she did- with pride. When I graduated college, I realized something:

I was broke.

I mean *super* broke. I didn't understand. I did **everything** I saw my mother do, but I was still in this inescapable black hole of *suck* and I didn't see a way out of it. Turns out, she was doing all that stuff just to survive. There *was* no extra money anywhere. If there were any savings, it wasn't enough to enjoy life- it was there to avoid complete financial disaster. Now I would never criticize what she did for us, but when I became an adult, I realized that a crucial part of our finances was completely absent:

"Investing."

I didn't even *hear* this word until I was 18 and it was used in the wrong context. I was at some pyramid scheme meeting that I got dragged into by an ex-girlfriend. I was told to "invest in yourself." That meeting started me down a journey that would destroy countless relationships and waste 10 years of my life chasing get-rich-quick schemes. But it was *exciting!* I never knew I could actually have a lifestyle like the people on tv. The *possibility* was enough. I believed in the dream.

In hindsight, I'm glad I went. It at least introduced me to what my life *could* be. The point of telling you all of this was to show you that I was desperate for a solution. I knew something was wrong with a system where my mother couldn't get ahead despite working two jobs. Here is the problem: I could spend all day talking about the virtues of my hard-working mother and all her moral highlights and Christian values. However, **none** of these things have anything to do with money. The main reason why we never got ahead financially is because we only **saved** our money. We never utilized the one thing that actually *grows* your money: **investing**.

Pull out a dollar from your wallet or purse. Look at it. Imagine this dollar as a soldier whose only mission is to fight on the battlefield to get more dollars. You are the proud general of this noble soldier. You direct your soldier where to go and send it into the battlefield. If your soldier succeeds, you **gain** another dollar and increase your fighting power. If your soldier loses, you **lose** that dollar and your ability to fight is decreased. The more soldiers you have, the more unstoppable you and your army become. If you lose all your soldiers or choose not to use them, you must fight on the battlefield alone by yourself- where you could easily be overwhelmed.

Saving without investing is like keeping all your soldiers on base while *you* go the front lines. It doesn't matter how many weapons you can carry or how skilled you are. Alone on the battlefield, you WILL lose. It's just a matter of time. Time is **against** you when you fight alone. It doesn't matter how much of a badass you think you are.

You will eventually get **tired**.
You will eventually get **burned out**.
You will eventually get **old**.

You may have to retire and retreat from the battlefield before you ever reach your goal. Unfortunately, this is how most Americans will live their lives.

Investing without saving is just as reckless. If you empty your base and deploy every soldier, there's a chance all of them could get wiped out in one battle. Now you have no defenses for your base **and** you'll still have to go fight **alone** until you are forced to retreat.

Investing AND saving is the most intelligent strategy. You send a portion of your soldiers to fight and you keep a portion of your soldiers on base. If your soldiers on the battlefield are successful, you add to your forces. If your soldiers on the battlefield lose, at least you have soldiers on base to help defend yourself. However, your battlefield soldiers will **win** more often than they lose. As they increase their numbers, you can gain serious ground towards your goals. Again, it's just a matter of time. But now, time is in **your favor**. It doesn't matter how incompetent or unskilled you are. As long as you're smart enough to let your money fight to get more money-

You will eventually do **less** work.
You will have **more** time to focus on the important things.
You will eventually become financially independent.

My analogies can get out of control, but the main point is something you've probably heard before:

"Don't work for money. Make your money work for you."

By that, I *specifically* mean it must gain a percentage of return through compound interest or through profit by **passive income**. But I'm willing to bet that you've heard this statement so many times that it's lost its punch. It's overused, so people overlook the powerful truth it contains. After all, how many times have you been told to "diet and exercise?" I don't know about you, but I tune out when I hear that phrase. So let me put it another way:

Your job is to keep enough soldiers in the base for defense and send the rest to the battlefield for offense.

It's perfectly fine to work for money. You need it, don't you? So let's not get caught up in popular sayings. It doesn't matter what you do for income. Just take the extra amount that you have after paying your bills (and building up your emergency savings) and invest it. Send your soldiers to the various battlefields (aka stocks, bonds, mutual funds and ETFs) and let them do the fighting for you. Sometimes you win. Sometimes you lose. However, long term, you are more likely to win more than you lose. **Most importantly**, you will make money with your job **AND** your investments. After your investments gain you a large amount of money, you will be able to stop working at your job. So, in my opinion, the saying should go more like this:

Make your money work for you so that you don't *have* to work for money.

Again, the problem is that most of us were never taught to invest. We were taught to save and save and keep on saving. I would argue that my family saved better than most. So why weren't any of us millionaires?

Saving gives you peace of mind, but no *growth*.

It's good to save. In fact, you **absolutely** need it for your emergency savings. If you have no savings, you won't be able to handle life's little inconveniences- like needing a new set of tires. If you're always at the risk of running out of money, you won't risk what little money you *do* have in the stock market. That's a good thing- because you shouldn't put money in the stock market without having built up emergency savings first.

However, saving without investing is a terrible idea. Right now, as of March 2021, banks are paying roughly half of a percent in interest. You heard me. That's 0.5%. Let me show you how that would work:

If you're 25 and you were able to put $100 a month towards in a savings account paying 0.5%, it would make you a millionaire at:

125 years old.

You probably won't be around when you finally become a millionaire, but at least your grandkids would appreciate your sacrifice. The truth is that technically, you could become wealthy by saving alone. You'll just be too dead to enjoy it.

This brings up something you probably haven't ever considered. Sure it would take a ridiculously long time to reach 1 million dollars by saving, but did it ever really cross your mind that it was *technically* possible? Were you aware that you could **automatically** become a millionaire just by putting $100 a month away for a long time? You can! It is seriously **that** easy. Now we just need to fix the interest rate and maybe we can get you to millionaire status while you're still alive.

If you're 25 and you were able to put $100 a month towards a brokerage (stock market) account *averaging* 10%, it would make you a millionaire at:

71 years old.

I can already hear you. "71 Years Old?! That's still too old! I won't be dead but I might as well be!" First of all, that's insensitive. Seventy-one is a perfectly good age to be a millionaire. Furthermore, you'd also miss the point. The amount of money you put in *didn't change*. Simply increasing the interest rate saved you **53 YEARS.** You didn't do anything *different*. You just found a **better** place to put your money. You put your soldiers on the battlefield instead of leaving them on base. Doing something simple over a long period of time can produce powerful results. Still don't believe me?

- If you are 25 today (March 2021) and I invested $100 in the stock market every month since you were born, I would have about **$92,000** RIGHT NOW.

- If I invested $50 a month, then I'd have **$46,000**

- If I invested $25 a month, then I'd have **$23,000**

What if your parents had done this when you were born? How would your life be different? How much would it change your life if you could log into your account *right now* and see a balance of $92,000 staring back at you? Think about that. We'll take it a step further. Let's say I didn't cash out and I let the money continue to work for you until you were 50 years old:

- At $100 a month, you'd have **$1,444,000**

- At $50 a month, you'd have **$720,000**

- At $25 a month, you'd have **$360,000**

If you don't remember anything else from this book, remember this one thing:

TIME IS MORE IMPORTANT THAN MONEY.

If you have a lot of time, it doesn't take a lot of money. The reverse is also true. If you have little time, it takes a **lot** of money. I'll show you:

- I'm 42. If I want to have 1 million dollars by 65, I'd have to put in $1000 a month.

- You're 25. If YOU want a million by 65, you only need to put in $200 a month.

- You're 21. To get to a million by 65, you only need to put in $130 a month.

- You're 18. To get to a million by 65, you only need to invest $100 a month.

- Your kid is 1. To have a million by 65, you only need to put in $20 a month.

The longer you wait, the harder it will become to reach financial independence. It will **always** be possible, but it will take more of a financial sacrifice. If you invest early or invest for your child, it doesn't take much of a sacrifice at all. It actually becomes easy. Do you know why?

Compound Interest.

This is one of those terms I heard in math class and remembered long enough to pass a quiz. However, it's probably the **single most important thing** that can help you achieve your financial goals. You hear a lot about stocks, options, real estate investing, owning a business and et cetera when it comes to becoming wealthy, but it isn't that complicated. It *really* isn't. You just need compound interest and a simple way to invest that helps you get roughly 8% per year. All those other things are great and in time you'll learn more about them. However, you **DON'T NEED ANYTHING COMPLICATED.** Compound interest can grow your money faster than you realize:

- It doesn't take a day off and it works while you sleep.
- Your money makes money without you having to do ANYTHING.
- The more years you let it work for you, the more money you make.

Again, this is the story of the Tortoise vs the Hare. You already know how it ends: The turtle wins. You already know the moral of the story:

Slow and Steady Wins the Race.

Let me ask you a question. With all my previous examples of how long it would take to become a millionaire,

Did it *matter* what your job was?

No, it **didn't**. I know a guy who worked in the back warehouse at a home improvement store who retired at 59. He had invested since his early twenties.

- ✓ Would you have to win the lottery or get a record deal or play pro sports? **NO.**
- ✓ Does it matter how many kids you have? **NO.**
- ✓ Does it matter if you grew up poor? **NO.**
- ✓ Do you have to be smart? Honestly, **NO. Not at all.** You'd probably be shocked (and disheartened) at the sheer amount of dumb rich people.

Can You Be a Millionaire?

YES.

Again, the **ONLY** thing you must do is **consistently** put your money into an investment that gets you roughly 10% per year. Fortunately for you and everyone who participates, there is a way to do this: **the stock market.** The stock market has produced more millionaires than real estate or inheritance. However, a lot of people don't even participate in it. Some people have retirement plans at work, but they don't know how it really works or what's in them.

There is a real apathy and fear of the stock market for the average working person in America. Only 55% of American adults own stocks. That means 45% **don't.** That may shock you. Maybe it doesn't. I tend not to get too moved by percentages, so here's what 45% looks like:

160 Million People.

160 *million* people are not participating in one of the few things that can make money while they sleep. That means all those people are sold on the idea of "work hard and save money." All of them are fighting **alone** on the battlefield. Folks, **that just doesn't work.** Any investor or anyone with a high-paying job will tell you that they actually work **less** compared to when they *didn't* invest and had *lower-*paying jobs.

The reason why people avoid the stock market is because they associate it with gambling. They hear about all the ways people have lost money and so they stay away. To be fair, if you knew a relative or a friend that lost thousands of dollars screwing around with stocks, you'd avoid it too. However, investing is not gambling and gambling is not investing. There's a very important term you need to know: **Managed Risk.**

Managed Risk vs Gambling

Managing your risk means that you have an established, trusted way to influence or control the outcome of a risky activity. **Gambling** means that you have **no control whatsoever.** Let me give you an example:

- Do you skydive with a parachute? That's managing risk.

- Do you skydive **without** a parachute? That's gambling.

The parachute is an established, trusted tool that has made the very dangerous activity of jumping out of a plane safe. Can you still get hurt? Yes, but nowhere near as bad as if you *didn't* have a parachute. Is it guaranteed to work? No. One in every thousand parachutes malfunctions. That means parachutes work 99.9% of the time. For the 0.1% when it doesn't, this is why you have a **reserve** parachute. Jumping out of a plane with no parachute reverses those odds. Could you survive? Yes, you *could*. Ten or so other people have done it. Feeling lucky?

For all you non-daredevils, we're going to manage our risk and influence the outcome of our investments so that we succeed more than we fail. Remember this moving forward:

Stock Market = Investing with Managed Risk
Las Vegas = Gambling

Why is it not so risky? Because you're going to invest in publicly traded companies. That means **everything** about these companies is public information. You will have access to **all** their financial information to help you make good decisions. Now let's look at the first way we're going to manage risk: **The Index Fund.**

CHAPTER SIXTEEN
Put Your Money to Work in an Index Fund

1. Low-cost Index Funds are the best way for beginners to earn money with the stock market.
2. You don't have to pick winners with Index Fund. Just invest in the entire stock market.
3. With Index Funds, you aren't trying to beat the market. You match it.

If you want to grow your money and eventually become wealthy, the **stock market** is one of the best ways to do it. Sure, there's real estate, but you can get started with $50 in the stock market. $50 won't get you far in real estate. So let's start by addressing the elephant in the room:

"The stock market is risky. I work too hard for my money and I don't want to lose it."

You're exactly right. You *do* work too hard to lose it. If you believe what TV and the movies tell you about the stock market, you'll **absolutely** think that stocks have these wildly unpredictable swings in value and can suddenly lose their value overnight. It's true that *some* stocks can do that, but other stocks barely change their value at all. Why is that? And what is a stock?

A share of stock is just *one* small piece of *one* company.

When a company needs to raise a whole lot of money, they sell a portion of their company to the public through a **stock offering**. This is what it means when you hear of a company "going public" or having an IPO (Initial Public Offering). The portion they are willing to sell to the public gets divided into millions (and sometimes *billions*) of individual pieces called **shares**. When you buy a share of a company's stock, you now own a tiny piece of the company.

When it comes to how it performs (and whether it goes up or down), that mostly depends on that *one* company itself. Some companies are good, some are bad, and some are popular. The bad ones are the ones we hear about in the news because fortunes are lost and gained in a short period of time. The good ones are super boring. They're just not newsworthy. They're usually old companies that are really big like Wells Fargo and Walmart. Then there are popular stocks like Google, Amazon, and Tesla. They seem to grow so fast that you regret not buying them years ago when you had the chance. These are all individual companies that each have their own stock and their own performance.

So where does the "market" in the stock market come from? You know what a market is, right? Maybe you think of a flea market or a farmer's market. One sells random items and the other sells produce. It's all the same concept. People gather at these markets wanting to buy and sell the stuff they're interested in. The bigger the market, the more people show up. The stock market is just a bunch of people showing up to buy and sell the stocks of individual companies. Trust me, you already know how this works. Investment professionals and financial news programs can definitely make it seem complicated, but fundamentally it's simple.

The stock market is just like a marathon. There will be winners and losers. There will be participants that drop out of the race. There will be participants that get disqualified. Some will get caught cheating. Some will start strong but finish last and some will start slow and end up in the top ten.

But what if we could bet on the marathon **itself**?

What if we get paid based on the *average* of the participants who cross the finish line vs the ones that don't? That would be a no-brainer. We know that **most** are going to cross the finish line. Some participants end up *walking* through the finish line, but they still finish. Plus, several participants will perform really well- even if they're not the winner. The only way you could lose the bet is if there are more losers than winners. Would you take that bet? Of course you would. You understand how marathons work. When you bet on the **entire** marathon, you're only concerned about the **majority** of the participants. You don't really care about *individual* athletes. Got it? In that case:

Welcome to Index Fund Investing.

Index fund investing (also called **Passive Investing**) means that you **never** have to worry about picking individual companies. John Bogle is the founder of the Vanguard Group and creator of the first index fund marketed to retail investors. I bring him up because he has a great quote about index fund investing vs picking stocks.

"Why try to find the needle in the haystack when you can buy the whole haystack?"

Makes sense to me. With index fund investing:

- You don't have to be a stock market guru.
- You don't have to know a ton of financial terms and strategies.
- You don't suddenly need to watch hours of Bloomberg.
- You don't have to read a bunch of books about beating the market.
- You don't have to do anything complicated.
- Just invest your money consistently and **go live your life.**

It's probably the **easiest** and **lowest-risk** way to invest in the stock market- because you're investing in the *entire* stock market vs individual companies. Think about it:

- Can a company go out of business? **YES**. Any money invested is gone **forever**.

- Can the *entire* stock market go out of business? **NO**. It can *crash*, but it doesn't close its doors for good. As long as you keep your money in, it can recover. Historically, it has **ALWAYS** recovered.

With Index Fund investing, your return will be whatever the *entire* stock market does. If the entire stock market goes up, your money goes up. If it goes down, your money goes down. You will never *beat* the market, but you will also never do *worse* than the market. You will simply **match** the market. Turns out, it's really, really hard to beat the market consistently. Most professional money managers can't do it. I'm serious: Dozens of professional money managers who study, trade and analyze stocks single every day *lose* to a **completely brainless strategy**. You don't have to be smart. You just have to consistently put your money in an index fund. Here are some more benefits:

- They allow you to invest in the biggest companies at one time.
- An Index fund isn't a company. It can't suddenly lose all of its value.
- It protects from large losses if bad news hits a certain company or industry.
- You really can't get more diversified than 500 companies.
- Takes a lot of the guesswork and the stress out of picking individual stocks.

What is an Index Fund?

It's a mixture of stocks designed to match the performance of a financial market index.

Huh? What's a "financial market index?" Don't worry- you've heard of financial indexes before. Maybe you've heard of:

1. The S&P 500
2. The Dow Jones Industrial Average (DJIA) or sometimes called "The Dow"
3. NASDAQ

There are others, but you've probably heard of at least one of these when you listen to the news or anytime you hear people talk about financial stuff. Here's what they really mean:

The Standard & Poor's (S&P) 500 Index:

This is an average of the 500 biggest publicly traded companies' performances. The reason people like to talk about it is because it's a quick way to see how "big business" is doing. Big businesses are considered "Large Cap" companies. The "Cap" stands for **market capitalization**- the number of outstanding shares times the share price of their stock. (We'll talk about this more later). Large Cap companies are billion-dollar businesses that have a ton of employees. You've probably heard of most of them. These are established companies that have likely been around for a long time. You won't find a lot of growth here because the companies in this index are already big- like Walmart. Can Walmart get any bigger than it already is? Probably not. They're everywhere. This index has historically averaged 10% since the index began in 1926. Does that mean you'll get 10% guaranteed? No.

- Since 1980, it's been 9.2%, BUT
- Since 2001, it's been 5.90%.

What does that mean for you?

It means your average return will still be higher than a savings account will ever pay you.

Seriously, don't overthink this.

The Dow Jones Industrial Average (DJIA):

This is an average of 30 of the biggest publicly traded companies- but not *the* biggest 30. As you can imagine, these companies are huge: McDonald's, Nike, Microsoft, Johnson & Johnson, etc. Since it only has 30 companies, a lot of financial professionals feel it doesn't adequately represent the overall health of businesses in the United States. You'd think that the historical average would be significantly different from the S&P 500, right? Nope. Since 1919, It's averaged about 9.2%.

- Since 1980, it's been 9.3%
- Since 2001, it's been 5.83%

Pretty similar, right? Again, the goal is to beat the terrible rates from bank savings accounts. This index would serve that purpose as well.

The NASDAQ Composite or "Nasdaq" (pronounced "naz-dak"):

NASDAQ is an **exchange,** just like the **New York Stock Exchange** (NYSE). An exchange is just another way to say *'market.'* You don't have to worry about knowing that right now. All you need to know is that the NASDAQ Composite is an index of the 100 largest companies in terms of market capitalization. Again, capitalization = outstanding shares of stock x share price. I promise you we'll come back to this capitalization stuff. The point I'm trying to make here is that this index has the biggest 100 companies, so it's a decent indicator of how American business is doing overall. The biggest difference with the Nasdaq Composite is that it tends to have more information technology companies in its index. Since 1999, it's averaged around 9%. Again, that doesn't mean *you'll* get 9%. Why?

The Stock Market Goes Up and Down

This sounds obvious. I realize that. However, the truth is that the stock market goes up **MORE** than it goes down **over long periods of time.** This is why I keep talking about turtles and averages and a 20-year investment plan. There **absolutely** will be years where you will NOT get a 10% return. It might be 40%, but it also might be -10%. I can **guarantee** you that there will be times that you *lose* money in the short term. There will be some oil crisis in Saudi Arabia or some financial news that will freak out the stock market and everybody will lose their minds. This happens every couple of months, **Every. Single. Year.**

I'm not saying that you should ignore the news. I'm pointing out that news cycles are inherently focused on the **short term.** News focuses on what is happening today, or this week, or in the next month. It's entirely possible to turn on the TV and hear this:

"The Dow suffered its worst single-day decline since the Great Depression."

That sounds really, *really* bad. Most people hear this and think they need to get the heck out of the stock market ASAP and stuff all of their cash under their mattress. What if the news said this instead:

"The Dow suffered its worst single-day decline since the Great Depression, **but it's still up 30% since last year."**

Not so bad now, right? Hearing this, you might feel irritated that you lost money, but you only lost *some* of the money that you had already gained. In fact, you're still up 30%. It's not that bad. Now, what if they said this:

"The Dow suffered its worst single-day decline since the Great Depression, but it's still up 30% since last year **and is still on track to average 9% annually since the Great Depression."**

That doesn't seem bad at all. You would likely do *nothing* with this information. You might not even have any feelings towards this news one way or the other. Unfortunately, **no one** reports financial news this way. It's just too…boring. That's why **YOU** have to be focused on the long term vs. the short term.

So How Do You Invest in an Index?

It's actually pretty easy. All you have to do is open a **brokerage** account. You have a bank account, right? Whether you physically went to the bank or opened it online, you probably had to provide some ID and give them some cash to open your account. Opening a brokerage account works basically the same way. It's just more likely that you'll open your account online or through your phone. You've probably heard of:

Fidelity
E-Trade
Robinhood
TD Ameritrade
WeBull
Vanguard
Interactive Brokers

If you've never heard of them, don't worry. It's not important that you know who they are. You only need to know what they do. They allow you to buy stocks and index funds through your phone or your computer. We'll come back to these companies frequently as we discuss buying and selling stocks, but for now, just know that these are the "banks" we're going to use to buy an index fund.

Every one of these brokerages carries a fund that tracks the S&P 500 and the Dow. Not all of them have one that tracks Nasdaq. That doesn't really matter. I'm going to suggest that you pick the **S&P 500**. Why? Remember the marathon example earlier? Your chances are better if you have 500 participants vs 30 or 100. *That* is why. If you look online to see which one is best, you'll see decent arguments for each of the three.

Something to keep in mind; the S&P 500, the Dow, and Nasdaq are indexes that are used to measure how businesses are doing overall. They are measurement tools, not actual products you can buy. So some of these brokerages will **make** an index **fund** that you *can* buy. They do this by putting all the stocks that are in these indexes into a single fund. When you buy this fund, you are not buying individual stocks. You are buying a fund **that contains a mixture of individual stocks**. The fund owns the stocks and you own the fund. Have I lost you yet? Here's another way of thinking about it:

Let's say you like Starburst candy- especially the strawberry and cherry flavors (the red flavors). You're not crazy about the orange and lemon flavors, but you'll tolerate them. You know that the only way to get the red flavors is to buy a regular pack of Starburst. Therefore, one pack of Starburst is a **variety pack of flavors**. You know that out of a pack of 12 pieces, you'll likely get about 3 pieces of each flavor. That means that 25% of each flavor is represented in a pack of Starburst. Now imagine a 50oz bag of Starburst. There are 288 pieces in that bag (I counted), but you'll still have the 25% representation of each flavor. But what if there were 288 flavors? If it was an "every flavor" bag, you'd get **one piece of each flavor** in a 50 oz bag. Each piece represents 0.03% of the total amount of flavors in the bag. But you're not buying an "every flavor bag." You're buying a *variety* bag. You wouldn't likely get one of each flavor. There would be **more** of the popular flavors and **less** of the others. In that case, you wouldn't get every flavor. Some flavors would be left out to make room for more popular flavors.

That being said, do you have control over what flavors get put into a Starburst pack or 50oz bag? Nope. Mars Inc., the company that makes Starburst, makes that decision and puts their most popular flavors in the individual packs and the 50oz bags. They decide how many of each flavor goes into the pack or the bag. You don't buy a bag of only the flavors you want. You buy the variety pack or the variety bag and just let the lemon pieces get super hard in the back of a drawer somewhere.

Index funds are like the 50oz bags. You don't choose what's in them. You just buy the whole bag. The benefit is that you can buy ONE bag instead of buying one unique flavor 288 times. You know that the variety bag will have *enough* of the flavors you want, so you don't care about all the details and percentages and flavor representations. You just want some candy.

My Starburst connoisseurs are probably getting irked right now. They know that it's entirely possible to get a bag of "all pink" or all red starbursts and they hate this analogy. But I did it on purpose. Buying **all of one flavor** is like buying an individual company's stock. You're just a little ahead of me. That's the next chapter.

That being said, each brokerage will name its index funds a little differently. It's their product after all, so they'll name it in a way that stands out from the competition while still being clear about what it is. Let me give you an example:

- Fidelity's S&P 500 fund = Fidelity® 500 Index Fund (FXAIX)
- Vanguard's S&P 500 fund = Vanguard 500 Index Fund (VFINX)

See those letters in parentheses? Those are the **stock symbols** (or **ticker symbols**) for the funds. It's the easiest way to find the fund or stock you're looking for. Funds and stocks don't share symbols, so if you type in "FXAIX", the only fund that's going to pop up is the Fidelity® 500 Index Fund. Cool? That being said, don't go to Vanguard.com looking for Fidelity's stuff and vice versa. Even if you find it, there's likely an additional fee. You wouldn't buy a Coke out of a Pepsi machine, right? Even if you could, Pepsi might make you pay more for the *convenience* of getting a Coke out of one of their machines. It's just like using your debit card at a random ATM. You'll get charged a fee because it's not your bank. Same principle.

Here are two other funds:
"The Dow" = SPDR Dow Jones Industrial Average ETF (DIA)
Nasdaq =The Invesco QQQ ETF (QQQ)

These funds are available through multiple brokerages, so you don't have to worry so much about being charged extra fees. However, **these aren't the only two.** There are **multiple** funds that track the Dow.

There are other funds that track Nasdaq, but that's currently the most popular one.

Fidelity and Vanguard are the most popular funds for everyday people like you and me. Why? It's because they're two of the most well-known brokerages and they have the lowest fees. Let's talk about fees for a second. It's more important than you realize.

Fees Steal Your Wealth Forever

You already know the feeling. You got paid on a Friday, spent a little too much at the bar, and got hit with a fee from your bank on Monday. You know it's your fault, but it still pisses you off. The only good thing (if you could even call it a good thing) is that the fee of $40 or whatever is fixed and it happens **once**. The bank can't charge you any more than that for *one* mistake. It's in the bank's disclosures.

What if I told you about a type of fee that would take your money for as long as you have the account- whether you make a mistake or not? Oh, it definitely exists. For index funds, it's called an **expense ratio**. I'm going to talk a lot about this, but the short version is that **anything over 0.2% is bad**. Ok. Moving on.

An expense ratio is like the maintenance fee for your checking account. It is the cost to manage the fund. Unlike banks, however, there is nothing you can do to get rid of it. You must pay it. Therefore, your main goal should be to find an index fund with the lowest expense ratio possible.

This would be a good time to mention that index funds aren't the only type of funds out there. There are a ton of them. All these funds attempt to do certain things and cater to different situations and different people. There are bond funds, funds that have stocks and bonds, and funds that change over time to help people with their retirement goals. If the place you work for has a 401k, you've probably seen something like this- that is if you've ever looked at all the paperwork they gave you. The first time I saw that paperwork, I didn't know what I was looking at. The point here is that the more some administrator needs to manipulate the fund, the more maintenance has to be done- which drives up the expense ratio.

For example, let's say you saw a commercial on tv for a brokerage called T.RowePrice and they're advertising a Retirement date fund. This fund owns riskier, more profitable stuff when you're younger, then switches to owning less risky, more income-producing stuff as you get older. You think that's kind of cool. You don't even have to think or plan or anything! However, **you will pay** for this convenience. After all, *someone* has to go in and do all the buying and selling for this fund to do what you expect it to do. That person or persons deserve to be paid for their time and effort. It's their job. Their payment is charged to the fund and now your expense ratio goes **up**.

You may not think that's a big deal. It is. I'll show you. Remember the Vanguard 500 Index (VFINX) I talked about before? Let's compare it to the Retirement date fund.

- ✓ T.RowePrice Retirement Fund expense ratio = 0.71%
- ✓ Vanguard 500 Index expense ratio = 0.14%

It doesn't look that bad when you see the percentages. After all, they're both under one percent. It couldn't be all that bad, right? Let's say you put in $1000 to get started and put $100 every month until you retired. You're 25 now, so you'd retire in 40 years. We'll use the stock market's historic average of 10% as your expected interest rate. After 40 years:

- With the T.RowePrice Retirement Fund, you'd have $513,946.
- With the Vanguard 500 Index, you'd have $604,720.

So what happened? **Fees** happened. You would have paid **$115,535 in fees** with T.RowePrice. Think about that. They would take **six figures** for the convenience of managing your account. It doesn't make sense. How does 0.71% end up taking 15% of all your money? Compound Interest, my friend. It can work for you or *against* you.

In contrast, Vanguard would have only charged you $24,761. That's still a good chunk of change, but it's nowhere near as bad as T.RowePrice. What if I told you there was a fund that would only charge you $7,180 and earn you $622,300? It's another fund from Vanguard called the **Vanguard 500 Index Admiral Shares.** "Admiral Shares" just means you have to open your account with a higher dollar amount. Right now, that amount is $3,000. Don't have $3,000? Don't worry. **Start where you are** and you can convert it to Admiral Shares once your account reaches $3,000.

Keeping your fees low is **SUPER IMPORTANT**. I'm going to show you *again*:

T.RowePrice Retirement Fund = $513,946
Vanguard 500 Index Admiral Shares = $633,300
Difference = **$119,354**

Just by changing *who* you put your money with, you could have earned an **additional $119,354.** When you stop to think about that- it's just **insane**. I don't mean to be dramatic, but that is a life-changing amount of money. Don't give it away. Do your homework. Get the lowest fees possible. Right now, Fidelity and Vanguard have index fund fees as low as 0.04%. Please take advantage. By the way, if you really like the idea of someone changing your fund to fit your retirement goals, Vanguard offers a Target Retirement Fund that only charges 0.15% (as of the time of this writing). It always pays to shop around.

What's the Difference Between a Fund and a Mutual Fund?

There is no difference. To be fair, I've simplified some of the terminologies in this book to make them easily understandable. When I first started, some of the financial terms and phrases made me feel dumb and I felt intimidated. I don't want you to feel the same way, but I don't want to oversimplify things to the point that I'm teaching you the wrong thing. That being said, every time I've said the word *fund*, I'm actually talking about a *mutual fund*. So:

Fund (simplified term) = Mutual Fund (actual term)

Nothing else is different. A mutual fund still works like the variety bag of Starburst- it's just a **container** that you can put financial assets in. We touched on this earlier, but a mutual fund can contain stocks, bonds, money market instruments, real estate, or several other financial assets. If you start digging around and looking up different types of mutual funds, you will see all the information you need to know about that mutual fund. For example, you'll probably see the following terms on the page:

Fund Overview
A summary of all the important info.

Objective
What the fund aims to accomplish. In the index fund we've been talking about, the objective would be to track the performance of the S&P 500 index.

Strategy
How it uses a combination of assets (in our case, stocks) to achieve the goals and the percentages of each asset (like 80% stocks and 20% bonds)

Risk
This lets you know how risky this mutual fund is. More risk = More reward. Any mutual fund with a bunch of stocks in it will be riskier than a mutual fund full of government savings bonds like the ones your grandma gave you when you were five.

Expense Ratio (Exp. Ratio)
This is the fee we've been talking about. Make sure it's below 0.2%. In fact, try to find something around 0.05%.

Minimum to Invest
Some mutual funds require that you start your account with a predetermined amount. Some don't. In general, the ones that require you to start with $3,000 or more give you a lower expense ratio.

NAV
This is how much one share costs. Again, this is NOT a share of stock. This is **one** share of the fund. The price is adjusted **once a day** and it *stays* that price until the end of the next day. It doesn't go up and down throughout the day like stocks do. Keep in mind that different funds have different prices. Even though the Fidelity® 500 Index fund (FXAIX) and the Vanguard 500 Index Fund (VFINX) both track the S&P 500 Index, as of the time of my writing this, Fidelity has a NAV of $139.84 and Vanguard has a NAV of $371.06. This does **NOT** mean that Vanguard is twice as valuable or somehow more profitable. It just means that Fidelity offers a cheaper way to get in. However, it's important to realize that an investment of $1,000 will perform *almost exactly the same* way because they **both** track the S&P 500.

Top 10 Holdings
Remember the Starburst bag? These are the most popular flavors. The fund will have a higher percentage of these companies versus other companies.

Overall Rating
This is almost like a Yelp or Google review. Different financial reporting companies and/or news sites can rate the fund. A high rating doesn't guarantee great performance and a low rating doesn't guarantee poor performance. It's important that you pick a fund based on **your** goals and **your** needs. Ratings can help inform your decision, but they shouldn't be the only thing you look at.

What's the Difference Between a Mutual Fund and an ETF?

Great question! There is **one big difference** between the two:

An ETF can be traded like a share of stock.

Hop back up to the NAV section. Remember when I said that the price is adjusted once a day? Well, **the price of an ETF does go up and down throughout the day** just like a share of stock does. Since the price changes, it allows you to jump in or out whenever you want. You could buy one share in the morning and then sell it by that afternoon for a profit (or a loss). This is called **day trading** and I DON'T recommend doing this, by the way.

ETFs typically don't have account minimums and *may* be cheaper to buy into. As of right now, ETFs are very popular. There's an ETF for almost anything you can think of. There's an ETF for:

- Marijuana stocks
- Obesity-related stocks (it's gone now. It didn't last long lol)
- Millennial based interests and trends
- Buzz US Sentiment = made up of the most talked-about companies on social media
- Video Games = made up of companies that make video games or are in the gaming industry

If you have an interest, there's sure to be some random ETF that will scratch your itch. Would I personally invest in these? No. Why? Because the average expense ratio of these particular ETFs is close to 0.7%. It doesn't matter how cool or convenient something looks. That expense ratio is too expensive and will eventually rob me of my wealth. Are you starting to see how you can get duped into buying something trendy? **Don't be someone else's sucker**. If you're *really* interested in these types of companies and industries, either buy the individual stocks or find an ETF with an expense ratio under 0.2%. **The guidelines don't change.**

So yes, you can buy an S&P 500 index mutual fund OR an S&P 500 Index ETF. When it comes to index investing, it doesn't really matter because most people who buy them are "**Buy and Hold**" investors. That just means you're not trying to make a short-term profit. This is also what I've been preaching this whole book. You should be investing for the long term, not trying to make a quick buck. I'm sure you've heard the phrase "buy low and sell high." This book is NOT telling you to do that. If anything, I'm more of a "Buy Low and Buy *Some More* Low" kind of investor. Obviously, you can do whatever you want. Just get the basics down first.

Boosting Your Return with Dividend Reinvestment

Another **huge** benefit of index fund investing is that you get **dividends**. Dividends are basically free money that you get just for owning shares of a fund or a stock. We'll talk more about dividends in the next chapter and break down how it works, but for now, just know that it's free money and that you don't have to do anything extra to get it. If you have an index fund, you'll get a notification that you got a dividend for some random, low amount. It'll be for $2.57 or something like that. This amount is deposited into your brokerage account as cash money. So now you can go buy some coffee. Or…

….You could **reinvest** the dividend. Seriously, don't buy coffee with it. You can choose to have your dividends automatically reinvested into the index fund. This is a good thing. Remember all that talk about compound interest? Well, dividends are free money **on top of that**. Think about dividends like fees **in reverse**. Remember, compound interest works for you or against you. With fees, it works against you because you're losing money that could be earning interest. With dividends, you're **gaining** money that earns **additional** interest. Both fees and dividends seem small individually, but over the course of 20 years, they can make a **massive** difference. Your brokerage should have some setting that allows you to reinvest your dividends. It's usually not the default setting, so you'll need to find the setting and change it yourself.

CHAPTER SEVENTEEN
Growth vs Value Stocks, Dividends, & Bonds

1. Own stocks to grow your money. Own bonds to preserve your money and get income.
2. Growth stocks can make you a lot of money but usually pay no dividends. Value stocks probably won't make you a lot of money, but will usually pay dividends.
3. Bonds are less risky than stocks, but the tradeoff is a lower return at a fixed amount.

An Overview That You Shouldn't Skip

Before we get too far down the rabbit hole with investing in individual companies, I wanted to give you a (not so) quick overview of the different ways you could do it. Trust me, I wanted to jump right in, but there are a few terms and phrases that will keep popping up and I didn't want that to slow you down. This chapter will help me get to the point faster moving forward. That being said, we talked about it briefly in the previous chapter, but let's go over what stock is again:

**A Share of Stock is Just a Small a Piece of a Company.
You can buy it, own it, sell it or give it away.**

When people talk about "buying stock," they're actually talking about the *process* of buying shares of a company's stock through a brokerage. The shares that are available to buy and sell are called **common stock.** We don't have to get technical. Just understand that companies use two primary ways to get money from the public:

1. Equity (stocks)
2. Debt (bonds)

A company's **equity** is its ownership value. By selling the equity to you (the public), the company gets money directly from you in exchange for the price you pay per share. Now you own a portion of the company and the company has more money to grow and buy stuff. If the company does great, you share in their profit and your stock's dollar value goes up. It could go up **12,000%**! That happened with Amazon. On the other hand, if the company is unprofitable, your stock's dollar value goes down. It could do down to **zero**. That happened with a company called Enron (Look it up. That story is *crazy*.) It's natural for companies to have periods of going up versus going down. How frequently that happens is called **volatility**. A stock with **low volatility** means that it doesn't have big changes in its share price. A stock with **high volatility** means that it could lose 20% of its value *overnight*.

A company's **debt** is sold to the public in the form of **bonds.** Did you ever get one of those government savings bonds as a kid? Well, this works the same way. Companies sell bonds with a promise to pay you back with interest. They'll tell you the interest rate upfront and how long you have to wait to get paid back- similar to CD from a bank. It's one of the few investments where there are few surprises. As long as the company doesn't go under, you should get your money back with interest. It's that simple. Even if the company does go under, as a debt holder, you get first dibs on whatever money the company raises after selling all their stuff (aka liquidation). Of course, bonds are nowhere near as sexy as stocks.

With bonds, you can't make more money than what you were promised upfront. You could still sell to someone else for a profit, but there's no unlimited growth potential like there is with stocks. That's not a bad thing though. Bonds are seen as a less risky investment because companies will pay their debt to stay in business. You have to pay your rent to stay in your house or apartment, right? Well, companies have to pay their debt or else they'll have consequences too. Your stock value may not go up, but it's very likely that they'll make their debt/bond payments because it's an obligation. It's very possible that a company's stock price goes down while the bondholders *still* get their payments. Since the payout and the interest are known from the beginning, a lot of people who invest in bonds do it because they use the interest income as **passive income.** Remember talking about passive income? That was like 100 pages ago.

To be fair, stocks can provide passive income as well through **dividends.** We'll talk more about that later, but it basically means that a company will pay you cash just for owning the stock. It's really cool.

Growth Stocks vs Value Stocks

Let's step back for a moment. We've been talking a lot about buying stocks, but what is important for you to consider is that you're buying *companies*. Your goal is to buy stock in high-quality *companies* that have done well in the past and that you believe will do well in the future. This means that you are not **only** trying to "buy low and sell high." You're buying a company that you believe will be a good investment for years to come, not just the immediate future. Again, I know this isn't the way everyone does it, but my goal for you is to gain more money than you lose. Over time, you'll have a ton of money-unless you gamble it all away trying to chase overnight success and other people's returns. That being said, when you're looking at different companies, they typically fall into one of two types: **Growth & Value.**

Growth Companies

Growth is kind of obvious. The company is relatively new and it wants to use all of its profits to grow aggressively. This type of company usually has a new technology or a new way of doing something old. They tend to **disrupt** existing ways of doing everyday things by using that new technology to make things more efficient, easier, or just plain better. Apple and Tesla are good examples of growth companies. Apple isn't new, but it's constantly seeking to disrupt the way you buy music and entertainment. It still has some room to grow, but it's getting so big that people aren't seeing it as primarily a growth company anymore. Tesla, by comparison, is far more aggressive right now. Every dollar of profit goes right back into growing the company even *faster*. They're attempting to expand internationally and a lot of people feel they have a lot of room to grow. Tesla's share price was hovering around $200 in October of 2019. Now it's worth $3,000. (They did a 5 for 1 stock split, so the current price of one share is around $600 today). By the time you read this book, there's no telling how much higher they could go.

This is the number #1 advantage of growth companies; they could go on a tear and increase over 1,000% in a very short period of time. Read that again: one *thousand* percent. That means the $100 you put in just to dip your toes into the stock market turned into $1,000. You did **nothing**. This is why growth companies are all over the news. They tend to make regular people into millionaires and millionaires into multi-millionaires. They're also very popular. They seem to have an air of excitement surrounding them and they usually have a charismatic CEO that almost seems like a rock star.

Does it mean that all the excitement is warranted? **No**. Does it mean that all of its financial stats are healthy and positioned for success? **No**. Does it mean that the current stock price accurately reflects the current value of the company? **No**. Does it mean that they have a monopoly or some type of super competitive edge that makes all this excitement and hype justified? Again, **NO**. Those things could be true, but the company's stock might be "going to the moon" **just on hype**.

Don't be fooled. Popular companies with rock star CEOs have also crashed **spectacularly**. It happened with WeWork in 2019 and Nikola in 2020. Both were seen as cutting edge. Both were seen as the future. Unfortunately, both had charismatic CEOs that got caught misrepresenting the details of their businesses (aka lying). Nikola saw its share price go from $70 to $13 at one point. Right now it's hovering around $11. WeWork was supposed to go public in 2019 but *didn't even make it*. They went from being valued at 47 BILLION dollars to discussing bankruptcy options in just **six weeks.** They released a documentary about it. Watch it when you get a chance.

This is the number #1 disadvantage of growth companies; they could be massive success stories or massive flops. Everyone wishes they got in when Amazon first went public. Ditto for Netflix. But nobody remembers Pets.com or Webvan. All of these companies all came out around the same time- kind of like your high school graduating class. Just think of some of your classmates. Some of the ones you just *knew* would do well are struggling now, while a few of the dumb jocks went out and started million-dollar businesses. People can change. Companies can change too. You just never know. **No one** can guess right- not even the experts.

Case in point- people forget that Amazon originally was an online bookstore and Netflix used to mail DVDs to your house. A child today wouldn't even recognize the older versions of these companies. **Nobody** knew that Amazon would become an online Walmart and **a lot of people** were surprised when Netflix started streaming content. These companies **changed** over time. They adapted and thrived. But you couldn't have known what they were going to do in the future when they first went public 20+ years ago. So cut yourself a break and stop looking at those "If you had invested $10,000 in 'X' company 20 years ago, you'd be a millionaire!" articles. Hindsight is always 20/20. It's not productive to regret the past when the answer only became clear *recently*. Don't take those articles seriously. They're just going to make you second-guess yourself and encourage you to take unnecessary risks.

Value Companies
This title isn't as obvious as "growth." This doesn't mean that these companies are "cheap." It really just means that they're really big, older companies with no real room for huge growth. It also means that their **valuations** are below the average stock in the S&P and/or that their stock price may be lower than analysts feel it *should* be. Bottom line, these companies aren't exciting and no one is in a rush to buy them. Think about toilet paper. Is your blood pumping yet? Are you fidgeting in your chair waiting for the next exciting cotton swab from Johnson & Johnson? Are you thrilled about Clorox? Of course you aren't.

Welcome to Value Companies.

This is the number 1# disadvantage of value companies: they're boring. They don't have much momentum (or much interest) and since they're worth billions of dollars, the price doesn't really move too far up or too far down from where it was yesterday (or even last year). It's like dumping a cup of water into the ocean. You and some friends could spend a lifetime dumping your cups, but the ocean won't move much. The share price of value companies should slowly inch up over time, but it won't be anywhere near the excitement of a 1,000% return. It's probably closer to 4% to 8%. Again, if you invested $10,000 in Clorox years ago and your friend invested the same amount in Tesla, you'd still be shopping at Walmart and he might be on a yacht somewhere. That's not due to Tesla being a *better* company, it's due to Tesla's focus on fast growth and innovation vs Clorox's focus on modest profit.

What's important to remember here is that these value companies usually have more to offer than just a shot at getting rich quick. They are typically far more **stable** than growth companies because they're so old and big. In the world of investing, **stability is worth its weight in gold**. For some of us, we take comfort in lower-risk, reliable investments that grow *a little* or lose *a little* at any given time. It's far easier to plan for things like retirement. If that's the case, I'm probably not keen on the idea of losing 20% of all my money *overnight*. Think about it: Who would be more responsible with a $100 bill? An 18-year-old or an 80-year-old? Exactly. The 80-year-old would look to *preserve* the money while gaining a modest, but respectable amount of interest. The 18-year-old would YOLO it into oblivion. In other words, the 80-year-old would never want to lose the original $100 value while the 18-year-old would feel far more comfortable making risky bets. In a nutshell, that's the difference between growth and value. However, value stocks offer something most growth stocks don't: **Dividends**.

This is the #1 advantage of value companies. Remember earlier when we talked about how Tesla uses **all** their profit to make their company grow faster? Well, what if you're *already* big? You obviously don't need to use all of your profit to grow. Also, you know no one's excited about cleaning products and toilet paper. So a lot of these large companies **give** a portion of their profit back to shareholders in the form of **dividends**. It's just profit divided up and given back to the people who invest in the company's stock.

That means you have the potential to get paid **twice** with one stock. Wait, twice? How is that possible? Here's how:

#1. **Capital Gains** is the term for the profit you get when the stock increases in value. If you invested $100 in a company and your investment doubles to $200, you would have $100 worth of capital gains. In other words, you **gained capital**.

#2. The **Dividend** is the profit that is divided up and paid out to shareholders. The amount of the divided is announced periodically, but companies who pay dividends attempt to keep their payouts around the same amount to attract income investors (people who invest to get **passive income**). Dividends are usually paid out quarterly. The dividend is paid directly to your brokerage account as cash. You can withdraw the cash as income or you can use it to buy more shares of the company's stock.

Let's look at an example. In 2020, Exxon (stock ticker symbol: XOM) saw its share price go from $32.74 at its lowest and $41.22 at its highest. That's not that big of a difference. Even more interesting is that the $32.74 "low" was only because there was a huge drop in demand because of the pandemic AND a dispute within the oil-producing companies. At the end of the year, the vaccines starting to roll out and everybody was excited about eventually traveling again. However, even with all that drama, the difference was **still** less than $10.

- If you had invested around $100 at the lowest price, that would have bought you 3 shares for a total of **$98.22**.
- At the end of the year when the price went to $41.22, you would have a profit of **$8.48** per share.
- Since you have 3 shares, your total profit is **$25.44**.
- With your initial investment, you would have **$123.66** by the end of the year.

We can all agree that a profit of $25.44 is not enough to change your life, but it is still a **really good** 26% return. In the world of investing, that's **huge**.

Even better, Exxon paid out a **dividend** of $3.48 per share in 2020. That means for every share you owned, you got an additional $3.48 paid back to you in **cash**. You owned three shares, so you received $10.44. If you add your dividend to your capital gains, you earned $28.92 for every share of Exxon that you owned. You got paid **twice**. *Now* your return is 29%. That's really, *really* good. The best part about dividends is that it doesn't matter if you had a lot of capital gains. Let's say you only had a $1 increase in share value from $32.74 to $33.74. That's not great, but you would likely *still* get a dividend. It may not be $3.48, but it'll be close. And you didn't have to do *any* work to get it.

Using Dividends for Passive Income

What if you had 30 shares instead of 3? That would have gotten you **$104.40** in dividends. That's not a whole lot of money. But what if you had 300 shares? Now you'd have **$1,044** in dividends. That's better, but you can't exactly live off of that. But what if you had 3,000 shares? Now you'd make **$10,440** just for owning the stock. Divided monthly, that's **$870** a month that you didn't have to work for. This is one great way to create **passive income**. Remember- you need your passive income to equal or exceed your expenses to become financially independent.

However, that would require that you own $98,200 worth of Exxon stock. This is why dividend income is better suited for when you get closer to retirement. The goal isn't to get 3,000 shares of a dividend-paying stock *today*, it's to **end up** with 3,000 or more shares **by the time you retire**. Trust me, you'll get there if you consistently invest every month. Also, by **reinvesting** your dividends when you're younger, you automatically buy more shares. More shares = more capital gains and more dividends.

You Can Also Invest in a Company with Bonds

We're not going to spend too much time on bonds because you're probably under the age of 30. Why does that matter? Here's the quick version:

- ✓ Stocks = *Grow* Money through *unlimited* capital gains & dividends
- ✓ Bonds = *Earn* or *Preserve* Money through *fixed* **coupon payments** and repayment of principal at **maturity**.

If you have more than 20 years left until you retire, you should be focused on **equities**: index funds and stocks. You have time to ride the ups and the downs of the market- which has historically averaged close to 10% annually.

However, if you have *less* than 20 years left until you retire, you may want to add bonds to your investment strategy. The closer you get to retirement, the less time you have to wait for the market to recover. How most investors do this is by slowly increasing their ownership of bonds in their **portfolios**.

A **portfolio** is just a fancy way of saying *all the investments I own*. Every time you say it at a social gathering, people will suddenly think you're smarter and that you know what wine pairs best with smoked gouda.

Anyway, bonds are best used to preserve your money and earn some **passive income** in the form of interest (the coupon payments). There are honestly **a lot** of other ways people use bonds (and stocks as well), but the purpose of this book is to give you the basics. If you want to be the next bond king or an options trader, you'll need to learn that stuff on your own. M'kay?

Bonds are an IOU. You are letting the company **borrow** a fixed amount of money for a fixed period of time. In exchange, they'll give you a fixed amount of interest- either annually or a couple of times a year. The amount of money, the period of time, the interest rate, and the payment frequency are all told to you upfront. There is no guessing here. This makes bond investing excellent for **capital preservation**- making sure that you don't lose money. If you're close to retirement, capital preservation is WAY more important than investing in some brand new company with an unproven track record. Here are some terms you'll need to know if you're considering buying bonds:

- o **Face Amount** = the fixed amount of money you invest ($1,000, $2,000, etc.)
- o **Maturity** = the fixed period of time (i.e. 1 year, 2 years, 5 years, etc.)
- o **Coupon rate** = the fixed interest rate (also known as **yield** or **nominal yield**)
- o **Coupon** = the dollar value of the interest payment and the payment frequency

Here's an example: You buy a **5-year maturity** bond with a $1,000 **face amount** and a 4% **coupon rate** that pays a **coupon** of $20 twice a year.

In this example, you'd get $40 a year for each of the 5 years for a total of $200 in interest payments. At the end of the five years, you get your $1,000 back. You now have $1,200. What's that you say? Not impressed? Too slow? Well, that's the point. If you're investing in bonds, you're no longer looking for growth. You just don't want to *lose* any money. Bonds are a good way to accomplish this.

Using Bonds for Passive Income

Just like with dividends, you can own multiple bonds to build up your passive income. If you owned $100,000 worth of 5-year bonds, you'd make $4,000 per year in coupon payments. That's only $333 per month in passive income, but if you were to **add** that to the $870 in monthly dividend income from our earlier example, now you'd have **$1,203** in monthly passive income. Are you starting to see how you can build up your passive income to where you **no longer have to work for money**?

If your portfolio reached 1 million dollars by the time you retired, you could use dividend stocks and bonds to produce an average 5% return on your money. That would be **$50,000 per year**. I explained at the beginning of the book that you needed become to be a millionaire to create income that you don't have to work for. **Dividends and Bonds** are a great way to do it.

Bonds vs. Certificates of Deposit (CDs)

Bonds and CDs basically work the same way. You put in a fixed amount of money and you get interest after waiting for a fixed period of time. The biggest difference is *who* is asking for the money: Companies vs. Government vs. Banks.

Bank Certificates of Deposit (CDs)
Risk = **None**. You are **absolutely** getting your money back with the interest you were promised. Your CD cannot be closed unless you cash it out early. In that case, you'll lose a portion of the interest you've earned up to that point. Even if the bank goes out of business, FDIC insurance will kick in and you still get ALL of your money back AND any interest you've gained up to $250,000 (as of March 2021).

Reward = Lol. Seriously, it's pretty low. You're looking at interest rates that are currently hovering around 1%. You know the saying, "No Risk, No Reward"? That definitely applies here. The only reason you'd even open a CD is because you're waiting for a better investment opportunity.

Government Bonds

Risk = low. You are fairly certain to get your money back, but that's not a guarantee. You've probably seen one before. It's that weird, oversized dollar bill-looking thing you got from your grandmother in 5ᵗʰ grade. That's technically a **Savings Bond**, but it works the same way. You're loaning the government money. Either way, the government is going to give you your money back, so there isn't a lot of risk here.

Reward = not much better than bank CDs (right now at least). Depending on the maturity, the interest rates are actually **worse** than what you could get at a bank. Here's the thing though: **interest rates can change**. In September of 1981, a 10-year government bond paid **15.82%**. That didn't just randomly happen. There were other things happening in the economy that drove the interest rate up that high. However, a high government bond rate doesn't necessarily mean things are awesome and everybody's happy. There's a good chance it's because of some economic disaster.

Corporate Bonds

Risk = medium to high. Depending on the company offering the bond, it could range from being *less risky* than stocks to *just as risky* as stocks. As a general rule, the higher the coupon/interest rate, the riskier it is. Keep in mind that bonds are not guaranteed. You could still lose some or all your money if the company goes under. In that scenario, you would be entitled to a portion of the company's **liquidation**. Liquidation is the process of selling all the company's assets to pay off debt. Since bonds are debt, you would be first in line to get your fair share of the liquidation. That doesn't mean you'll get all your money back, but you may get some. In contrast, if you own stock in that company, you'll likely get **zero**.

Fortunately for investors, there are three **bond rating systems** that help you understand how risky bonds are. We won't get into the nitty-gritty, but it's sort of like the grades in school: AAA is excellent, AA is pretty good, A is good, BBB is acceptable, and anything lower than that is questionable and high risk. The higher the grade, the lower the risk and the lower the return. The lower the grade, the higher the risk and the higher the return. The grades I referenced were from the Standard & Poor's Rating system. (Remember them? They're the same Standard & Poor's from the S&P 500.)

Call Risk

Additionally, the company may decide to close your bond before it matures. Why would they do that? Think about it. The bond is an IOU with an interest rate. Let's say the going rate for bonds is around 5%. You buy the bond at 5%. Then all of a sudden, there's some random drama in the bond markets and now the going rate is 2%. You're not worried, you still own the bond at 5% for a couple more years. Remember, the conditions of your bond are **fixed and cannot change** as long as you own it. However, the company doesn't want to keep paying you 5% when they now can pay 2% on new bonds. So sometimes companies will **call** bonds with higher interest. When your bond gets called, that's bad news for you. It means that they close you out, pay you all the interest they owe up to that point, give you your money back, and wipe their hands clean of you. Whatever plans you had for your interest payments are now canceled. Worse yet, if you want to buy another bond, you'll now only get 2%. It's not great, but it can happen.

Reward = Pretty decent. Right now the average corporate bond rate is hovering around 3% (as of March 2021). That's at least better than government bonds or bank CDs. If capital preservation is what you're aiming to do, this should achieve your goal. Also, once we get into the higher rates, you can start using bond interest payments as **passive income**. At 3%, you're going to need a lot of money invested in bonds to make a real dent though. You'd need a million dollars in bonds at 3% just to make $30,000 a year.

Before you freak out, that's not really a problem. Remember that people who invest heavily in bonds are close to retirement. If you spend your first 20 or so years investing in index funds and/or stocks, you would have hundreds of thousands of dollars saved up. You could then begin cashing out your stocks and buying more bonds. So no, you don't need to worry about going out and buying one million dollars worth of bonds anytime soon. Invest in the stock market for a long time, then **slowly** increase your bond holdings as you get older. Make sense?

Again, this isn't everything about bonds. These are the basics. Sometimes bonds cost less than the face amount and sometimes they cost more. I'm not going to go into all that in this book. If you're interested in bond investing, do a little more research. Some people really like them. Depending on your risk tolerance and investment strategy, they may be a good fit for you.

CHAPTER EIGHTEEN
Invest By Using What You Already Know

1.   Don't speculate or gamble with your money. Develop a strategy and stick with it.
2.   Find and buy stocks that are "on sale." You'll get a profit when it goes back to the regular price.
3.   Use free or paid research tools and do your homework before you invest.

Now we're going to take a look at buying individual stocks. We discussed the advantages of index investing, but there is one **major** downside: your return will be the *average* of all the winners AND losers. That return is still close to an impressive 10% historically, but what if you had invested in an index fund and your idiot buddy from high school invested in Amazon when it first went public? You'd probably feel pretty pissed. His strategy (if you can even call it that) got him a 1,000% return. You bet on the race, while he bet on the **winner**. More risk means more reward. You know you should never compare your results with anyone else, but let's be honest. We're human. We don't like the idea of someone having a 1,000% return while we got 10%. It doesn't seem fair. However, if your idiot buddy *lost* all his money gambling on some meme stock, you would feel pretty smart. Your 10% turtle strategy was best, after all.

This highlights the difference between **Passive Investing** and **Active Investing**. We mentioned passive investing before in the chapter on index funds. It's passive because you're not messing around with all the stocks in the fund. You just **passively** invest in the fund itself. Active investing means **you** are buying and selling individual stocks yourself. You are **actively** managing your own portfolio. You're attempting to beat the market using a combination of experience, analysis, and dumb luck. This is how your friend from high school got a 1,000% return.

This is the risk (and the dilemma) with investing in individual companies. Even when you have a good strategy and achieve a respectable return, there will always be some reckless idiot who will get lucky and leave you in the dust. What you *should* do in this situation is curb your fear of missing out (FOMO) and stick to your strategy. You *should* know that no one gets lucky forever. Unfortunately, what you're *likely* to do is jump on the bandwagon with whatever stock is hot at the moment and **lose a bunch of money**. That is why you need to read the following sentences over and over:

The stock market is NOT a casino.
Do NOT gamble with your money.

Yes, there are people who treat it like a casino. Yes, there are people who are willing to risk their life savings on some crazy YOLO strategy. Yes, there are people who attempt to profit with day trading. And yes, there are professionals (and amateurs) who use various strategies to make a ton of profit seemingly overnight. However, I strongly suggest **not** using those strategies unless you're comfortable losing money.

Don't invest in something *just because-*

- Other people made money with it.
- Some internet guru told you to.
- They're talking about it on the news.
- A financial advisor told you to.
- You have a "hunch."

DO YOUR **OWN** RESEARCH.

Folks, **this is serious**. People do desperate things when they lose a lot of money. The stock market (and the world) is full of risky companies and people trying to make a quick buck. The CEOs of these companies will straight up **LIE** to the government, their investors, and **everyone** if it means they can pump up their stock prices. The truth about buying individual stocks is that your investment can go to **zero** if you're not careful. Individual stocks are like fire. Fire is very useful, but **don't play with it-** *especially* if you don't know what you're doing. This is not a game and you can get seriously burned.

So, what I'm going to do for the rest of this chapter is show you how to invest in individual companies without putting yourself on fire. The good news is that you probably already know how to do it. Fair warning: this is going to be a super long analogy.

The "Manager's Special" Strategy

You're familiar with the manager's special at the grocery store, right? Don't act like you don't know what I'm talking about. It's that old meat, old yogurt, and old bread that's going to expire *tomorrow* and the store is trying to get rid of it *today* before they are legally obligated to throw it out. It's the store's last chance at making a profit. However, since it's close to expiration, they know you won't buy it at full price. So they'll offer a **discount** to encourage you to buy it. Grocery stores will usually mix these manager's specials in with the regular-priced stuff. They'll put a brightly colored sticker on it so you know it's about to expire.

However, a lot of times there's a section in the store around the back where they put all or most of their manager's specials. Once you start shopping in the back of the store, you'll start to realize that some shoppers *go straight there* as soon as they enter the store. If they don't find what they want, they look for "Buy One, Get One Free" (BOGO) deals, 2-for-1 specials, or they use the pack of coupons in their wallet or purse to get a discount.

You're probably visualizing some stressed-out, middle-aged mother pushing an overloaded shopping cart with 5 kids running around her. Nobody is jealous of her situation. Nobody. But what you *can't* see is that she most likely saved 30% off the same groceries you bought at full price. If you're only buying one or two things, that might be a difference of $2. However, with a cart full of groceries, that difference can be closer to $100. That means you paid **$100 more** than she did for **the same stuff**. Do I have your attention yet?

Your goal is to be just like her…with stocks.

You're going to treat the stock market like a trip to the grocery store. If you know how to get a good deal shopping for groceries, you're already ahead of the game. Here's why- If you're a bargain hunter, you know that prices **change**. Sometimes the things you really want are regularly priced, and sometimes they go on sale. Sometimes the things you *don't* want (and aren't even looking for) are *such a good deal* that you end up buying them anyway.

That means that pack of Oreos you've been eyeballing isn't "worth" $5, it's just **priced** at $5 *right now*. If it were *worth* $5, it would *always* be $5 *no matter what*. However, there's a good chance that you could come back on the weekend and it will be **on sale** for $4. Some of you would buy a pack then, but the frugal warriors will *wait*. They know that *eventually* those Oreos will have a "Buy One, Get One Free" promotion. How do they know? It's because they've seen it several times before. They understand that every two months or so, a good buying opportunity presents itself. When the BOGO promotion finally arrives, they don't just buy one pack, they buy **four**. Some will buy as many as the store policy allows. So let's look at the numbers:

- ✓ Regular price = $5 per bag = **$0** saved per pack
- ✓ Sale price = $4 per bag = **$1** saved per pack
- ✓ BOGO price = $2.50 per bag = **$2.50** saved per pack

Maybe these numbers don't impress you, but what if you could **sell** these Oreo packs **back to the grocery store at the current price**? That means that if you don't eat them, these packs sitting in your pantry are worth real money. Now you have an **incentive** to buy as *many* as you possibly can as *cheaply* as you possibly can. You already know that the **regular price** is $5. Even if you take all three prices into consideration, the **average of those prices** is $3.83. If you can get the packs at $2.50 a pack, your profit will **average** $1.33 per bag. That also means that you don't want to pay more than $3.83 for a pack or you risk *losing* money when you try to sell it back. Still with me? You are working with three assumptions:

1. The price is *regularly* $5.
2. Randomly, it's *on sale* for $4.
3. Every two months, there's a BOGO offer that makes it $2.50.

- If you buy a pack at $5, you won't make any profit selling and you'll lose money if it's any cheaper. You've bought them at the highest price. You might as well just eat them.

- If you buy at $4, you'll make a dollar when the price is $5, make zero when it's randomly on sale, and *lose* money during the BOGO.

- At $2.50, you'll profit anywhere from $1.50 to $2.50 **most of the time**. During the BOGO promotion, you won't make any money selling, BUT you should *probably* use this opportunity to **buy some more**. Buying more cheap packs **guarantees** a profit **regardless** of whether it goes back to regular price OR goes on sale. Got it?

I know this sounds like your typical "buy low, sell high" strategy you've heard a million times, but it's deeper than that. What I'm explaining is called:

Reversion to the Mean.

This means that no matter how high or how low the price of something gets, it will **eventually** return to the long-term average of all those prices. It's like a rubber band. No matter how far you stretch it out or how much you squeeze it in, it will typically snap back to its original, or average, state. In other words, it will **revert** to the **mean**.

In our case, that average is $3.83. That means that buying a pack of Oreos *below* that price will *most likely* mean a profit when I choose to sell it. Conversely, buying a pack *above* that price will *most likely* mean a loss. Reversion to the Mean is just a way to help you understand *how much* you should be paying for your investments in order to make a profit. It's also a way to help you manage the **risk** involved with investing in things that go up and down in price.

So, am I saying that Reversion to the Mean is a sure thing? Absolutely not. Prices don't exist in a vacuum and nothing stays the same forever. Things change. Situations change. Let's throw in some real-world stuff so you can see what I mean.

Let's say that Nabisco, the company that owns Oreo, reported that they're suffering from a national shortage of cocoa. There was a massive fire in Brazil somewhere and the cocoa output was reduced by a third. What do you think will happen to the price of Oreos? Exactly- it will go up. Now your favorite cookie costs $7 a pack. If you already had a bunch of packs you bought at $2.50 in your pantry, you're stoked. You'll make a whopping **$5.50 profit** per pack. That's a 220% return! Even if you bought it at the regular price, you'll still make a $2 profit per bag at a 40% return. That's still an awesome return, but which would you prefer: a 40% profit or a 220% profit? But wait- could the price of Oreos go even *higher*? Should I:

A.   Wait and see if the cocoa shortage thing gets worse and drives up the price?
B.   Sell right now!

The answer is: Who knows? The truth is that the fire in Brazil may have actually only destroyed a quarter of cocoa output- and it's only going to be for a few months. Most likely, the price will go back to normal. However, if the fire's damage is permanent, the price will come down some, but it likely won't go back to $5. It may only go back down to $5.75. After all, cocoa will cost more now. Nabisco will have to raise their price or make smaller packs for the same price. **My decision to wait or sell would depend on how much I paid for the Oreos originally**. If I only paid $2.50 a pack, you'd better believe I'm selling.

As an investor, the **last** thing you'd want to do in this situation is **buy** packs of Oreos. However, some people would **speculate**(aka gamble) that the fire in Brazil is so bad that Nabisco will *stop* making Oreos. That means that any Oreos already made will become scarce. These **speculators** know that scarcity will drive up the price and go from store to store attempting to buy up all the Oreos. We actually saw this exact thing happen during the pandemic with toilet paper. Remember that? Toilet paper was scarce. That's how weird things got. Anyway, speculating is not something I recommend. Why? Because:

Speculating is NOT investing. It's gambling.

This is how you get burned. The nature of speculating the price of anything means that there's a **time window** that will provide the best returns. If you buy in or cash out at the wrong time, you could lose a TON of money. There is a real chance that Nabisco's plan to stop making Oreos is a rumor. Rumors are still very powerful. Even with no evidence whatsoever, the fear of missing out (FOMO) will make the average person attempt to hoard a bunch of Oreos. No store will have them in stock. This scarcity will drive up the price. It could get as high as $10 a pack. That doesn't matter because you won't be able to find them anywhere. Speculators might put their packs of Oreos on Amazon and eBay for as much as $25 a pack. People **will** buy them. They're operating off the fear that they'll never eat another Oreo again. Speculators who bought at $10 are raking in the dough. They're making an **$18 profit** per pack. That's an insane 357% return! Everything will go great until....

...Nabisco puts out a statement in the news saying that the rumor is untrue and that Oreo production is 95% on schedule. They've found another cocoa producer in Switzerland that will allow them to keep prices low and they see no real impact to their ability to give inventory to the stores. What do you think will happen to the price of Oreos now? You're right. It'll go back to the regular price **as soon as** the cookies start appearing on the shelves.

If you're a speculator, you're in a race **against time**. You have to get rid of a garage full of 400 packs of Oreos- and **fast**. No one is going to pay $25 a pack now. You lower your price to $20, then $18, then $15. You manage to get rid of about 100 packs at an average price of $17. You paid $10. You profited $700 at $7 per pack.

That's not bad, but ultimately, you can't sell anymore online and you'll have to sell to the grocery store at the current price of $5. You have 300 packs left. You sell the rest for $1,500. But remember: You spent $10. Those 300 packs **cost** you $3,000. So here's how you did:

- ✓   Sold 100 packs at $17 average cost = +$1,700
- ✓   Sold 300 packs at $5 grocery store cost = +$1,500
  - ▪   Total Sales = +$3,200

- ✓   Bought 400 packs at $10 individual cost = -$4,000
  - ▪   Total Profit = **-$800**

So for all that hard work, hustling, scheming and depriving regular people out of their Oreos, **you lost $800**. You **lost** it because you jumped on the bandwagon of people **speculating on prices**. Sometimes you win, but **most** times you lose. If you had done your homework, you would have known that buying a pack of Oreos above $3.83 lowered your chance for profit. The moral of the story is- **Don't be a speculator. Be an investor.**

Here's another situation. Let's say that CNN did some investigative journalism and they found a ton of rat feces at one of the Nabisco plants where they make Oreos. The fallout is so bad that Nabisco has to recall a whole bunch of packs of Oreos and it's all over the news. What do you think will happen to the price of Oreos now? Yep, it plummets. They'll probably reduce the regular price to $3 a pack AND will have "buy one get one free" promotions **nearly every day**. Now you can get a pack of potentially doo-doo infested cookies for $1.50 a pack. Any takers? No? No matter how much you paid for a pack of Oreos, you're faced with a conundrum. Do you:

A.   Wait and hope that the price of Oreos goes back up?
B.   Get rid of all your Oreos and cut your losses?

The answer to that probably depends on **how much you paid for them** and **what you think will happen in the future**. Do you really think that people will stop eating Oreos forever? Let's be real. There's no way that's happening. So what do you do?

A.   Buy some more!

I can hear you now. "Are you crazy?! You just said that there was doo-doo in the cookies! Why on earth would you suggest buying even more of them!?" Well, it's because **I did my own research** and realized that only *some* of the cookies were affected. There are several Nabisco plants and only **one** had the issue. So although popular opinion isn't great for Oreo right now, the **fact** is that most of the cookies on the shelves are perfectly safe to eat. The ones that have doo-doo in them were taken off the shelves before the story even aired. The public is **over-reacting.**

The result is that I now can buy as many $1.50 packs of Oreos as I want.

When all the drama dies down (and it *will* die down) the price of Oreos will **revert** back to an average price of $3.83. Unless Nabisco goes out of business, I'll profit- no matter what happens.

This is now officially the longest analogy I've ever written. I'm sure you got the point, but in the chance you didn't, just replace "packs of Oreos" with "shares of Nabisco Stock" and it's basically the same thing. See? This stuff isn't hard. You already know how to find a good deal at a grocery store. Do the same thing with individual stocks. If you want the technical term, it's called:

Value Investing.

Value Investing means that you **never** pay full price for anything- *ever*. You do your *own* research and determine what price you'll buy any given stock and then you **wait** until the price is the price YOU think will make you the most profit down the road. You've already seen this in action with our Oreo example. We determined that the **average** between the highest price and the lowest price gave us a target price that we could use to help us make decisions.

Of course, you're grown and you can do whatever you want. I can't tell the future and anything can happen. But can you see how value investing can help you make decisions? If you've ever heard of Warren Buffett, he's generally known as a value investor. Watch some videos on him. Pick the ones where he's talking to college students or beginning investors. He prefers to **buy** and enter the market when everyone else wants to **sell** and exit the market. His biggest thing is to "be greedy when others are fearful and fearful when others are greedy." Jack Bogle, the founder of Vanguard, talks about Reversion to the Mean a lot in his books. Also, keep in mind:

Value Investing Works Best with Value Stocks, Not Growth Stocks.

Growth stocks tend to move steady upward (or steady downward). Growth stocks can be stuck in a range for a period of time (often referred to as **range-bound**), but it's not likely to last for long. If you try to use averages to wait for a good price to buy, you might never get your chance. Growth stocks can be like a runaway train. If you *choose* to miss the train because you think it's slightly too expensive, you may be forced to pay **way** more down the line. This has happened to me several times and I still kick myself. However, the reverse is also true. Growth stocks can also be like a derailing train. If you choose to hop on because you think you got a good price, you'll be in for the ride of your life and hopefully you can escape before it crashes. This has also happened to me and I've lost money.

Value stocks have prices that **tend to stay in the same range for a long time**. For example, from July 2016 to January 2020, Exxon's stock price ranged from around $67 at its lowest to around $95 at its highest. For four years, it stayed within a $30 price range and had an average price of $81. That is, until the pandemic. The combined shock of the pandemic and a dispute between the oil-producing companies caused the price to go down to close to $32. So let me ask you: What do you think the price of Exxon stock will go back to? Will it ever reach its average of $81 again? Who knows? But I can tell you that by March 12, 2021, it had climbed back to $61. Talking about Oreos is a good way to explain what *could* happen, but I wanted to show you an example of something that *actually* happened so you can see for yourself. Okay, it's time for a major disclaimer:

Value Investing isn't just about finding averages.

My goal is to slowly introduce different investment ideas and strategies to you. I tend to oversimplify first, then move on to the more complicated parts. The truth is that the "value" in value investing is determined using **fundamental analysis** to determine whether or not a stock is **underpriced**. We can obviously use common sense to see that some things are cheaper than they normally are, but the analysis helps us to understand that sometimes things get cheaper **for good reason**. If that's the case, we wouldn't get an underpriced deal that we could profit from later. We would instead get an *accurately* priced stock that is now cheaper because **fundamentally** the business is no longer as valuable as it once was. I'll give you an example:

Do you remember K-Mart? Some of you do. At one point, it was more popular than Walmart. If you owned K-Mart stock back then, you were doing well; it was $121 per share. Would you want to own K-Mart stock now? No, you would not. It's currently priced at 26 *cents* a share. What happened? Well, look around you. Do you see any K-Marts? Nope. Most of them are gone. Walmart and Target had better business models and the competition destroyed K-Mart. If you had only used averages to buy K-Mart stock, you could have potentially made money in the short term, but you would have lost everything in the long term.

That's why it's ALWAYS important to make sure that you're investing in **good** companies. That means that they were good **yesterday**, they're good **today**, and they're projected to be good **for the foreseeable future**. Well, how can you possibly know all that stuff? Fortunately, you have access to that **fundamental analysis** that I keep talking about.

Everything About a Company's Stock Is Public Information

It's true. You can go to Yahoo Finance (finance.yahoo.com), type in a company's name or stock (or ticker) symbol and see WAY more information about that company than you were probably prepared for or know what to do with. You'll see all types of charts, graphs, and numbers. Some of them may make sense. You won't have a clue about other stuff. That's ok. As you learn more about investing, things will get clearer. Here are some of the more important and more common terms that you should know in the beginning.

EPS (Earnings Per Share): **This is a measure of profitability.** It's the company's profit divided by the number of outstanding shares of stock. **This should be a positive number**. The reason you want to know this is because it helps you compare the stock of similar companies. If Home Depot's stock was $313 a share and Lowes was $194 a share, it might be confusing. They're both home improvement stores with a similar experience, so why is their stock price so different? It may be because Home Depot's earnings per share is 11.94 and Lowe's is 7.75. Home Depot has a higher earnings per share, so it is considered to be more profitable. In that case, Home Depot's higher share price may be justified. There are other factors to consider, but EPS can help make comparing similar companies easier.

P/E (Price to Earnings) **Ratio: This is a measure of valuing a company**. It's the price of the stock divided by the earnings per share (EPS). Investors use this number to get an idea if the price of the stock is too high, too low, or just right. To get an idea of where that number should be when you're doing your research, the average of the S&P500

has historically been around 14. How you would say that in conversation would be:

> "It's trading at 14 times its earnings."

When you say it out loud, it sounds kind of high. Why would something be 14 times what it earns? What does that even mean? It means that the relationship of the price of the stock *compared* to the company's earnings is getting influenced by the outlook for the future. Investors are beginning to **speculate** on the future of the company and are driving up the price with less regard to the company's business fundamentals. If earnings are the main driving force behind a company growing bigger, then the P/E should be a low number. A low number means that the money coming in and the price of the stock are in step with one another. That makes sense, right? The company you're investing in **should be earning money**. Therefore, it's generally thought that stocks below the S&P's historical P/E average have a **healthier** relationship between their earnings and their stock price. They're considered a better value than stocks above the average.

On the other hand, stocks above the average are considered "expensive." There is *less* of a relationship between earnings and the stock price. Investors may be bidding up the price of the stock based on other factors **besides** earnings. Higher than average P/E ratios may also be the result of a booming market (also called a **bull** market), the industry the company is in (like Tech), or the feeling that the company is a game-changer with a really bright future.

Right now, we're seeing a booming market. Home Depot's stock has a P/E ratio of 26. Lowe's is at 25. Apple is at 35. However, Tesla is at **1,070**. What? How does it get *that* high if everything else is in the two digits? It means that Tesla is a tech company in a booming market AND investors really, **really** think that it's a game-changer that will grow into a huge company in the future.

What's important to realize is that because the P/E is so high, Tesla stock is currently priced **as if the future is already here**. The high P/E reflects the attitude that Tesla's success is **guaranteed**, so why not just go ahead and give it that future price? Right now, it's valued at more than Toyota, Volkswagen, Daimler, General Motors, BMW, Honda, Hyundai and Ford **combined**. At such a high P/E (or **valuation**), investors are betting that Tesla will be the most profitable car manufacturer in the **world**. Is that possible? Maybe. However, if Tesla doesn't live up to investors' expectations (and speculations), the stock price could fall pretty fast.

The question I want you to consider is this: If a stock is being **currently** priced for what investors *think* it will be 5 years **in the future**, will you grow your money significantly by investing in it **today**?

52 Week Range: the lowest price and the highest price for the past year. You could look at this to try to determine a range but be careful. There might be a significant event that made the price go up or go down in a way that's not normal for the stock. Currently, that event is the pandemic.

Ex-Dividend Date. You have to own the stock **before** this date to get paid the dividend. So don't think you're just going to buy the stock to get the dividend and then sell it after you get paid. They already knew people would try that.

1 Year Target Estimate: what analysts think the price will be in a year if everything about the company keeps operating the way it does presently. Obviously, no one knows the future. Take this with a grain of salt.

Fair Value: what analysts feel is the "appropriate" price of the stock based on the company's earnings and growth rate. Not all analysts are going to agree on this number. I tend to check at least two different sources to make sure that everyone is in the same ballpark.

Overwhelmed yet? Well, don't stress out. I don't expect you to memorize any of this stuff right now. I just want to get you started. There is a ton more information available to any investor who wants to do extensive research on any company's stock. All that information is free. That's a good thing. Unfortunately, when you're starting out, it can be really difficult to understand and interpret what that information **means**. Here's the good news: There are tools available to the beginning investor that presents all that information in a simple way. These tools are like using a calculator vs trying to remember a bunch of formulas and having to "show your work" in math class.

Use Stock Research Tools to Help You Make Better Decisions

You are not alone when it comes to making investment decisions. There are so many tools, websites, forums, and social media groups that I can't even count them all. Once you enter the world of investing, you will meet so many people who each have their own favorite research software or app or service. A lot of these services have a limited service that's free. If you want the entire service, you're going to have to pay a monthly or yearly subscription. The cool thing about these tools is that they're not all that different from what Wall Street professionals use. This can be a good and bad thing. It's good that you have the tools professionals have. It's bad when you have NO clue of what you're looking at. You may get intimidated and decide that investing isn't for you. This is absolutely untrue and it's why I spend so much time using Oreo analogies and being silly. It's not hard. **Don't believe anyone who tells you it is.** There are definitely levels of mastery, but it's okay to be a beginner.

You're probably going to find a good amount of analysis and research tools in the brokerage service you use. Remember: you'll need to open a brokerage account to buy stocks. Robinhood, WeBull, Vanguard, Fidelity, TD Ameritrade, and Interactive Brokers all have some level of analysis that you can look at. TD Ameritrade also has an impressive educational component that's completely free for account holders. However, if you'd like to dig deeper, I recommend:

Yahoo Finance
Investor's Business Daily
Value Line
Simply Wall St.

I've used these services and I have gotten good results with them. There are plenty of others but be careful. Research tools and stock-picking services are two **different** things. A lot of the services advertised on the internet are **stock-picking services** and can get kind of spammy. You'll sign up for a free account, and then they'll spam you every single day to try to get you to buy a membership or some kind of exclusive stock-picking club or whatever. Even if you purchase a subscription, they'll harass you to upgrade to some *higher*-priced service. These companies have fairly high-pressure sales tactics and they make you feel that you'll miss out on some life-changing opportunity or some massive discount if you don't act by midnight *tonight*.

The information they provide is genuine, but it's expensive. Any money you pay for stock picks takes away from your profit as an investor. Worse yet, you can pay the money for a stock pick and the stock tanks. I'm *currently* in the red for a stock that was recommended by one of these services. I'm confident I'll make my money back, but the point is that **there are no guarantees with the stock market**. Losing money is bad enough. *Paying* someone to lose money is infuriating. We'll talk more about these services in the chapter on "Helpers."

What I Specifically Look For When Grocery Shopping for a Company's Stock:

- ✓ **Valuation**: This is what I look at first. I want to get a good deal. If the company is undervalued by 25% or more of its **fair value**, I start digging around more. Personally, I'm not interested in anything that isn't on sale.

- ✓ **Share Price & News:** I want to see what the current price is and if there are any news events that are affecting the price of the stock. Did the company have some unexpected good or bad news? I want to know how that affected the stock. If it's bad news, the price will likely come down. This is exactly what I'm after: a cheaper price. However, I need to make sure that the bad news isn't so bad that the stock price is likely to continue falling.

- ✓ **Insider Trading Volume:** I want to know if the people running the company are buying or selling shares. They are required to disclose anytime they buy or sell company stock. It's not necessarily a bad thing if officers and executives are selling shares, but if there are **way** more insiders selling than buying, to me that means something is up. It may mean that they feel that the price is high enough to cash out. Either way, I don't want to buy when everyone else is selling. If they're buying shares, they may think it's at a good price.

- ✓ **Future Growth**: I want to make sure that the company is forecasted to increase its earnings over the next 3 years. I would expect a double-digit increase for a growth company and a high single-digit increase for a large company.

✓ **Financial Health:** Just like you need cash to pay your bills, so do companies. And just like you can pay some of your bills with a credit card, eventually you're going to have to use your cash to pay down your debt. I want to make sure the company I'm looking at has enough cash to cover them for at least a year. 1 year is considered **short-term.** Their short-term **assets** (cash, buildings, and equipment) value needs to be a higher number than their short-term **liabilities** (debt). Otherwise, they're highly leveraged. This means they have too much debt. You know from personal experience that having too much debt means you're spending a lot of money on interest and payments. Some debt is ok. Too much is bad.

✓ **Does It Make Sense:** This isn't something you're going to find on research tools. I just like to ask myself if this price makes sense based on my understanding of the company and the industry. I don't know everything, so I tend to invest in things I understand. When the pandemic crushed the demand for oil, the price went down. Makes sense. When the vaccines started rolling out, the price for oil started going up. That makes sense too. Then I see that the stock prices for oil companies were more than twice as high before the pandemic. So that means the price isn't even halfway back to where it used to be. That makes even more sense because we're not back to normal yet. If I buy today, before we've even gotten halfway back to pre-pandemic levels, I'm likely to make a profit. Even if it only gets to 75% of pre-pandemic levels, I'll still make a profit. Cool. I'll buy some oil stocks. That was my thinking. I still checked all the other fundamentals, but it made sense. As of today (April 2021), my return is over 50% on oil stocks. When the things I buy make sense, I usually make a good return. When I don't understand what's going on and I'm just hoping to get lucky, I typically lose money. All these facts and stats and stuff are good, but it needs to make sense to you.

Don't Discount Your Personal Experience

If you work at one of these companies or you if have experience with this company as a vendor or customer, you will have a better understanding of that company. That's an **advantage**. I used to drive for Lyft. I signed up for another company as well, but I just felt that Lyft delivered a better experience for the customer. I got a bonus, had a good experience with the company, had fun driving people all over the city, and even started reading up on the co-founders. When the pandemic hit and all the rideshare companies lost business, I had a good feeling that Lyft would recover. Sure enough, they did. However, it wasn't just a guess. I had plenty of customers tell me during their rides that they thought Lyft gave them a better overall customer experience than other rideshare companies. Turns out I wasn't the only one who felt that way. I did company research **just by talking to people**. Lyft stock is now one of the best performers in my portfolio.

CHAPTER NINETEEN
How to Buy Stocks

1.   Pick an online stock broker that's simple and doesn't have fees. Fees reduce your return.
2.   Choose a broker that gives you access to limit, market, and stop orders.
3.   Use "stop" orders to protect against excessive losses.

Alright, it's *go time*. I've spent an entire book lecturing you about everything with a dollar sign in front of it, but now it's time to actually buy something. Are you excited? You should be. The first thing we're going to do is open a brokerage account. Don't worry. I'll walk you through it.

Picking a Stock Broker

Brokerage accounts are offered by online stock **brokers**. Most brokers offer similar features and services, but **the most important is that there are no trading or commission fees for buying or selling shares.** If you learn nothing else from this book, know that fees eventually rob you of your wealth. Other than that, you should pick something that you like and is relatively easy to use. Here are a few of the current popular brokers, but it's not a complete list by any means.

For Passive Investors Who Want Index Funds, Mutual Funds, ETFs and Retirement Plans:

✓   Vanguard

For Passive and Active Investors Who Want Access to Everything:

✓ Fidelity
✓ TD Ameritrade
✓ Charles Schwab

For Passive and Active Investors Who Prefer being with One Company for Banking & Stocks:

✓ JP Morgan Chase/Chase Bank
✓ Merrill Edge/ Bank of America

For Active Investors Who Want to Pick Stocks Using an App or Desktop:

✓ Robinhood
✓ WeBull
✓ E*Trade

If you're looking for recommendations, I believe the best one for beginners overall is TD Ameritrade. They have a lot of educational tools that are free for their users. Other than that, each of the others caters to specific types of investors. If you want to pick stocks, don't go to Vanguard. If you want a low-cost index fund or ETF, don't sign up on Robinhood. Once you know what your investment goals are, it will be easier to choose a broker that caters to those goals.

Opening a Brokerage Account

Now that you've picked a broker, go to their website or use their app and open an account. They're going to ask you for some information about who you are and how you intend to use the account. Don't stress over these questions. Most of them are required by **FINRA**, the government Financial Industry Regulating Agency. Every broker has to ask them.

Funding Your Brokerage Account

After you finish typing in all your personal info, your account will be open and you will have a brokerage account number. It might be called a "money market fund" or a holding account. It doesn't really matter what they name it. You just need to know that it will hold whatever money you use to buy and sell stocks. However, your new account will obviously have $0 when you first open it. You know you can't do anything with $0, so you'll need to fund your new account by putting money into it.

Unless you opened your account with Chase or Bank of America, you can't just go to a physical location and deposit money into your brokerage account. You'll need to **link** an existing checking or savings account to your new account and **transfer** some money. It doesn't matter who you have your checking account with. You just need to tell your broker what that account is so you can transfer money into and out of your brokerage account whenever you want. You only have to do this once. The link will always be accessible to your brokerage account unless you decide to remove it.

Once your bank account is linked to your brokerage account, you will initiate the transfer **from your brokerage account**. Your brokerage account setup will probably walk you through this entire process. It will probably take a couple of days to verify who you are and transfer the money from your bank account, but once that's done, you're ready to start investing!

Buying Your First Index Fund or Stock

Now that you have money in your brokerage account, you can buy something. Just to make it clear, buying something through your brokerage is always a two-step process:

1. Transfer money into your brokerage account.
2. Use the money from your brokerage account to buy stuff.

Got it? Transferring money into your brokerage account doesn't mean you've bought any stocks. Your money just sits there until you buy something with it. You don't have to buy something just because you put money in it. If you want, you could even set up your brokerage account to automatically transfer a set amount from your bank account every month. One thing to keep in mind: it'll take a couple of days for the money you transfer to show up in your brokerage account. If you're trying to jump on some hot stock tip and you have no money in your account, you'll have to sit on your thumbs for 1-3 business days waiting for a transfer to complete. If you don't like the sound of that, it might be a good idea to keep some money in your holding account so that you can buy things without having to wait.

Depending on how much money you transferred, you may be limited to what you can buy. It's kind of like being in a store. You have money to buy stuff, but that doesn't necessarily mean you can buy anything you want. Everything has a price and you can only buy what you can afford. If you only transferred $100, you can only buy shares of stock or fund shares that are $100 or less.

Let's say the first stock you want to buy is Amazon (AMZN) stock. You could either type in the stock symbol AMZN or the word "Amazon" into the search field. You see that the cost for one share is around $3,400. Well, unless you have that amount, you're not buying Amazon stock today.

However, some brokers allow you to do **Fractional Investing**. It means that you'll be allowed to purchase $100 *worth* of Amazon stock. You will then own 0.029 of 1 share, or roughly 3%, of one share. That's not a bad thing by any means. It's still yours. If Amazon stock doubles next month, your investment will double as well. Fractional Investing just allows you to participate in a company's stock at a lower price entry point. It's really a good thing for expensive stocks like Google and Amazon.

Index Funds, Mutual Funds, and ETFs may not have the ability to do Fractional Investing. For example, if you look up Fidelity's S&P 500 fund (FXAIX), the current price is near $150. You will most likely need the entire $150 to buy one share. If you only have $100 in your brokerage account, you'll need to transfer in some more money using your bank account link.

Placing An Order to Buy or Sell

So, you've opened your account and you've found something you want to buy. Now you need to place an order. There are two main ways to do this. You can buy something at the current price **right now** OR you can buy something once it reaches a target price.

> #1. Buy/Sell right now at **current** price = a **Market Order**
> #2. Buy/Sell once it reaches a **target** price = a **Limit Order**

There are other types of orders, but they are simply variations of these two. Understand how these two work first, and then you'll understand why you may want to use the other variations.

Market Order
This is the simplest, fastest way to buy and sell something. This is like the "add to cart" button on a website. Once you click or press "buy," you'll then need to enter the number of shares you'd like to buy, then submit. Ta-da! You're done. Your order will be filled as soon as possible at the market rate. Your broker confirms that the order is completed and the money is taken out of your brokerage account. You now own the number of shares you purchased. If you want to sell those shares later, you'd do the exact same thing. Click or press "sell," enter the number of shares you want to sell, then submit. The money from the sale goes back into your brokerage account.

The only drawback with using Market Orders is that the price you pay is dynamic: it's **always** moving. The market isn't going to wait around and reserve the price you like just because you started an order. Thousands (maybe millions) of people are trying to buy and sell that company's stock during market hours. It's like a bidding war every second. There are no price guarantees and the price you pay will likely be different from what you saw on the screen when you hit buy. Usually, it's not more than a few cents, but it could be a few dollars difference. You're placing an order that must *wait* to be fulfilled. That order *seems* like it's filled immediately because of modern technology, but technically it's in line with other orders. As people bid on the price, there's a chance that the price is higher by the time your order is fulfilled.

Imagine going to the grocery store. You get a gallon of milk. When you take it off the shelf, it's $2. You get in line at checkout and wait for the cashier. There are a few people ahead of you. By the time you get to the cashier, the milk is now $2.15. With market orders, you have no choice but to pay it. When you stepped in line, you committed to buying the milk. You might be irritated, but that's how market orders work. The price can change up until the moment your order is fulfilled.

Bottom line: You complete the transaction as soon as possible, but you may end up paying a few cents (or dollars) **more** than you anticipated when you **buy** and getting a price per share **less** than you anticipated when you **sell**.

Limit Order
This allows you to specify the **exact price** you want- whether you're buying or selling. Your order will **not** be placed and fulfilled until the price you specified is reached. Your brokerage account will place a **hold** on the money needed to purchase the shares- you can't use it because you're committing to buy the shares once your price is reached. However, the transaction doesn't complete until the limit order executes. You can cancel the order at any time before this happens and the hold is released from your money- allowing you to spend it again. If the price doesn't reach what you specify, nothing happens and your order will cancel at the end of the day by default (unless you choose a later expiration date).

Imagine going back to the grocery store. You're not in the mood to screw around with spontaneous prices this time. You're not paying one penny over $2. You stand in the "I'm only going to pay $2" checkout line. When the cashier turns on her light, that's the sign that the milk is now $2. You checkout. You paid exactly $2. You're happy. But what happens if the price never goes back down to $2? You might be standing there for a long time. Worse, the longer you stand there, the more you'll potentially pay for the milk. When closing time comes, you have to leave with no milk. You're free to try again tomorrow, but there's no guarantee you'll ever get your milk for $2.

This is the main drawback with limit orders. If your exact price isn't reached, nothing will happen. Maybe you were confident that prices would go down, but they never did. Maybe it got really, really close. It doesn't matter. If your price isn't reached, you walk away empty-handed. If this is a part of your strategy to be patient, that's a good thing. Perhaps you've done your homework and you feel that the price will eventually lower to your price point. That's totally fine. However, no one can tell the future and you might be waiting a very long time. It might not ever happen. That being said, limit orders are a very useful tool. You can use them in a couple of different ways:

- You can purposely underbid (or overbid) the price of a stock. If for whatever reason the stock reaches that price- even temporarily- you got the price you wanted. If it doesn't, you don't mind. You were just trying to get a good deal or make a good profit. Stock prices "dip" and "spike" all the time. Why not take advantage?

- You can make sure that you're paying the price closest to the one you see on the screen. If you see that a stock is at a good price, set your limit price close to the current price so that your order is filled quickly. Don't nickel and dime and risk the chance that your order won't trigger.

- You can have a limit order stay in place until you cancel it. This is called a **Good-Till-Cancelled** (GTC) limit order. If you're buying, you'd put in a price that you're hoping to pay after a significant price drop. If you're selling, you'd put in the price that you're hoping to sell for.

Bottom Line: You can use limit orders as a way to buy **now** with more control, or you can use them to try to get a deal **later**.

Stop-Loss and Stop-Limit Orders

These are the other variations on the market and limit order that we talked about a while back. These give you a little more control over how and when you buy or sell shares:

- A **Stop-Loss** order is a type of **Market** Order – order filled at market price.
- A **Stop-Limit** order is a type of **Limit** Order – order filled at your price.

The "**stop**" is simply a trigger. Once a stock's price decreases or increases beyond a price you specify, the stop **then** executes a market or limit order. Think about it like a tripwire for a trap: once the wire is tripped, something happens. In a stop-loss order, the trap activates immediately. In a stop-limit order, a second condition must be met to activate the trap.

You would use stop-loss and stop-limit orders if you wanted to protect yourself from a sudden drop in a stock's price. Companies get bad news all the time and sometimes it's out of their control. Supply issues, social unrest, regional conflict, environmental disasters and company scandals can make prices plummet. If you're like most of us, you don't have time to watch financial news all day. You could set this up **in advance** to make sure that you don't have huge losses when you're not paying attention. You don't want to realize too late that the stock lost 30% during the day's trading session.

You could also use stop-loss and stop-limit orders to protect any gains that you earned. Let's say you invested in a company's stock that went from $10 to $30. That's an amazing 200% return! You'd be excited, but you'd also want to protect that return. You could set a stop-loss or stop-limit order to execute if the share price ever fell below $25. That way, you could still keep around a 175% return.

Stop-Loss Order
A stop-loss order would be like automatically getting ejected from a crashing plane once it reaches an unsafe altitude. It's a failsafe that you plan in advance. If the plane is flying normally, it will never activate. However, if the plane ever decreases to an unsafe altitude, the "stop" will trigger and you're ejected immediately. It doesn't matter if you're flying over the ocean or a volcano- you're getting ejected **immediately**.

Stop-loss orders execute a market order as soon the stock's price reaches a number you set. You might think this is like a limit order, but it's different. Once the stop is activated, it triggers a market order that will buy or sell shares **as soon as possible**. Just like with a regular market order, you **don't** control the *exact* price per share. You're just trying to execute the trade **asap**.

Stop-Limit Order
Continuing with the plane analogy, a stop-limit order would *prepare* for ejection once an unsafe altitude is reached but would **wait** until a secondary condition is met **before** ejecting you. That secondary condition could be that you're over trees or over land that's *not* a volcano. Again, it's about control. If you're going to be ejected, you'd

at least like to be ejected in the most favorable way. However, if you specify that you get ejected over trees and you never fly over trees, nothing happens. You'll remain on the plane.

Stop-limit orders execute a limit order as soon the stock's price reaches a number you set. This is like a limit order with 2 triggers: the **stop-limit price** and the **limit price**. **Both** triggers must happen before the order executes. Once the stop-limit price is reached, it triggers a limit order that will buy or sell shares **as soon as the desired limit price is reached**. Just like with a regular limit order, **nothing happens** if you don't reach your desired price.

In general, don't make your stop-limit price and your limit price the same number. Give it a little breathing room; at least a 10-20% difference in price. If the price is coming down really fast, you want to give your brokerage time to process the two triggers:

1.   The stop-limit price that places the limit order.
2.   The fulfillment and execution of the limit order.

If the stop-limit price and the limit price are the same dollar amount, the stop-limit will trigger, but there's a chance that the resulting limit order *won't* trigger. Remember, ordering stocks is not instantaneous. Someone has to buy whatever you want to sell and you have to wait in line behind other orders that already exist. The stop-limit will **create** a new limit order that previously did not exist. Now you're in line. However, the price could have *already* gone lower than the limit price by the time this new order gets its turn in line. You would be too late; your order won't execute because the price you specified was never reached when it was active.

Bottom Line:
*   Stop-Loss – Guarantees* execution, but zero control over price.
*   Stop-Limit – Guarantees* control over price, but not execution.

*Stop orders work as expected under normal conditions, but there are no guarantees in the stock market. When there are extreme movements in a stock's price, weird stuff happens. Remember, for every buyer, there must be a seller and vice versa. Hitting the sell button is **not** a guarantee that you can cash out. Try not to invest heavily in anything that is extremely volatile or speculative.

Important Note About Ordering Outside Regular Trading Hours

The stock market is not open 24-7. It has regular trading hours from 9:30 am to 4 pm Monday through Friday. There are also **extended trading hours** before 9:30 am and after 4 pm. Orders can execute during these extended hours, but there are additional risks. The biggest risk is that the price of market orders can be significantly different from what you expect. It's called **spread**, and without boring you to death, it basically means that there is less bidding available to get you the price you expect. Since there's less bidding, your order may fulfill at undesirable prices. Market orders will function more as you expect during regular trading hours.

Limit orders will also execute in a way that makes sense during regular trading hours. Things can get complicated when you try to use limit orders outside of that time. Even if you set up your limit order to last longer than the end of the current business day, it doesn't mean that it's active during extended hours, non-trading hours or the weekend.

Congratulations! You own stock now!
Unless you didn't actually *buy* anything.

So up until this point, I've focused more on *how* to buy stocks vs the potential elephant in the room: your fear of buying stocks and potentially losing money. You know buying stocks is a good thing, but you haven't gotten around to it. There is definitely a psychological resistance to do something you (or your family) haven't really embraced before. It's hard. I grew up broke/lower middle income, so I definitely had a scarcity mindset when it came to money. I've always been interested in studying investing, but actually putting my money at risk was a whole different ball game. I've said this before, but your emotions are your #1 enemy. If you find yourself hesitating, you may be scared or holding on to some bad programming from your childhood. Just ask yourself:

Is It the **Fear of Losing Money**? If so:

✓   Have I done my due diligence (research)?

✓ Am I confident that this is a great value at a great price with growth potential?

✓ Does my gut tell me that this is a good idea?

✓ Do I have inside information that leads me to believe my actions are justified?

✓ What's the realistic downside? (Look at the 52-week **low**)

✓ What's the realistic upside? (Look at the 52-week **high**)

✓ Is my decision based on data or my emotions?

✓ Do I feel rushed or anxious?

Is It FOMO- the **Fear of Missing Out**?

✓ What if a stock does well in the future and I didn't buy it when I had the chance?

✓ What if everyone else makes more money than me?

✓ What if everyone else is investing in a "hot" stock but my research and my gut say not to? Do they know something I don't? (They don't.)

If you're **afraid of losing money**, consider this:

- Doing research is the best way to manage your risk. Being informed means you're not guessing. It's just like school. If you do your homework, odds are you won't fail the test.

- You'll know if it's a good value based on its fair price vs. its market price. If the current stock price is 20%-50% lower than its fair price, try to find the reason why. You may have found yourself a great deal.

- Your gut is a powerful tool. Don't rely on it entirely, but don't disregard it.

- If you have experience with the company as a customer, vendor, or employee, you know things the average person doesn't. Use that to your advantage.

- You'll know the realistic upside based on historical

performance, how close the current price is to the 52-week high, the fair price being higher than the market price, and earnings expectations for the next 3 years.

- We all fear the extreme downside: losing all our money. However, you can look around you and see companies that have been around for decades. The bigger the company you invest in, the less likely you'll lose all your money. Walmart isn't going anywhere anytime soon.

- Emotions make you chase money. Data helps you make money. Emotions and your money need to keep a healthy distance so that you can keep a cool head whether things are going great or going terrible. Remember, in the long run, the stock market never loses.

- If you feel rushed or anxious about buying or selling something, STOP. Go get lunch, go for a walk, or talk to someone you trust and who will encourage you. You must feel confident about your choices. If you're not confident, do more research or invest in another opportunity.

  If you're **afraid of missing out**, consider this:

- No one, and I *mean* **NO ONE**, knows the future. Sometimes you get lucky. Sometimes others get lucky. That's just how it goes. It has nothing to do with your intelligence. Do your own research and be an investor for the long term. Speculators and gamblers will eventually lose most of their gains. I've seen this time and time again.

- It doesn't matter how much other people are making. What are *your* goals? Are you wanting to get out of debt? Buy a house? Create passive income? Other peoples' success has nothing to do with your own. It's certainly tough to deal with because we tend to compare ourselves to other people. Save yourself the headache. Focus on **you**.

- There will always be a "hot" stock or investment vehicle that seems to make millionaires overnight. The painful truth is that the time to buy was yesterday, **not today**. If you buy today, you're likely going to deal with a painful loss as the value eventually drops back to normal levels.

- Check out the Fear and Greed Index on cnn.com. If it's showing "Extreme Greed," it's probably a sign that the market is overheated and people are gambling with their money. If you feel you absolutely have to buy something, buy with an amount you're willing to lose. Conversely, if it shows "Extreme Fear," that's your cue to buy aggressively. Everyone is selling, so things will be cheaper for you to buy. You should still do your research, but remember what Warren Buffet says: "Be greedy when others are fearful and be fearful when others are greedy."

General Tips to Overcome Fear and Doubt in Investing:

✓ Investing your money in stocks, mutual funds, and ETFs **doesn't** mean you *spent* it. $500 in your checking account has the same value as $500 in an index fund. It's not *gone*. You only moved it to a place where it has a better chance to grow. It's true that you could lose value, but it's also true that you could **gain** value. Most importantly, you can sell it and put it back in your checking account any time you want. **You are in control.**

✓ If your research and your gut say buy it, **buy it.**

✓ If your research and your gut say don't buy it, **don't buy it.**

✓ It doesn't matter what everyone else is doing. Your choices are your own and you have to live with your decisions. People love to shout from the rooftops about their successes while keeping their failures buried under their basement. Keep that in mind when you're browsing through social media.

✓ If you've done your research and genuinely feel that you've found a **great** company at a **great** price **at or near a market bottom** with **plenty of room for growth, buy as much as you can afford.**

✓ Be confident about your choices! If you've found a gold mine, don't just fill your pockets, **bring a dump truck**. If you still have doubts, just buy smaller amounts **consistently over time**.

✓ Be **consistent**. Make a budget and **take action** every month. However, you don't have to spend all of your budget in one day. You could spend a certain dollar amount every week, split your budget between multiple stocks, or buy the same stock throughout the month as the price goes up and down.

✓ If you feel like the price is going down too fast or is too high, **wait**. You don't want to buy something and then have regret as the price drops and you lose money.

✓ **Do not attempt to time the market.** Literally **no one** is consistently good at this- not even the experts. If you find yourself stressing out about *when* to buy, try:

Dollar-Cost Averaging

If you consistently use a fixed dollar amount to buy a stock over time as it goes up and down, you will likely have an average cost that is **less** than the current price. Why? Because you'll buy more of the stock when it's cheaper and less of the stock when it's more expensive. It's an effective way to invest long-term because it avoids the emotional roller coaster of trying to time the market. It also avoids the stress of buyer's remorse and/or FOMO. And with fractional investing, you never have to worry about what the stock price is. Just put in the same amount every month. You could even set up your brokerage account to automatically take money out of your bank account purchase a certain stock, index fund, or ETF every month.

If this all this stock picking, analysis, and research stuff *still* seem risky or too much of a pain in the butt, may I present to you...

The "No Work, No Stress, No Thinking" Strategy

This is the **ultimate** slacker investment plan. There are just 4 steps:

1. Buy an S&P 500 based Index fund.

2. Set up your account to purchase the same amount every month automatically.
3. Choose to automatically reinvest your dividends.
4. Go play video games.

Think this won't work? I've said this before and I'll say it again: this strategy amazingly beats industry professionals **nearly every year.** You don't have to take my word for it. It's actually very difficult to consistently beat the return of the S&P 500. It works for you because you're not actively screwing with it.

Most of the mistakes individual investors make come from doing **too much** with their portfolios. You won't get to participate in the massive gains of some hot tech company, but you'll avoid the massive losses of picking a loser. It's less risky, too. If any one of those 500 companies goes out of business, it'll be replaced with another one automatically. You don't have to do anything. Truthfully, the more you invest, you'll quickly learn that the best strategy is to buy your shares, then **do nothing**. You'll make *way* more money this way.

CHAPTER TWENTY
Retirement Plans: 401Ks and IRAs

1. If you have a 401K, put the maximum salary percentage that your employer will match.
2. 401Ks and Traditional IRAs let you grow your money and pay the taxes when you retire.
3. Roth IRAs let you pay the taxes now and pay no taxes when you retire.

Now that you know all the basics of stocks, mutual funds and ETFs, it's time to talk about retirement stuff. If you're 25, you're nowhere close to even thinking about retirement and you probably don't care. I know I didn't care about it back then. Of course, now I wish that I did, but that's not your problem. Even if you couldn't care less and think you have plenty of time, take advantage of this stuff **today**. I guarantee that your future self will appreciate it.

Sidenote: I want to take a few seconds to talk about Social Security. A lot of you already know what it is and how it works. If you have a job, you pay into Social Security. You don't have a choice. It doesn't matter where you work or how long you work there. If you have a job, your contributions to Social Security go to an account linked to your Social Security number. You don't have to worry or think about it. When you reach a certain age, you can collect payment based on how many total years you worked and how much you contributed to Social Security. I bring this up now because this idea of "**contributing**" to some fund, whether you have a choice or not, is the fundamental way retirement plans work. Got it?

Anyway, 401Ks and IRAs (Individual Retirement Accounts) are a way to save money on taxes. That is their whole purpose. They are tax-advantaged methods of growing your money. How can they help? It's simple. Any time you make money from investing, that money is called **capital gains**. After all, you gained capital, right? Capital gains are considered income. You get taxed on your income. That's why it's called income tax. You must pay income tax every year. You already know that your job will take it out automatically.

What you may *not* know is that your banks and your stock broker report your interest income and capital gains to the IRS and send you a notice of how much you earned. Since they already reported it to the IRS, you can't hide this income and pretend it doesn't exist. You cannot get out of paying taxes.

When it comes to your investments, any fees or money taken out reduce the effect of compound interest and rob you of your future wealth. Remember how we talked about expense ratios for ETFs and mutual funds? Remember how much money you **lose** over time by choosing a fund with high fees? Taxes work the same way. They blunt the effects of compound interest and can end up costing you tens of thousands of dollars.

Let's say you saved up $10,000 and put it in an index fund that got a 10% return that year. You made $1,000 in interest for a total of $11,000. However, you have to pay 25% in taxes on that interest, so after the tax fee of $250, your total now is $10,750 *after* taxes.

Let's say you make a 10% return again next year. You made $1,075 in interest for a new total of $11,825. You pay your 25% in taxes on the $1,075, so the new total is $11,556.25 *after* taxes.

At the end of the two years, you **made** $12,100 but were only allowed to **keep** $11,556.25. You **lose** $543.75 to taxes. Worse, this money you lost can no longer gain interest. This is how your compound interest is weakened and your wealth is taken.

Unfortunately, you **must** pay taxes. You may have lost money, but so did everybody else. Every citizen has an obligation to pay taxes and you can go to jail attempting to avoid them. But what if there was a way to **delay** paying taxes until later? Like *way* later? 401Ks and IRAs let you do that.

Qualified Retirement Plans

401Ks and IRAs belong to a long list of **qualified retirement plans.** These plans are ways the government helps you to save for retirement by giving you flexibility on **when** you pay your taxes. That doesn't sound like a big deal, but it's a **huge** deal. If you don't have to pay taxes every year, your money can continue to grow without interruption or fees. All the interest you earn will earn interest the next year. Compound interest can work its magic and you could end up with tens of thousands **more** by the time you retire. So, what's the catch?

After-Tax and Pre-Tax (Before Tax)

You will need to choose between two options for when you pay your taxes:

- o   **Option #1:** Pay your taxes upfront. Your investments will grow **after-tax.**
- o   **Option# 2:** Your investments will grow **pre-tax.** Pay your taxes **when you retire.**

Confused yet? Go grab or look up one of your recent pay stubs from work. Look at the gross pay, then look at the amount on the check. The gross amount is **pre-tax** and the amount you got paid was **after-tax.** It sucks to get that money taken out, but come tax season, you probably won't owe any money. If anything, you'll get a **refund.**

However, if you could somehow get paid the gross amount, come tax season, you'll have to pay the taxes on all that money you made that year- **at once.** That means you'll have a tax **bill** that may be several thousand dollars. However, it's not the end of the world if you know it's coming. This is how businesses and independent contractors get paid.

That's the basic difference between **pre-tax** and **after-tax.** Here's how 401Ks and IRAs fit into those two choices:

Pre-tax: 401K & Traditional IRA

After-tax: Roth IRA

This means 401Ks and Traditional IRAs **don't** pay any taxes until you retire or you cash it out. Roth IRAs have taxes taken out upfront, so when you retire, your money is tax-free because you've already paid taxes on that income. If we were to use your check as an example again:

- 401K & Traditional IRA contributions come out of your gross, or **pre-tax** pay.
- Roth IRA contributions come out of the amount on your check, **after-tax.**

What? There are two different IRAs? Yes, there are. There are some 401Ks that are after-tax as well. Everybody's tax situation is a little different, so having options is a good thing. We'll come back later to discuss tax stuff, but for now, let's jump right into:

A Not So Brief History of the 401K

Once upon a time, 401Ks were a perk for the executives that worked at a company. Everybody got a pension, but the execs got a 401K: a **second** retirement plan **on top of** their pension. Not only were you guaranteed income from your pension when you retired, but you would also have a nice little nest egg by way of your 401k investments. Sounds pretty awesome, right? What? Don't know what a pension is? I don't blame you. They barely exist anymore.

Pensions were an employee benefit guaranteed to any employee that completed the required years of service. Once you completed those years, you were guaranteed a monthly retirement income that was calculated using your highest earning years with the company and factored in with your years of service. At most, this gave you about half of your salary every year. You didn't have to manage a portfolio. If there were stocks involved, you didn't pick them. In fact, you didn't do anything to manage any aspect of your pension. These big companies had pension funds and pension fund managers whose primary job was to find investments that would return enough profit to pay for all these pensions. These companies had full-time, professional investors at their disposal that would research hundreds of companies in the search for investments that offered a good balance between growth and risk.

The employee benefited from these professionals and could focus on doing their jobs without being burdened with the responsibility of *also* focusing on their retirement. If you worked for the government, you likely paid a portion of your paycheck to a pension fund until you retired or left the company. However, most private companies didn't require employee contributions at all. If you served your years, you just *got* it. Once you were old enough, a check showed up in the mail without you having to do anything. It was that simple.

Well, somewhere down the line, big companies started seeing pensions as a drag on their bottom line. Giving someone a pension means that you have to pay them until they die. Folks, some people live a *long* time. And some big companies have hired thousands and thousands of people during their existence. I'm sure those companies *want* you to have a long life, but they're just not keen on footing the bill until thousands of people kick the bucket. So sometime around the '80s, companies slowly began phasing out pension plans. It was a cost-saving measure that instantly benefitted stock prices but ultimately cost the average worker.

However, companies knew that employees loved pensions. They knew they couldn't get rid of them without pissing off millions of workers, so they came up with a brilliant idea: Why not give the 401Ks to the workers instead of the pensions? Millions of workers were told that their pensions were going to be replaced by 401Ks. To circumvent the inevitable angry outcry from employees, the big companies would offer an "employee match" where they would match employee contributions dollar for dollar up to a certain percentage of their salary.

That meant that for every dollar an employee put in, the company would put in a dollar as well. Now the account would have two dollars. The employee could effectively double their retirement money by using this "new" 401K retirement plan. Even better, their 401Ks wouldn't be taxed until they retired. The employees were all in (but even if they weren't, they didn't have a choice).

And just like that, pensions started dying and *employees* become responsible for their own retirement. Regular people who had no clue about the stock market suddenly had to make decisions about their investments and how to manage their retirement portfolios. A lot of people struggled and lost money. Others didn't even participate because of the complexity and their unfamiliarity with the stock market. Some people left their jobs and totally forgot about their 401Ks. Still others needed to change careers and were suddenly faced with a bunch of requirements and deadlines about the 401K they had with their *now* former employer. Millions of dollars in unnecessary fees and IRS penalties were paid as retirement plans became tax burdens.

To be fair, some companies continued to offer pensions and other companies did a very good job of educating their employees on how to maximize their 401Ks; including how to navigate transferring 401Ks into Individual Retirement Accounts (IRAs) without fees and penalties. However, the **point** is that companies *ditched* the responsibility for taking care of employee retirement and placed that duty back onto the employees in the form of an **optional** plan. Since the plan was optional, a whole lot of employees never signed up. As of today, April 2021, 57% of all workers **do not participate in 401Ks.**

These days, companies may or may not even match your 401K contribution anymore, but you're still 100% responsible for your own retirement. In a way, it's good that you have control. On the other hand, giving control to regular people who don't know what they're doing is a surefire way to ensure their failure.

So, if you want to know why that old person is greeting you at Walmart or working with high schoolers at Wendy's, *that's* why. They don't have a choice. They don't have enough income to pay their bills, so they have to work anywhere that will accept them. I've seen the financial hardship that's currently facing retirees. Living a long time means that you could run out of money with no way to get income. You don't want to have to deal with that when you get older.

Manage Your 401K the Right Way

Your 401K plan from your employer probably doesn't give you access to the entire stock market. In fact, I'm willing to bet it doesn't. This means that you may not be able to pick the exact stocks, mutual funds, and ETFs that you might prefer. More than likely, you'll have access to a handful of mutual funds and ETFs with names like:

Aggressive Growth Fund
Aggressive Balanced Fund
Balanced Growth Fund
Technology Industry Sector Fund
Large-Cap ETF
Mid-Cap Balanced Fund
Small-Cap ETF
And so on, and so on.

Folks, the names of these products have **nothing to do with how they will actually perform**. Trust me. I know countless people who have had these types of accounts for years and barely made any money. It's almost criminal. Do you want to know why they didn't make money?

Fees.

These funds have notoriously high fees and expense ratios. We've talked about expense ratios, but we haven't really talked about fees. The reason is that it's easy to find no-fee options as an individual investor, but with your employer-based 401K, there's no competition. You must choose from what's available in your employer's plan. When it comes to the fund options your employer offers you, beware of **load**. Load means fees- typically sales commissions. I have no idea why it's called 'load', but you don't want it. It comes in a few different flavors and they're all bad:

- **Front (End) Load**: a fee you pay upfront when you buy a share of the fund.
- **Back (End) Load:** a fee you pay when you sell a share of the fund.

So if you were to choose a fund with a front-end load and a high expense ratio, you would be charged a percentage of your entire holdings every year **and** you'd be charged every time you contributed to the fund. You could easily spend more money on fees than the money you earn from your investments. The sad part is that your investments are making money, but most of that money is going to the fund managers, not you.

Ignore all those cleverly named funds. Choose an **index fund** or **ETF** based on the S&P 500 or the Dow with a low expense ratio at or below 0.2%. It's also important that the fund you pick is a **No-Load** fund. Fees destroy your wealth. Pay as little as possible.

Take Advantage of Employer Matching Contributions

This is probably the single biggest advantage of a 401K. It's truly a powerful thing if you use it wisely. We touched on it before, but it means that your employer will match your contributions dollar for dollar until you reach a certain percentage of your salary; usually between 3% and 5%.

That means if you make $30,000 a year, you could put $1,500 (5% of your salary) into your 401k and your employer would **match** your contributions with the $1,500 that they **give** you. Now you have $3,000. **It is literally free money**. The only catch is that you have to hang around for a few years to *keep* that free money. Once you've completed the required years of service, you are considered **vested**. If you leave or quit after that point, you keep all the money. If you leave *before* being vested, you forfeit the money they gave you, but you get to keep any money you put in it.

Take Advantage of Pre-Tax Investment Growth

Remember, 401K contributions are pre-tax. They come out of your **gross** pay, not the amount on your paycheck. Most people assume that contributions come out of their "check." This is a common misunderstanding that makes people not want to participate in their 401Ks. Your contributions come out of your **pay**, not your check. The difference is important. Here's why.

Still have that paycheck stub handy? Look at all the deductions and taxes and stuff. Do you pay for health insurance through your job? You'll probably see an amount listed on your pay stub. Do you pay for life insurance through your job? You might see that amount too. The reason I bring this up is because these amounts are both **pre-tax** deductions. You pay federal, state, and Social Security taxes on what's *left*. The result is your paycheck.

If you contribute to your 401K, your contribution will be listed in that column with your health and life insurance. Those are your **pre-tax** contributions. You only pay income tax on what's *left*. That means you end up paying **fewer taxes** if you contribute to your 401K. Paying fewer taxes means you get to keep **more of your check**. You will end up having to pay taxes on the money in your 401K, but only when you cash it out or retire.

So yes, hearing that you must sacrifice a portion of your pay to participate in a 401K doesn't sound great, but you really won't lose as much as you think because you'll be taxed on your gross pay **minus** all the pre-tax deductions. This means that if you agree to contribute 5% of your pay, that 5% comes out of your gross pay, not your net pay (the amount on your paycheck). Run the numbers for yourself using a "take-home pay calculator" that you can freely find on the internet. The difference in the amount of your paycheck won't be as bad as you think.

"Maxing Out Your 401K"

You may have heard this phrase listening to a financial show or reading some financial website. It's good advice, but it could mean one of two things:

1. You have reached the salary percentage limit that your employer will match.
2. You have reached the dollar amount limit that you can contribute.

Your job's matching contributions aren't unlimited. They're not trying to give you too much free money, so they'll set a matching cap at a certain percentage of your salary. Usually, that's between 3% and 5%. Obviously, the higher, the better. It means more free money. Let's say you earn $30,000 and the matching cap is 5%. Your company will match your contributions up to $1,500 (5% of your salary) but will no longer match if you decide to contribute more.

There is also an annual contribution cap on 401Ks. You can't contribute 100% of your salary even if you wanted to. That's not controlled by your job; it's a limit imposed by the government. As of 2021, that limit is $19,500 if you're under 50 and $25,500 if you're over 50.

So if you earned $30,000 and wanted to **fully** max out your 401K, you'd contribute $19,500. Your employer will max out their contribution at $1,500 (5% of your salary). Your total contributions will be $21,000. Congratulations! Now you just have to figure out to pay rent and eat.

Seriously, you probably don't want to fully max out your 401K. It's just not very realistic. Most financial experts and websites are likely suggesting that you contribute the highest percentage of your salary that your employer will match. That makes perfect sense. I just wanted to give you some clarity. When it comes to financial stuff, it's easy to get lost in all the "good advice" floating around. The details are important.

401Ks can provide the perfect storm for your retirement savings. If done correctly, it can significantly boost your efforts to become financially independent. Here are six ways your 401K can be great:

1. Free Money from Your Company's Match.
2. Capital Gains from your Index Fund investments.
3. Dividend Reinvestments provide more free money.
4. Compound Interest means #1 through #3 make you even more money.
5. Low/No Fees means you keep most of your money.
6. Tax-Deferred Growth means your money grows tax-free until you retire.

Unfortunately, this is how **most** people do it:

1. They don't max out the employer match (or participate at all).
2. They choose some randomly named fund that doesn't perform.
3. They don't choose to reinvest their dividends (or know that they can).
4. There is less money earned for compound interest to work.
5. They choose funds for how they sound and end up paying crazy high fees.
6. They cash out their 401K before they retire and pay taxes **and** IRS penalties.

Most people don't choose poor performance. They just aren't aware there's a better way. I've always been smart enough to know the basics of money, but the details that I didn't know would trip me up every single time. By the time I truly understood how it worked, I had already lost money and was hesitant to try again. I believe this is the experience of most working Americans. We all know enough to be dangerous, but the solutions marketed to us end up hurting us more than helping us. I'll hop off my soapbox now.

Individual Retirement Accounts (IRAs)

IRAs work basically the same way 401Ks do. You can make tax-deferred contributions every year up to a certain dollar amount and you pay the taxes once you retire. Or you can choose to contribute after-tax and not have to pay taxes when you retire. That sounds simple, but in practice, it can get a little tricky. You must set it up correctly or else you'll have to deal with the headache of fixing it later. So why would you have an IRA if you already have a 401K? The quick answer is: you could, but you probably wouldn't.

401Ks are only available to people who are employed. Also, their employers have to offer 401K retirement plans as part of their benefits package. If you're a rideshare driver, "paid under the table" worker, freelancer, independent operator, etc, you are **not** an employee. You are an **independent contractor**. You can't get an employer-based 401K. Even if you're employed, a lot of small businesses don't offer 401K plans to their employees. So what do you do? There are plenty of things you can do, but let's start with opening an IRA.

Remember all those online brokers we talked about before? Well, not all of them are going to work for this. You're going to need a full-service broker to open an IRA account. Just for clarity: **it is literally called an IRA account**. It's **not** a regular account and it doesn't go by any other name. Robinhood and some of the app-based brokers designed for millennials and Gen Z won't cut it. Here are a few good options:

TD Ameritrade
Vanguard
Fidelity
Charles Schwab

If you've already used one of these services to buy stocks, then great.

Login and open a new IRA account. It'll be easy. If you've been using Robinhood, CashApp, or a similar app-based broker, you'll need to complete a new profile with another company before you can open an IRA. Once you start the new account process, you'll have to make a choice: A **Traditional** IRA or a **Roth** IRA.

Traditional IRAs - The Pre-Tax Retirement Plan

By this point, you know what pre-tax and after-tax mean. However, it's easy when you have a job because your employer takes out your contributions on your behalf. But how do you do it when you don't have a job? How do make your contributions pre-tax if your employer isn't doing it? The answer is:

Your tax return.

I can hear you now: "Huh? What does my tax return have to do with my IRA?" It has everything to do with it because it's the only way you can make your contributions pre-tax. Here's how it works:

1. You make money as an independent contractor (or a business).
2. You get a 1099-MISC or a 1099-NEC form saying how much you made.
3. You type in your amounts into your tax preparation software.
4. You have a panic attack when you see how much you owe to the IRS.
5. You type in your contributions to your Traditional IRA for that tax year.
6. The amount you owe goes down.
7. You calm down and figure out what other deductions you're going to use.

You make your contributions pre-tax by **filing your taxes**. You don't have to pay income tax (yet) on any money you put in a qualified tax plan. An IRA is a qualified tax plan, so you get to **deduct** the total amount of your contributions from your total income. Now you're off the hook for the taxes amount until you retire. If you feel like you're going to make a lot of money as an independent contractor and you want to lower your tax bill every year, this might be the way to go.

Another great benefit of Traditional IRAs is that you are allowed to make a contribution until Tax Day of the *next* year. That means if you're doing your tax return for 2021, you have until April 15, 2022, to make a contribution for tax year 2021. The reason you'd do this is because of step #4 above.

Roth IRAs - The After-Tax Retirement Plan

Roth IRAs are a little easier to understand and deal with. Money put into Roth IRAs is considered after-tax because you can't deduct contributions. When you do your tax return, here's how it'll work:

1. You make money as an independent contractor (or a business).
2. You get a 1099-MISC or a 1099-NEC form saying how much you made.
3. You type in your amounts into your tax preparation software.
4. You have a panic attack when you see how much you owe to the IRS.
5. You type in your contributions to your Roth IRA for that tax year.
6. The amount you owe **barely** goes down (if it goes down at all)
7. Your panic attack isn't going anywhere. You'd better figure out what other deductions you're going to use.

You make your contributions after-tax by **filing your taxes** and **not getting a deduction.** You are choosing to pay the taxes now instead of later, so your contributions will still be treated as **income**. However, you may still get a tax credit for making contributions. Tax credits aren't the same as deductions. The government offers tax credits as incentives for people to save for their retirement. They are not guaranteed and they can go away at any time. For the sake of clarity, assume that you will **not** lower your tax bill by making Roth IRA contributions.

However, the benefit is that now when you retire, you don't have to pay taxes. You already paid them, so the money is all yours. No planning or tax-wrangling is necessary. If you're the kind of person that likes to keep things simple, this might be the best way for you.

Finish Opening Your IRA Account

Now you can finish setting up your IRA account with whatever broker you chose. The good thing about most brokers is that they will guide you on how to set up your account properly once you've decided on whether to choose a Traditional or Roth IRA. Most IRA accounts don't have minimum balances, so you may not have to immediately put money in it. You can, but it's not a huge deal right now. However, you do need to know that there is definitely a maximum amount you can contribute every year.

Contribution Limits

As of 2021, you are only allowed to contribute **$6,000 per year**, whether you opened a Traditional IRA or Roth IRA. Again, don't stress too much about it. Your broker will likely warn you if you're in danger of exceeding your allowable contribution and will keep track of your amounts for you.

If you're older than 50, the max is **$7,000 per year**. That may not apply to you, but maybe you'll want to go harass your parents about it. You're never too old to learn something new.

Don't Cash Out Until You Retire

This is where everybody screws up. I've done it too, so you'll get no judgment from me. Unless it's an absolute emergency, **do not cash out your 401K or your IRA.** It's super tempting to see your retirement savings as a way to start a new business, take a nice vacation, or just take a few months off to "find yourself," but trust me, it isn't worth it. Find some other way to do that stuff. Cashing out retirement plans is expensive, as in you could lose nearly *20% of all your 401K or IRA money* expensive.

Early Withdrawal Penalty

If you cash out your 401K or your IRA, you'll have to deal with a 10% penalty. Your job or your brokerage will most likely withhold this 10%, but even if they don't, you'll pay it when you file your taxes. It may not seem like a lot when you only have a couple hundred dollars saved up, but when your account reaches the thousands, you could be throwing a good chunk of money away.

Income Tax

Also, the money you got from cashing out is no longer tax-advantaged and you'll have to pay income tax on the entire amount of your retirement plan. That could easily be another 10-25% of your money.

As an entrepreneur who at times can be simultaneously rebellious and unreasonable, I understand why you might want to cash out your retirement plan when you leave your job (or when your job leaves you). I like revenge and sticking it to the man just as much as anyone else, but in this case, you're only sticking it to yourself. If you have ambitions to start a business or travel or take a break from work, you might be better served by selling some personal items, lowering your expenses, or getting a loan. That way your retirement investments can continue working for you in the background while you focus on the other important areas of your life. It may seem silly to take out a loan when you have retirement cash, but the best thing you can do with your retirement savings is to leave it alone. **Pretend it doesn't exist.** Don't make rash decisions with your retirement money. Think it through and explore other alternatives.

CHAPTER TWENTY-ONE
Tax Stuff: Skip at Your Own Risk

There are three things that will rob you of your potential wealth as you journey down the path to financial independence:

1. Fees
2. Taxes
3. Inflation

You have the **most** control of your fees, **some** control over your taxes, and **no** control over inflation. Let's focus on what we can control. We've already talked about fees, so let's talk taxes.

Tax Brackets: Getting to the Point of Pre-Tax Contributions

We spent a lot of time in the last chapter talking about what pre-tax contributions are and how they work, but we didn't really go into *why* you would do it in the first place. The whole point of waiting until you retire to collect your money when you retire is that you're most likely going to be in a **lower** tax bracket, which means you would pay less in taxes. You may have heard about tax brackets before. A lot of people have the wrong idea about them because they haven't really looked at them. So here they are:

2020 Federal Income Tax Brackets and Rates for Single Filers, Married Couples Filing Jointly, and Heads of Households

Rate	For Single Individuals	For Married Individuals Filing Joint Returns	For Heads of Households
10%	Up to $9,875	Up to $19,750	Up to $14,100
12%	$9,876 to $40,125	$19,751 to $80,250	$14,101 to $53,700
22%	$40,126 to $85,525	$80,251 to $171,050	$53,701 to $85,500
24%	$85,526 to $163,300	$171,051 to $326,600	$85,501 to $163,300
32%	$163,301 to $207,350	$326,601 to $414,700	$163,301 to $207,350
35%	$207,351 to $518,400	$414,701 to $622,050	$207,351 to $518,400
37%	$518,401 or more	$622,051 or more	$518,401 or more
Source: Internal Revenue Service			

These are the most current tax brackets. Remember, this is the government we're talking about, so these brackets could change if a new law is passed. Glance over it real quick. The idea is that if you make less money, you pay fewer taxes. If you make more money, you pay more taxes. When you retire, your income will go down because you'll only have retirement savings and Social Security as income. That would put you in a lower tax bracket than you were when you were working.

Let's say the most you made in your working career was $75,000 per year. While you were working, your income would have been subject to a 22% tax bracket; meaning that you would owe $16,500 per year in income taxes. When you retire, let's say you receive $40,000 per year from Social Security and retirement investments (That's realistic, but your situation will obviously be different). Since you earn less, now your income is subject to a 12% income tax. So let me now ask you a question:

If you saved up to a million dollars in your retirement accounts, would you want to pay a **22%** tax or a **12%** tax?

Well, obviously you'd want to pay fewer taxes, so the answer is 12%. But take a look at the actual numbers:

22% tax rate on 1 Million = **$220,000**
12% tax rate on 1 Million = **$120,000**

You'd save **$100,000** just by dropping to a lower tax bracket. That's a whole lot of money. *This* is why you'd want to wait until you retire before collecting a bunch of taxable income.

If you had a Roth IRA, you wouldn't have to pay any taxes at all. You paid the taxes **upfront**. If you had a million dollars in a traditional IRA when you retired, it had the benefit of growing tax-deferred. You would likely have less in your Roth IRA account because you paid taxes the whole time. Also, you would have likely been in a **higher tax bracke**t when you paid those taxes because you were working.

This is where you need to plan. A Traditional IRA could *potentially* put more money in your pocket *if* you actually go to a lower tax bracket. I say, "if" because it depends on how much your income is during retirement. Saving up to a million dollars means you did really well with your investments. You could potentially end up in a **higher** tax bracket. Also, unless you retire on December 31st, your income doesn't just instantly drop; you'll likely have a combination of Social Security payments along with whatever income you made with your job until the day you retired. That means you'll likely be in a higher tax bracket until the *next* tax year.

You would need to **wait** before you could take full advantage of being in a lower tax bracket. How long would you need to wait? Well, this is where I stop talking and advise you to talk to a tax professional about your retirement goals. I can't possibly know your situation, your income, or your goals. Talking to someone in person can help guide you into properly taking retirement money out of your retirement accounts so that you don't pay too many taxes. Tax law changes all the time. There is no way that what I'm writing today will remain unchanged for the next 40 years. Traditional IRAs can save you thousands in taxes *if* you plan and *if* you do it the right way.

Or just use a Roth IRA and don't worry about it. Just sayin'.

Save Fees and Taxes by Buying and Holding Stocks

Here's another big one. A lot of people new(and not so new) to stock investing are consumed with this idea of "buy low, sell high." That isn't bad advice, but it's too oversimplified to be good advice for every person and every situation. It focuses too much on short-term gain and trying to time the market. Like I said before, no one is consistently good at timing the market. You are likely to lose more than you gain. It can be exciting, but it is equally stressful.

Long-term investing is the best strategy for regular people who have jobs and families and other stuff to do. If you want to be a professional trader that sits at home all day looking at your three-monitor setup with a bunch of stock charts, that's your business.

I am a "buy and hold" investor. That means my goal is to buy a good company at a great price and hold it indefinitely. If the price of the stock goes lower, I don't want to sell. I want to **buy more**. As long as the company is fundamentally strong, I benefit by getting as many shares as I possibly can at a great price. If for some reason the company starts to become uncompetitive or poorly run (remember the K-Mart example?), *that's* when I sell my shares, because it's **no longer a good company compared to other companies.** Also, I don't want to always sell a bunch of stuff because I'll have to pay taxes on that money. Remember capital gains? Well, there are-

Taxes on Capital Gains

If I ever choose to sell my stock, it will be **after at least one year**. After a year, the taxes I pay on any profit (capital gains) will be less than if I sold it before a year. The idea is that the government wants to encourage people to be long-term investors and not short-term traders. Think it doesn't make a difference? Here are the taxes you have to pay when you make money on a stock you've owned for less than a year:

2020 Federal Income Tax Brackets and Rates - Short Term Capital Gains

Rate	For Single Individuals	For Married Individuals Filing Joint Returns	For Heads of Households
10%	Up to $9,875	Up to $19,750	Up to $14,100
12%	$9,876 to $40,125	$19,751 to $80,250	$14,101 to $53,700
22%	$40,126 to $85,525	$80,251 to $171,050	$53,701 to $85,500
24%	$85,526 to $163,300	$171,051 to $326,600	$85,501 to $163,300
32%	$163,301 to $207,350	$326,601 to $414,700	$163,301 to $207,350
35%	$207,351 to $518,400	$414,701 to $622,050	$207,351 to $518,400
37%	$518,401 or more	$622,051 or more	$518,401 or more
Source: Internal Revenue Service			

I can already hear you: "Wait a minute. Isn't this the same thing you showed me earlier?" Yeah, it is. Selling your stocks gave you income, so you have to pay income tax. Nothing changed just because you bought and sold stocks. Income is income. And before you start thinking you only have to pay 10% on anything under $9,875, that tax bracket isn't for *individual* transactions; it's for what you made that **entire year**. That means **all** your income; your job, your profits, your side hustles, and anything else that made you money. Now let's see what happens when you hold your stocks longer than a year:

2020 Federal Income Tax Brackets and Rates - Long Term Capital Gains

Rate	For Single Individuals	For Married Individuals Filing Joint Returns	For Heads of Households
0%	Up to $40,000	Up to $80,000	Up to $53,600
15%	$40,126 to $441,450	$80,001 to $496,600	$53,601 to $469,050
20%	$441,451 and over	$496,601 and over	$469,051 and over
Source: Internal Revenue Service			

Are you starting to see the benefit of waiting at least a year? If your total income for the year is under $40,000, you don't have to pay capital gains taxes at all. Currently, the **most** you can pay is a 20% tax for long-term capital gains. However, for short-term investments, that almost doubles at **37%**. Let's say you got lucky and made $100,000 in something that got crazy hot like GameStop or DogeCoin. You had a feeling that the party wouldn't last forever, so you sold it 6 months after you bought it. You made a huge profit and you feel pretty awesome...until you get a tax bill for **$24,000** next year.

Did you remember to put some money aside for taxes? Or did you spend your $100,000 on a new car or a boat or something? Either way, you'd better find a way to pony up $24,000 or the IRS is going to make your life miserable. This is how celebrities and day traders get in trouble. **Taxes will always reduce your income**. If you had held on to your investment for at least a year, you would have only paid $15,000 next year. It's still a big bill of course, but you save **$9,000**.

Don't Buy and Sell Stocks Too Much AKA Don't Trade Stocks

Buying and selling stocks is obviously fine. I'm saying that you should avoid buying stocks with the intention to sell them in under a year. Sure, you might make money doing it, but you're creating a bigger and bigger tax bill for next year. Even if your broker doesn't charge you fees to sell, you still have to pay taxes. Most people don't plan for their tax bills. A lot of people don't even think about them when they invest. Having no tax plan is a terrible, *terrible* plan. Don't get caught trying to keep up with everybody on social media that's "making money." Getting income from investing is just one part of the equation. Taxes and fees can take your money away faster than you realize.

You Can Deduct Investment Losses Up to $3,000 a Year

Unfortunately, some of your stocks will lose money. Fortunately, you can deduct **realized** stock losses up to $3,000 a year. This is called a **Capital Loss**. "Realized" means that you actually sold the shares for less than you bought them. It doesn't count if your shares lost *value* while still in your brokerage account. You haven't sold it yet, so technically the share price could go back up, then back down, then back up, etc.

The really cool thing about this is that you can carry over a huge loss to later years. For example, if you invested $12,000 in Bitcoin and you sold it at $6,000, you had a $6,000 capital **loss**. However, you can only deduct up to $3,000 in losses for any given year. Fortunately, you can deduct the leftover $3,000 loss **next year.** Now you've deducted the entire $6,000 loss over the two years.

Don't take this to mean that you have a safety net. Consistently losing money investing means that you'll never be able to fully deduct your losses. It also means that you're a gambler, not an investor. The whole point of investing to make money, not lose it. Don't gamble with your money.

CHAPTER TWENTY-TWO
Cryptocurrency: Speculating vs. Investing

In my experience, cryptocurrency investors fall into two camps:

1. People who truly believe in the technological potential of blockchain.
2. People trying to get rich.

Most people are the latter. Since this book is about money, let's talk money. Here are a few terms that I'll use in this chapter:

*   **Crypto** = short for cryptocurrency. Sometimes used to talk about the cryptocurrency industry as a whole.

*   **Exchange** = a currency exchange for crypto. You can exchange the cryptocurrency you own for other types of cryptocurrency or for cash. Most exchanges also allow you to store your crypto like a bank account. Some of the larger exchanges allow you to store your cash as well for more convenient purchasing.

*   **Blockchain** = the technology behind cryptocurrency that allows for encrypted transactions on a ledger. If implemented correctly, this could solve tons of problems for any industry that needs to verify transactions.

*   **Correction** = when an asset like a stock, or in this case cryptocurrency, declines 10% or more in value. The thought is that corrections happen when assets get too overvalued

because of speculation and hype. The correction brings the asset to more realistic values.

- **Private Key** = an alphanumeric code that allows you to spend your cryptocurrency or send it to an exchange. Without it, you can't do anything.

- **Public Address** = an alphanumeric code that accepts deposits. Unlike bank accounts, sharing your public address is harmless. No one can use this code to spend your cryptocurrency. You must have a private key to do that.

- **Wallet** = this is where you keep your cryptocurrency. This "wallet" can exist:
    - as software on your personal computer
    - within the exchange where you keep your crypto
    - on a smart card
    - in an encrypted thumb drive
    - on an external hard drive
    - within a QR code on a printed piece of paper

Cryptocurrency has been around since 2010, but in 2017, the speculative return it brought **exploded**. People who bought them in those early years saw $50 investments turn into $20,000 in 2017. Others who came near the end of 2017 looking for their own quick fortune saw their investments plummet 90% or more 4 months later. Cryptocurrency has both gained and lost fortunes for people. I'm not exaggerating. Even in 2017, almost no professional investor in their right mind would call cryptocurrency "investments." However, by 2020, the returns were so high that people who had missed all the gains of 2017 demanded a piece of the action. Financial establishments that at one time called cryptocurrency a Ponzi scheme were now offering crypto in conventional investment products like ETFs. It's a classic case of "if you can't beat 'em, join 'em."

Now, in 2021, it's gotten even crazier. Investment performance could skyrocket 6,000% with a single tweet from Elon Musk (the founder of Tesla). DogeCoin, a popular cryptocurrency, was invented as a joke. Read that again. It was made because of a popular meme of the day involving a Shiba Inu dog. Even "doge" was misspelled purposely to be in line with the comedic tone of the meme. Nonetheless, if you had invested $1,000 on January 1, 2021, you would have had nearly $60,000 in value by April 15th just four months later. Seven days later, DogeCoin lost 50% from its high. You still would have had $30,000, but just imagine losing nearly **thirty grand** in a week.

That's cryptocurrency investing in a nutshell. Millions in dollars in wealth can be created in 6 months or *less*. An equal amount can be lost within a week. If the coin you invested in gets hot, it goes "to the moon." If you're sitting on the sidelines and don't participate, you sit by and watch all kinds of random people on social media turn $200 into $100,000. Everybody suddenly becomes an investment guru. If you are a traditional investor who believes in fundamental analysis, you can only scratch your head and watch as all the rules are tossed into a massive dumpster fire.

You can't be human and watch this without *some* fear of missing out. At some point, you're going to jump in. It's human nature and I completely understand that. I am not a crypto hater. I invested in 2017 as well. I invested $8,000 into various coins and saw my money triple to $24,000 in less than 4 months. Then, on Dec 19, 2017, everything came crashing down. I watched as my $24,000 dropped…

…to $17,000,
…then $12,000,
…then $9,000,
…then $7,000,
…then $4,000,
…and then eventually $1,200.

To this day, I don't want to calculate the amount of loss I had. It was (and still is) too painful. You can say whatever you want to say about how I should have cashed some profits or did this or did that, but the truth was that I was paralyzed by indecision. I had never made that kind of money that quickly before. The entire time it was going down, I held out hope that it would regain its value.

I looked to the crypto community for guidance on what to do. They are incredibly stubborn; they even coined the term **hodl** (hold on for dear life). Encouraged, I hodled and watched all my money evaporate. It was devastating. Not only that, I had to explain to my wife what happened. Anyone who's married knows that discussion is *worse* than losing the money. Fortunately, it did regain its value- **nearly four years later.** If you decided to buy crypto, you should understand this:

Cryptocurrency is not an investment. It's pure speculation.

It's like betting on a horse race that *never* ends. There will be massive winners and massive losers. Then those massive winners become massive losers while some other random participant becomes a massive winner. Some coins will cease to exist as 20 others take their place and **every** coin is attempting to be the next Bitcoin. That's the simple truth. Your ability to make money is entirely dependent on how popular the coin or token you're speculating on becomes. If a celebrity or influential person gets behind it, it's going to the moon. If not, who knows? I made the mistake of putting a significant amount of my savings into an unproven, risky, super-volatile asset that had no fundamental value. I've said multiple times in this book that you shouldn't gamble with your money. **This** is why.

You may argue that it was worth it because I eventually got back to $24,000. Perhaps, but in that same time frame, I made over $60,000 investing the old-fashioned way. Crypto has given me a massive return on my investment, but the time it took to go through the complete cycle of boom and bust- *back* to boom took so long that my regular investments performed better, not as a percentage of return but as a total dollar amount. It turns out that I'm way more confident investing in something that won't drop by 50% overnight, so I'm willing to invest more of my savings. That being said, put your money in crypto **at your own risk.**

However, I'm not going to act like speculation is pure evil. It's part of human nature and therefore part of the stock market. If people see a gold rush, they're going to rush towards the gold. It's obvious that it can produce massive returns. There are plenty of stocks that are just as speculative as cryptocurrency, so it's not necessarily fair to pick on crypto. It's just that **all** crypto is speculative whereas the stock market runs the gamut from extremely speculative to the risk equivalent of watching paint dry.

While I'm not a fan of speculating, I'm human and I speculate as well.

The trick is to manage it. You put just enough money to satisfy your curiosity so that if it does well, you can participate in the gains. If it doesn't do well, your losses aren't catastrophic. As someone who has participated in crypto for years, this is what I can tell you:

Timing is Everything.

Historically, when it comes to their dollar value, all cryptocurrencies tend to follow a pattern that has 3 parts:

1. A period of low to no growth,
2. followed by a massive increase of more than 200%,
3. then a sudden correction of 25% to 80%.

Then the cycle repeats. Your performance will depend on **when** you buy the cryptocurrency. If you buy during the first part, you will come out on top. Even if there was a massive correction, you'd still make a profit. However, the likelihood is that the first part consisted of early adopters who believed in the project or were hoping to find the next Bitcoin.

The average person is likely to jump in during the second part. Again, your performance depends on when you got in. If you bought it after everyone's been talking about it, you'll join in the fun and make some quick money. You'll wonder why you didn't do this sooner.

However, the third part is where most of everybody in part 2 gets burned. Everyone loses value, but most of the part 2 investors jumped in when the prices were already unreasonably high. Instead of looking at *why* the prices were rising, part 2 investors are just trying to ride the wave higher and higher. They didn't care about fundamentals or use cases or any of that crap. They just wanted some easy money. Unfortunately…

Crypto and Pump and Dump Go Hand in Hand.

It's the *Wolf of Wall Street* on steroids. If you haven't seen that movie, go see it before you put even one dollar in crypto. It's about penny stocks, but the concept is basically the same. "Pump and Dump" means to **artificially** inflate the price of something so it can be sold at higher prices for a profit. Unfortunately for everyone else, all that selling, or profit-taking, creates downward pressure on prices and causes the 25% to 80% correction.

It works something like this: a well-known celebrity, respected public figure, or some influencer promotes a cryptocurrency on social media. That endorsement makes people comfortable jumping in. To reinforce just how awesome this "investment" is, even more influencers talk about how much money they're making and post their returns on social media. Now even more people jump in. That particular crypto gets so popular that it gets on the mainstream news. Even **more** people jump in. Now your cousin and random people from high school are all posting all their crazy gains on social media. Now **you** jump in.

Now **everybody** is in. It's obviously suspicious and everybody knows it doesn't make any sense, but because it's making so much money, everyone overlooks it. "It can't be a scam if I'm making money, right?" Actually, those are the **best** scams because within about two weeks after hitting the mainstream news, that crypto will crash spectacularly.

All the people who started this pump now begin to dump, and they'll make **millions** of dollars doing so. All they had to do was get a celebrity endorsement, use hashtags and make some YouTube videos. They knew the asset was worthless, but as long as some sucker came along and bought it at a higher price, they would always profit. When the pumpers dump all at once, it crashes the value of the cryptocurrency. Meanwhile, the late buyers hold on to hope that the price will magically skyrocket again but watch in horror as all their money evaporates in 72 hours. This is why you:

Book Your Profits Along the Way.

If you've tripled or quadrupled your money, consider taking your initial investment out. For example, if you put in $1,000 and it rose to $3,000, cash out your initial $1,000 and leave the other $2,000 invested. This way you can still participate in any gains, but you don't lose any money if it crashes. This doesn't have to be an all-or-nothing scenario. Speculating can be fun but treat it like a trip to Vegas because that's essentially what it is.

Don't Be Greedy.

Have a plan to get out before you get in. I'm serious. Learn from my mistakes. If you see that you're losing more and more of your money every single day, don't just sit there. Take some or all of your initial investment out while you have a chance. This makes sense, but it's extremely hard to do in practice. Why? Because no one wants to miss out on another huge gain. What happens if you sell and it goes back up again? The better question is: What happens if you do nothing and it continues going down? There will always be opportunities in crypto. Don't feel like it's your only shot at striking it rich.

Don't Overestimate Your Intelligence.

It's easy to brag about making huge returns. There's something about making higher returns than professional investors that makes you feel brilliant. After all, you must know something they don't. **Stop**. You may be smart, but that's not the reason your cryptocurrency is increasing. You're riding the wave of public excitement. Be smart enough to get off before you crash into the rocks.

Use Established Exchanges & Don't Assume You Can Cash Out.

Crypto is still in its infancy. It's barely even 10 years old. It's still the Wild West out there and there are plenty of outlaws, charlatans, and straight-up criminals who will go to great lengths to take your money. Just because you made a 3,000% return doesn't mean you can cash out. What do I mean? I'm saying that the random website you put your credit card and bank account info into may be easily hacked or not even legit. There are well-respected, established cryptocurrency exchanges that handle billions of dollars in transactions every week. If you use:

Coinbase
Kraken
Binance (BinanceUS for US residents)

You can deposit and withdraw your money with confidence. If you're invested in crypto and you don't see your exchange in this list, it's not necessarily a bad thing. There are other respectable exchanges. These are just three of the most well-known (right now).

However, in order to take advantage of some new coin that isn't listed in the well-known exchanges, people dump their money into some fledgling exchange that was never meant to handle thousands of transactions every minute. If their website traffic gets too high, the site will crash. If thousands of people try to take their money out at one time, they will run out of money. Are you starting to get the picture? You only make money when you **realize** your gains. You must sell all (or a portion) of your holdings **AND** have the money in your account before you can celebrate. Gains on a screen mean **nothing**.

This happened to me. I had more than $2,000 invested in some no-name exchange because it was the only one that listed a cryptocurrency I read about. I knew it was bootleg because it **looked** bootleg, but I didn't care. I wanted 4,000% returns. Fortunately, something told me not to press my luck. I transferred my crypto out to another exchange. Four months later, the no-name exchange got hacked, lost everybody's crypto, and got shut down. Anyone who had their money with them lost everything. To this day, the owners of the exchange are trying to process partial refunds while juggling multiple lawsuits. Don't think it can't happen to you.

Security is Your Number One Priority.

Cryptocurrency is digital money, and anything digital can be hacked or stolen. There are countless ways criminals can steal from you or trick you into giving them your private keys and credentials. I get emails all the time that are supposedly from Coinbase. The scary thing is that they look **amazingly** legit.

Keep your private keys and your passwords in a safe place. Consider getting a hardware wallet to keep your crypto assets offline until you need to transfer them. Keeping your crypto on exchanges is generally considered a bad idea. Exchanges get hacked all the time. Some get hacked so bad that they go out of business and everyone who had accounts with them lose everything. This has happened at least 5 times before. There have also been smaller hacks that impact an exchange's ability to get send cash to users who sell their crypto. Just be careful.

To sum it all up: There's a chance that your speculation will pay off, but you'll sleep better at night with traditional investments. The unfortunate truth here is that there's a real chance that you never even get to use any of the advice in this chapter. The government can step in at any time and change everything. Keep this in mind.

CHAPTER TWENTY-THREE
Helpers Rob You of Your Wealth...For a Fee

1. Helpers offer reassurance or a "guarantee" of success for a fee.
2. Their solutions can potentially slow your journey to financial independence.
3. You don't need helpers to perform well in the market.
4. You have access to the same information the experts have.

Respected investors Warren Buffett, Charlie Munger, and John Bogle all make the point that people or services that offer to "help" you get increased returns will more likely **reduce** returns. Helpers **reduce** returns because you have to pay a fee in order to use their services. Those fees come out of your money; meaning that you now have **less** money to invest. Worse yet, the help that helpers offer often produces **lower** performance than what individual investors are able to achieve by themselves. The result is that you pay a fee to get a **lower** performance than you could get on your own. So let me ask:

- Would you pay a fee for someone to make you Kool-Aid that tastes *worse* than when you make it?

- Would you pay someone to help you cross a street safely only to end up getting hit by a bus?

- Would you pay for daycare only to have your kid covered in bumps and bruises when you pick them up?

Of course you wouldn't. You can do these things on your own just fine. If you *did* pay for something, the expectation is that they will do a **better** job than you. You assume that professionals, who are more experienced and knowledgeable than you, are asking for payment *in exchange* for desirable results that you **can't** get on your own. It seems ridiculous that anyone would ask for money and give you worse results than you can get on your own.

Unfortunately, that happens far more than you realize. Check out the chapter on index fund investing. What I said back there is true: Investing in an S&P 500 based index fund consistently produces better returns than professional fund managers. Look it up for yourself. Sure, there are occasional years when fund managers beat the S&P 500, but they can't do it *every* year. If you were to use an actively managed mutual fund with an expense ratio of 1.5% vs an index-based fund with an expense ratio of 0.015%, you are paying **100 times more fees** only to underperform the market.

So, *who* are the helpers? They are the:

- Expert stock recommendation subscriptions
- Active fund managers for mutual funds and ETFs
- Exclusive software offered by investment coaches
- Stock, Options, and Forex trading coaches
- Financial Advisors and Planners
- Newsletter memberships
- Economic Prediction Experts

Helpers Literally Make Money At Your Expense

The financial services industry is full of helpers that offer exclusive information or promise great returns for a fee. Helpers remind me of those tourist trap tour guides that hang out at cruise ship docks. They take advantage of the fact that you're in unfamiliar territory and charge you a fee to "show you around." It's only *after* you've paid a high fee for a mediocre experience that you realize that you could have hopped on a public bus and gotten the same experience for a fraction of the cost.

Helpers offer to consult, coach, and guide you with the promise of giving you a good experience or a guaranteed result. Folks, no one can guarantee anything. You don't need helpers to do well in the market. Helpers save **time**, not money. Using the tour guide example, helpers may not be so bad if you only have 3 hours at your destination. In that case, they would offer a legitimate service: They take you to the most popular destinations right away instead of you wandering around and wasting time. Additionally, you get to hang out with other tourists who are like-minded. That alone can increase your enjoyment of the helper's services. However, if you have plenty of time, or more importantly- **if you do your own research**- their services become **unnecessary**. When it comes to helpers, I'd like to imprint the following idea in your brain:

Anyone with money in unfamiliar territory is going to get ripped off.

That's the *nicer* way of saying:

"A fool and his money are soon parted."

Helpers take advantage of your **ignorance**. People get really mad at that word. It doesn't mean you're stupid; it just means that you are unfamiliar with something. No one *wants* to be ignorant; so people spend a lot of money to educate themselves. Most people inherently trust those that offer education and help them achieve their financial goals. Why *wouldn't* they? However:

- Is all training equal in quality? **No.**
- Is all training a good value? **No.**
- Is paying thousands of dollars for training a guarantee of great results? **No.**
- Is paying a small fee for information a guarantee of undesirable results? **No.**
- Does the reputation or experience of the trainer guarantee great results? **No.**

I was ignorant of investing concepts when I was younger. As a result, helpers took advantage of my ignorance and charged me thousands of dollars for their help. I definitely learned something, but most of what they taught me could have been found at the public library. If I had known better, I would have invested all the money that I paid helpers over the years into investment books and an index fund. My net worth would be **three times** what it is now.

However, I'm not mad. **You can't know what you haven't been exposed to.** There was no way I was going to learn this stuff from high school. I spent a lot of money to learn, but it has given me the knowledge to write this book and help you.

You Have Access to the Same Information the Experts Use

Years ago, you had to rely on a financial advisor and/or a human stockbroker to recommend stocks based on your investment goals. They had information you couldn't access or didn't know about. That's not the case anymore. Virtually all of the online and app-based brokers give you access to all the charts you could want to look at. A lot of these brokers don't even require that you have an account to look at a stock's historical performance.

Furthermore, you now have access to all the research tools the professionals use. Once you learn how to use these tools and read their reports, you minimize the need to rely on stock picking experts. Pick the stocks yourself based on *your* criteria and *your* investment goals. Here are some I've used in the past and would highly recommend. Each one of these has a stock screener that allows you to search for companies that have the qualities and the stats that you're looking for.

- **Yahoo Finance** is a completely free resource that gives you a ton of information about stocks. You can pay more for additional tools, but their most expensive subscription is currently $35 a month.

- **Investor's Business Daily (IBD)** is a subscription-based service that focuses on evaluating a stock and giving it a score. A high score means it's a healthy, high-quality company. A high score doesn't guarantee massive returns, but the stocks I've invested in with good scores have performed well for me. This currently costs $35 a month as well.

- **Value Line** is an annual membership service that also focuses on evaluating companies. This is one of the oldest and most well-known research services. I've used this in combination with Investor's Business Daily to search for companies to invest in. The evaluations they make are very thorough and will give you separate scores for a stock's performance, technical analysis, and investing safety. The most expensive and comprehensive plan is currently $795 a year, but they have other plans that are cheaper and more targeted.

- **Simply Wall St.** is a newer, more modern research tool that has a very good visual interface (AKA it looks better). It's far more visual in nature; the charts and graphs are simple, color-coded, and tell you what you need to know quickly without needing a cup of coffee to read through blocks of text. The most important chart is right at the top and can let you know if you need to investigate further or keep looking. I feel that beginners could get the most out of this one. Just know that the prices are not live; they're at least one business day old. The best part? It's currently $10 a month.

Here's the takeaway: Every one of these tools is currently being used by professional investors, but **not one of them costs more than $800 a year.** Compare that to the **$3,000** dollar stock picking services that are all over the internet. These services don't have any better information than the tools I listed. You're paying for them to do the work for you. However, it will cost you. A **lot**.

Get Help At The Lowest Cost Possible

Any fee associated with investing robs you of your potential wealth. You've heard me say that but let me give you a deeper explanation. What I mean is that every dollar you spend to make money becomes **one less dollar** that can earn compound interest. Your goal is to keep your fees and expenses as low as humanly possible so that compound interest can make you more money by the time you reach retirement. Put simply:

The more you spend to make money, the less money you have to earn interest.

There are hundreds, if not *thousands*, of people, services, products, newsletters, subscriptions, clubs, memberships, and societies that **all** promise increased investing returns for *whatever* investment that is.

Gold, real estate, cryptocurrency, forex, options trading, day trading-you name it; *each* has an **army** of people desperately trying to sell you a solution for better returns or offer you reassurance in the form of coaching, stock picking, research, and software.

These products and services aren't cheap; they can cost anywhere from $1,000 to $20,000 **per course**. Imagine paying $20,000 for the *opportunity* to make money investing. How do you profit by starting out $20,000 in the red? Amazingly enough, people do it all the time; because the creators of these courses offer you the *reassurance* that you'll **multiply** your investment. I say "reassurance" on purpose because they *can't* offer you a guarantee.

- Will you make your money back? **Maybe.**
- Will you multiply your investment? **Possibly.**
- Will you lose your investment? **Who knows?** No one knows the future.

That's why I keep saying that the stock market has *historically* returned 10%. I can't say that it *will* return 10% in the future. It may return more *or* less than 10%. I can read a chart just like everyone else, but I can't tell the future. No one can. So let me ask you this:

How much are you willing to pay to *feel* better about a future **no one** knows?

- You could buy an investment book for less than $20 OR
- You could spend $20,000 on a course taught by ex-Wall Street traders.

Which one is guaranteed to give you better results? **Neither.** Let's say person A reads the book and makes a $1,000 return. Person B has access to the $20,000 course and makes $10,000. The book would net you a $980 profit while the course would still leave you in **debt** for $10,000. Now, which would you choose?

Getting Help is Fine. Just Don't Overspend.

Wait a second. Isn't this book part of that "army" of helpers? Yes, it is. However, as far as fees go, this book is the equivalent of an index fund.

It's an affordable, basic solution that can provide great results. It's a cheap way to learn the ropes so that you can be successful on your own. You won't get one-on-one training or access to some expensive educational course, but you won't spend hundreds or thousands of dollars either.

Helpers aren't all bad. There are some phenomenal trainers and services that can save you time and kickstart your education. Even Warren Buffet had to learn from somewhere. Like I said, I've personally learned a lot from investment courses and seminars. It's undeniable that helpers can provide more than just information. They can give you:

- A sense of community and support
- A network of people who share information
- An accountability partner/coach that will push you to achieve your goals

Sometimes, just having someone you can talk to about investing is exciting. You don't have to spend money on a course to have an investment buddy but being around like-minded people is invigorating. It's cool to pursue your dreams with other people.

However, getting educated on how to become a great investor shouldn't cost a fortune. In my opinion, it's perfectly reasonable to pay a few hundred per year to learn or get access to research tools, but anything over $1,000 should raise an eyebrow. It doesn't automatically mean it's a rip-off, but tread carefully.

It doesn't matter what they tell you. There are **no** guarantees of making your investment back quickly. Besides, there are countless free resources from investment professionals on YouTube, TD Ameritrade, and the library (remember that place? It still exists). If you must pay for an investment coach or a mentor, understand that the more you spend upfront, the more impressive returns you'll have to make to get your investment back. Do yourself a favor and shop around first.

CHAPTER TWENTY-FOUR
Stay Away From Payday Loans & Timeshares

1. Stay away from predatory services and businesses.
2. Avoid paying money for redundant services.
3. Don't pay for the appearance of success.
4. For the love of all things Holy, don't buy a timeshare.

Predatory Businesses Thrive in Certain Zip Codes

You know exactly what I mean. The more brown people in your zip code, the more likely you'll see:

- Payday loan companies
  - Title Pawn services
  - Rent to Own stores
- Blood Donation centers

Stay Away From These Places. At. All. Costs. I cannot stress how much I **despise** these businesses. My biggest issue with them is that they've turned what *should* be a last resort that you use *only* when **absolutely necessary** into a business model that encourages you to come back **every week**.

I'm not saying there isn't a need for these services. For example, renting furniture makes perfect sense for military families and traveling professionals that move around frequently. However, renting **to own** furniture is a terrible idea that will have you spend as much as three times the cost of the item.

Blood donation is a service that benefits everybody and it's good for society. It's great that you're compensated for giving something that helps people. However, when you're encouraged to augment your pay with a weekly visit to the plasma center, that's a problem. Donating blood (or plasma) too frequently is potentially dangerous. Even with safeguards to make sure you don't overdo it, there's no telling how your body will react long term. You can unexpectedly experience blackouts and dizziness. Don't risk your health. It isn't worth it.

I don't have anything good to say about payday loans and title pawn companies. These companies are predatory lending at its **worst**. You can easily spend just as much in interest as the amount you borrowed. Imagine borrowing $100 and having to pay back $200. You don't have to imagine. It happens all the time. This is the closest thing to loan sharks that is legally allowed and these businesses monetize the financial desperation of poor communities. If you're going to these places, you're *already* in a bad situation. They will make it worse. Do yourself a favor and work on improving your credit, then petition to get these businesses removed from your communities.

Don't Buy Extended Warranties

Extended warranties aren't evil, but they're mostly an unnecessary service and expense. Most products have warranties that are already provided by the manufacturer. On top of that, if you used your credit card to buy the item, your credit card will most likely offer an extended warranty and/or purchase protection that covers theft and damages. Anytime someone tries to sell you an extended warranty, do a quick check of your credit card's benefits online or on your phone. You may be surprised to learn that you already have an extended warranty service for free. If you're curious about extended warranties for your car, check out the Auto Insurance section in the insurance chapter.

Owning a Timeshare Means Your Vacation Owns YOU

Timeshares have gone through a bit of a makeover these last several years. It's not called a timeshare anymore. It's "**vacation ownership**." Whoever thought of this phrase is a marketing genius. According to their sales pitch, by *owning* your vacation, you'll *never* have to pay to vacation with your family again. No more budgeting for vacation or paying for multiple days at a hotel. No sir! You'll be staying at a resort that you "own," saving thousands of dollars over several years! Don't want to stay at the same resort every year? No problem! They have a directory of hundreds of 5-star resorts you can stay at whenever you want! Isn't that great?!

It would be great if it were actually true. Sure, everyone tends to go on vacation every year. However, unless you have grandkids and plan to meet around the *same* time in the *same* place every year, most people vacation wherever, whenever and however they *want*. No one says, "Let's go on vacation!" and then chooses what's *available* from a list of participating resorts. No one except timeshare owners because that's how it will be for as long as you own it.

You are never free to choose *exactly* where you want to go. You choose from a directory of properties. If the place you want to visit doesn't participate in your timeshare's list of affiliated resorts, you're not going. If you still want to go to a non-participating property, you'll have to do it the old-fashioned way: paying for every night you stay there. Here's what a timeshare really is:

It's a room in a building that you own for one week of the year.

The room could be in a hotel, a condo, a resort, or a golf course community. Imagine if you could *sell* one of the rooms in your house to one person. Now imagine you could continue selling that **same** room for each week of the year to 51 **more** people. Those people would *legally* own your room for 1 week out of the year, but they're only allowed to stay during **their** week and they **can't** choose the week they want. You could charge them anywhere from $5,000 to $25,000 for that 1 week. That's expensive, but you'll offer them a loan that they can pay off in 10 years or so. And oh by the way, there's a maintenance fee of around $800 they'll have to pay every year to make sure your property looks beautiful.

This is the most genius and creative scheme I have ever seen.

- A timeshare building with 10 rooms,
- at $20,000 a room,
- with each room sold for each week (52 weeks).

You could collect one million dollars for **one** room. Your building has 10 rooms, so your total sales would be ten million dollars. You'd never have to worry about paying for maintenance because the people who bought the room pay maintenance fees of around $800 a year. $800 per room x 52 weeks x 10 rooms = $416,000. That's enough to get you a full-time staff to run the place. It's the perfect business.

However, it's not the perfect deal for consumers. The maintenance fee has to be paid every year whether you use it or not. If you don't pay it, the timeshare can foreclose on your 1 week and sell it to someone else. Part of their sales pitch is that you can give a timeshare to your kids like real estate. What you're actually giving your kids is a maintenance *bill* they have to pay every year. If they don't pay it, even for one year, they **lose** the timeshare. That means that the $20,000 you spent was basically for **nothing**.

Furthermore, you'll feel ripped off when you're making monthly payments and you can't travel to a place you want to. Timeshares use a complicated system of resort inventory that's kind of like the stock market. Everyone can put their timeshares in the "market" and trade their week for someone else's. You don't specifically have to trade yourself; the timeshare company manages that for everyone. You only have to "deposit" your week and request a week at the (participating) destination you want.

Regardless of what they say about points and flexibility, you are buying a room at a *specific* place for a *specific* week and that means your room's value is based on **amenities** and **demand**. Quite naturally, some locations are nicer and have a higher demand than others. If your timeshare is an old condo in Kentucky that looks more like a motel than a resort, it won't have the same amenities as someone else's 5-star resort on the beach in the Bahamas.

Unless you pay additional cash or forfeit future weeks of your timeshare, you ain't going to the Bahamas. Also, remember that you are buying a *specific* week of the year. If that week falls in the middle of winter when no one wants to travel, your Kentucky condo is now worth even *less* because there is **no demand** for winter travel to Kentucky.

Are you starting to see how this works? You're being sold freedom and luxury, but what you actually get are restrictions and frustration. Timeshares take advantage of people's desire to live lavishly and experience luxury. If they feel that they won't have any chance to afford an actual resort because it's too expensive, they'll buy a timeshare so they can at least experience "the good life" once a year.

And that's the problem. Timeshares are marketed to lower and middle-income families and couples who don't have the income to purchase vacation homes. You're being sold a lifestyle of success that you only get to enjoy for a week. There are far better options for traveling. My family has been involved with timeshares for decades. We've had a blast hanging out together using them and it saves a lot of money, but it's difficult to get everyone in the same place at the same time because of all the restrictions. If you absolutely have to get one, **never** pay full price. Say no to their first, second, and possibly their third offer. Every time you say no, you'll get a better deal. Just make sure you don't end up with a motel in Kentucky during the winter.

Just in case you're thinking that you can just sell it whenever you get tired of it, don't kid yourself. You won't able to sell it. **Ever**. A timeshare is next to impossible to sell because *it's a room in a building that you own for a week*. Once you say it out loud, it even *sounds* like a bad idea. Outside of a high-pressure environment, who in their right mind would buy one? Think about how you go about buying one. You are promised a free trip or gift card to sit through a four-hour presentation (with breakfast!) and 3 different salespeople. Do *you* have those types of resources? Are *you* going to make scrambled eggs and cinnamon buns for your prospective buyers? What can you do by yourself- put it on Craigslist? You'll most likely end up **giving** it back to the people you bought it from. They already know that a percentage of buyers will do exactly that. And no, you don't get your money back.

You might be asking how I know all of this stuff. Well, it's because I bought a timeshare and owned one for several years. My dumb behind bought a vacation over the phone from some telemarketer and went to Florida with some friends and coworkers. It was a great deal, but the catch was that I had to attend a timeshare presentation. I had no intention to buy anything, but they convinced me that it was an investment (you should know by now that it's not an investment). I bought a timeshare *with my girlfriend* (which is a topic for a whole other book) and took out a loan for thousands of dollars for what was basically a rundown condo in Florida. I paid hundreds of dollars in maintenance fees every year and only realized **after** I bought it that you can't go where you want when you want. There are a ton of rules that govern what you can do, who can go with you, where you can go, when you can go there, and on and on. It was nothing like they explained at their 4-hour presentation with terrible breakfast and stale muffins.

If you want my advice, go to the presentation, eat the free breakfast, get the free gift card or the free tickets to Disney World and then get the hell out of there. They won't like you, but who cares? They're not doing you any favors anyway. After all, they're trying to sell you a room in a building that you own for a week. Trust me, they have enough money to give you five gift cards and a gourmet breakfast. In fact, take a few extra muffins for yourself on the way out. They told you the presentation would take an hour and it took **four**. You deserve those muffins as compensation for your precious time.

CHAPTER TWENTY-FIVE
Pyramid Schemes Exploit Your Lack of Opportunity

Pyramid Schemes Are All the Same. Join At Your Own Risk.

I'm not here to bash the business "opportunity" that your cousin or family friend is involved in. I'm just going to tell you that I've been in and out of Multi-Level Marketing (MLM) companies for over 20 years and they're all the same. They have some idealistic goal of helping the little guy while charging insanely high prices for their products and services. The focus will always be on recruiting and *not* selling the thing you're supposed to be selling. The result is that you barely make money selling and spend 90% of your time going to meetings by *yourself* because you couldn't convince anyone to come with you.

If you join an MLM company that sells products, you are incentivized to buy over $1,000 worth of products **yourself** so that you qualify for some promotion or higher compensation potential for recruiting. However, your recruits are encouraged to buy over $1,000 worth of products **themselves**. Who do you sell *your* products to? **No one.** Other than the handful of items your family buys out of obligation and guilt, the majority will sit in your garage collecting dust for years.

I got involved with one when I was 18. By 19, I was a presenter for those opportunity meetings that we told people were job interviews. In the pursuit of getting rich quick, I damaged a relationship with a family member, ruined at least 3 friendships, broke off a relationship, and alienated a good number of my college classmates. This was all before I turned 20. I learned a lot of success principles that have genuinely helped me throughout the years. However, those principles would have been better applied to starting my own business.

I'm going to tell you what my college advisor told me 20 years ago. I didn't listen then, but hopefully you will. Learn how to be an entrepreneur. Start your own business, sell your own products, and own everything you're pushing on prospective customers. If you're good enough to do some random MLM company, you're good enough to run your own business. Don't drag people to some random business opportunity meeting in hopes that they'll believe the same hype you did. Make your own business opportunity and find people that will help you build your vision. You'll be far happier in the long run. That's what I did and now I'm proud to tell people what I do.

That was my quick pitch to get you to avoid pyramid schemes. However, if you are like how I was back then, there is **no way** four paragraphs are going to counteract all the hours, weeks and months of non-stop conference calls and Saturday team meetings. So, let me break it down so you understand just how deep I got into these things.

You Want to Talk About Pyramid Schemes? I Did the Presentations. I've been involved in **two** pyramid schemes since I was 18. I did the sales presentations for the first one. I typically did at least two presentations during the weekdays and one presentation every Saturday morning. Here's how it went down.

First, you come in thinking you're there for a job interview, but when you get there, there's a room full of people who look confused but don't want to cause a scene by cussing out the person that invited them.

Second, you get some attractive, well-dressed-looking person to come out and start the meeting. They only talk long enough to tell you that you're about to watch a video.

Third, a slick promotional video comes on. You'll see a bunch of expensive homes, cars, and boats. Everybody in this video is super successful. The CEO pulls up in a Lamborghini, steps out of the car in his power suit, and explains that **you** can have everything you just saw. Then you'll hear from a bunch of random "associates" who've achieved this amazing lifestyle. They will be a diverse mix of people to make it seem that minorities have a better chance to be successful in this company than in a regular job. I'm not joking. By the end of the video, you only have a smattering of what the hell this company actually does but you *do* understand that you could be **rich**.

Fourth, the lights come back up and I come out and explain the compensation package. I'm dressed in a nice suit. I'm young and Black. The implication is that if a barely 20-something-year-old *minority* can do it, **you should have no problem at all**. I explain to you how **easy** it is to move up in the company and that we won't treat you poorly like your old job did. We'll "take care of you" because it's a "team" and [insert other bull crap here].

All you have to do is bring people in. Those people will bring people in and those people will bring **even more** people in. Before you know it, you'll have a team of 300 people all making you money. You're going to be the proud owner of an **Independent Business Organization** with a team of *hundreds* of people across the United States! Don't have the experience to run a national company? You've only mopped the floor at McDonald's you say? **It doesn't matter!** Our company accepts everyone and gives them the success they *deserve*.

By the end of the presentation, you're foaming at the mouth in anticipation of all the inevitable riches you're going to get. You'll basically do whatever I tell you to do. It doesn't even matter what the company is selling (water filters). You don't care at this point. You just want to be **rich**. I've had people write me a check for $2,500 on the spot. (I'm not bragging. I'm actually ashamed of this. This was a horrible chapter in my life that I'm not proud of.)

My point is that I was *really* good at selling, but I spent so much money in training, seminars, and buying products to get monthly sales volume that I **lost** money over time. One training I went to cost $600. I drove all the way from Tennessee to Texas just to hear the CEO give us special training on how to become successful. Think about that. I **paid money** to hear the CEO speak. Why would the CEO charge his *own* workforce to train them? Wouldn't it be in his best interest to train us for free? Why would he want to make regular people spend that kind of money when he's **already rich?** So, let me ask you. Was the goal to help us succeed or was the goal to make him **even richer**?

Don't think that I'm just some bitter person who didn't put the work in. I was a superstar at my office. Yet I was broke. I was a broke superstar who did the opportunity presentations at the pyramid scheme meetings. **Let that sink in**. The people who were running these meetings were renting suits, cars, watches, and venues to get people to join this pyramid scheme. We were literally told to

"Fake It Until You Make It."

I'm not telling you to avoid pyramid schemes because I'm "negative" or because someone told me that they were bad. I'm telling you to avoid them because **I** was the guy doing the presentations and they **instructed** us to fake or exaggerate our success to convince people like you to join. In that "company," the joining fee was $99. That would buy you a kit that was basically an expensive brochure in a three-ring binder. It came shrink-wrapped. Most people never even opened it. We were told to do everything in our power to get the $99 the same night they attended a meeting. We were also told to take the people who showed interest into a separate area and tell them to write down all the names and contact information for their friends and family who might be interested. Surely you see the trick, right? It doesn't matter if you pay the joining fee or not. It doesn't matter if you quit the next day or the next month. As long as I can get you to hand over your personal contacts, I have an endless list of people I can market to. The company wouldn't have to spend *a single dollar* in advertising.

Oh and by the way, we **specifically** ran ads to target people who were unemployed. I wrote some of those ads **myself** and paid to have them published. The company gave us advertising templates to follow and scripts for us to say when people responded to the ad.

I worked in a pyramid scheme's office six days a week- all while attending college in the daytime.

I bought into this company 100%. There wasn't a single person in my circle of influence that didn't know what I did. It got to the point where friends and family started avoiding my calls. I didn't care. I was determined to become a millionaire **in a year** and I wasn't going to let their negativity hold me back.

Is any of this sounding familiar to you? If it does, **stop and think**. The fact is that you don't have to be a part of ANY pyramid scheme to be a business owner. I've been a small business owner for 13 years. I own my business name, print my own cards, rent my own business space, and hire my own contractors. I don't have to go through any "company" or get permission to do anything. That is what owning a business is. It's 100% risk and 100% reward. There is no "upline" or "downline" to protect you from failure. Either your business is good or it isn't. Either you address a need in the market or you don't. Whether you succeed *or* fail, it's **your fault.** I've had successes and I've had failures. I've learned from them all and gotten better. There is no shortcut and there are no guarantees.

I'm seeing a new type of pyramid scheme that's attached to legitimate financial products and cryptocurrencies. I get it. Forex and crypto can be complicated and it would be nice to have someone help you or manage that stuff for you. However, you should know by now that there is no such thing as a free lunch. You will have to pay fees for that help and **fees rob you of your wealth**, remember?

Here's the deal. If you want to trade Forex or get involved with cryptocurrency, **just do it yourself**. You can set up a forex brokerage account at TD Ameritrade or Forex.com. These two brokers charge low fees or **no fees at all**. TD Ameritrade will even teach you the basics for **FREE**. We've already talked about where and how you can buy cryptocurrency, but Coinbase has a very extensive educational component on its platform. As of today (April 2021), they will **GIVE** you **free cryptocurrency** for completing their training modules.

YOU DON'T NEED TO JOIN A COMPANY TO TRADE FOREX OR
OWN CRYPTOCURRENCY.

Also, in case you didn't read the chapter on Helpers, let me make this abundantly clear:

YOU DON'T NEED ANYONE ELSE TO MANAGE ASSETS ON
YOUR BEHALF.

I know plenty of people that trade forex and cryptocurrency. Some of them make a lot of money (I'm sure they have losses too but they're not as vocal about that). The point is that you can do it yourself and you should own your assets **yourself**. It's not hard and you'll **never** have to worry about what will happen to your assets should you leave the company. If you're involved in any other type of "bring people in and get free money" deals, I'm not going to judge you. I'm just going to *warn* you. There is nothing new under the sun. It's an old hustle with a new face.

    ✓   **Anytime the focus is recruiting rather than selling a product or service, you're in a pyramid scheme.**

    ✓   **Anytime the focus is recruiting people to "invest" money and there's NO product or service, you're in a Ponzi scheme.**

You might be saying, "Well, I know it's legit because I got paid" or, "I know somebody who got two thousand dollars and they only put in two hundred." Yes, people get paid in these schemes. That is what makes them the *best* kinds of schemes. If no one got paid, no one would fall for them and they wouldn't work. The people who start these *know* that they **must** have people like **you** to tell everyone about your good experience. Think about a casino. Why do the slot machines make a bunch of noise when someone hits the jackpot? It's to **attract other gamblers**.

By sounding the jackpot alarm, gamblers flock to the area in hopes of finding a "hot" machine. Even other people in the area who had *no intention* of gambling might *stop* whatever they're doing and *start* gambling. It's like moths to a flame. This saying is overused, so I think it's important to spell out that the moths are attracted to the very thing that burns them to death.

Pyramid and Ponzi schemes, by design, benefit the people who get in at the very beginning. The more time goes on and the more people that get involved, the less profitable it becomes for new associates/team members/independent business operators/fun managers/dream specialists/whatever the hell they're calling themselves. This is the fundamental flaw of pyramid and Ponzi schemes. The reason is simple math. **You will run out of people sooner than you think**. If your friends ask your other friends who you've already asked, who will you and your friends ask to join? What will you do then? Keep asking the people who turned you down the first, second and third time? Try to offer some type of incentive to join? Maybe you find a way to get paid, but can you **guarantee** that all your friends and family will get paid?

You can't. Eventually, somebody you care about is going to get burned.

The average person who joins a pyramid scheme will likely make less than a thousand dollars a year in **profit**. Profit is the **most important thing** in business. It's true that you can make a ton of money with pyramid schemes. However, if you spend *two* tons of money in the process, you still **lose** a ton of money.

Use Your Money for Actual Investments
Worse yet, the money you spend every month in membership fees, travel and training could easily be invested in an index fund. Over time and with compound interest, you could be missing out on some **huge** returns. Want some real numbers? Here you go.

My First Pyramid Scheme (1996-1998)
Membership = -$99
Product Orders = -$8,000
Training = -$1,500
Travel = -$750
Office Desk Rent = -$1,200

Total Expenses = -$11,549

Total Sales & Commissions= +$7,800

LOSS = -$3,749

If I had put the dollar amount of my total expenses into an S&P 500 index fund and done **NOTHING ELSE**, I would have had **$58,000** by the end of 2020. If I continued to let it sit there until I retire at 65, it could have been worth around **$500,000** (assuming a 10% return annually). At 72, I would have been a millionaire. This would be from **one** investment **one** time. You might think that's a long time to get a million dollars. Sure, it may be. However, it's **far** more of a sure thing than anything a pyramid scheme has to offer. Here's something you may not have considered:

Time is going to pass no matter what you do.

Seems obvious, right? Think deeper though. I could have found a way to hustle up $11,000 on my own and invested it. I wouldn't have had to do anything else. I could have gone back to school, got a new job, got married, etc. That whole time, the money in my index fund would have made more and more money **without me doing any work**. Instead, I spent years putting thousands of miles on my car and attending meeting after meeting until I pissed off all my friends and family. For all that hard work, that business **lost** me nearly $4,000. More importantly, I lost **time**. All those years I spent chasing my tail were gone. Even when I learned how to invest, I could never get those lost years back for compound interest to work on my behalf. In fact, the only thing I gained was a garage full of organic lotion, water filters and vitamin supplements.

You might be wondering how I got all that money to put into the pyramid scheme in the first place. $5,000 came from a family member who believed in me. For the rest, I used my credit cards and cash from a part-time job as a dishwasher at a restaurant. This is probably a good time to tell you to never borrow that kind of money from family members. My relationship with that person has never been the same since. This "business" also caused all kinds of problems with my college girlfriend. We weren't going to last anyway, but this business definitely hastened the destruction of that relationship.

You Don't Know What You Don't Know
Look. I know I'm being hard on pyramid schemes, but I don't want to be too hard on **you**. You are not at fault. You are only going off the information that's being provided to you. If following all the rules and going to school didn't work, pyramid schemes will seem like your **last** chance to keep your dreams alive.

That *right there* is the main problem I have with these schemes. Your disappointment and disillusion with society make you a **prime target** for these companies. They prey on you when you are at your lowest; during a divorce, when you're unemployed, after losing your car, after being looked over for a promotion or having some other disappointing life development. You are **desperate** for a solution and they offer an easy way out. All you have to do is pay a membership fee and recruit five people a month.

Folks, that is NOT a solution. It's just a tool. We already discussed this at the very beginning of the book. If you are in a situation where you can take advantage of a pyramid scheme as a *tool for gaining income*, that's fine. However, if you think this scheme is going to *solve* your problems, you're in for **a lot** of disappointment and damaged personal relationships. I can promise you that. Even if someone you know made money doing it, it doesn't mean it will work for you. At the end of the day, you'll be forced to wonder if it was all worth it.

The only positive thing that I can say is that pyramid schemes introduced me to the idea that I could be a millionaire. I never even *dreamed* that I could be rich, so someone telling me that **changed my life**. **No one** had said that to me before. It opened my mind to a possibility where I could **choose** my future and **escape** the inevitable collision course with mediocrity.

If I'm **surrounded** by *dozens* of people telling me that I can be wealthy, **I'm going to believe them without question**. Someone believing in you is **powerful**. If no one ever believed in you and told you that you could do great things, having a group of people suddenly tell you how awesome you are is **addictive**. You will come back night after night just to be around people that build you up instead of joking on you and tearing you down.

This is the unfortunate reality for countless poor and lower-middle-income families and individuals. If you've never been told that you can be wealthy, you're an **easy target** for any scammer that says you can. All they have to do is smile at you and show you a fancy car and an expensive watch. Think about that for a second. I was so desperate for success that I blindly followed a CEO in a Lamborghini **just because he had a luxury car**. I didn't need any other reason or proof. Once he said that I could have one too, I was hooked. I believed him because I **wanted** to believe him. I figured I could get one if I did everything he said. It never dawned on me that I could get it myself.

If you've never heard someone tell you that you can be wealthy, allow me to be the first.

You can be a millionaire.

That is not an exaggeration. That is not a lie. You only need time and consistent effort. You don't have to be famous, exceptional, or talented in any way. Outside of some basic education, you don't need anybody's help. You **certainly** don't need any pyramid scheme to do it. It's just simple math and compound interest over time.

The sad truth is that if somebody-ANYBODY- had shown the 18-year-old me a simple, legitimate way to become financially independent, there's *no way* I would have gotten so deep into this kind of company. I would have **known** there was another way. Sure, I definitely would have tried to speed up the process of becoming rich. I know me and there's no doubt about that. However, I legitimately saw this company as **my only hope for success.** Nothing else I saw around me with my family or my neighborhood or my college campus made me feel like I had a real shot at becoming wealthy. **Of course** I was going to join a pyramid scheme if it meant getting rich. At 19, I could already see that the "go to school and get a good job" argument had **serious** flaws.

The next time someone introduces you to an opportunity to get rich, ask yourself the following questions:

- Why would a rich person need *me and my broke friends and family* to help them build their business? Why do they need our money *at all*?

- If this is such a team effort, why doesn't my upline or sponsor place people under me to help me get started? How can we be a *team* if I'm 100% responsible for my own success?

- Why does everyone in the business have so much time to spend on conference calls and meetings if they're so busy? Why is so much time spent on motivating me and keeping me excited?

- Am I learning more about running a business or am I learning more about how to talk people into attending meetings?

- Why am I being charged for training if I'm already paying a monthly fee? Why do I have to pay for training when I'm part of a team "that's focused on my success"?

- Why does the company need my money if I'm working for myself? Why do I have to pay someone else to be an *independent* contractor? How many times a year do I have to pay to participate in this opportunity?

- Why does this person keep posting their expensive cars, clothes, and homes on social media? If *I* already had a million dollars, would I feel the need to post pictures of my belongings **every single day?**

- Does this business make more money helping me succeed or by selling products and training to me directly?

These pyramid schemes will tell you that people asking these questions are negative or are "haters." They'll give you specific training to deal with these types of objections without having to give direct answers. Here's what they'll tell you to say:

- "Don't worry about the membership fee. You'll make so much money that you'll pay it back with no problem."

- "You have to invest in yourself. There's no such thing as something for nothing."

- "[Insert Random Person's Name] made $10,000 last month part-time. Imagine what you could do if you put in full-time work!"

- "The joining fee is just a way to make sure you're committed and that we don't spend valuable time training someone who isn't serious. You're committed to your success, *aren't you?*"

- "You don't have to explain anything to anybody. Leave the talking to us. Your job is to get your recruits to a meeting at the office or with your sponsor/upline. We'll handle the rest."

I know this is what they say because I trained people on how to overcome objections. Before you say that this was all in the past and that things are different now, I've been invited to countless presentations from friends and family members over the years and I've been involved with another multi-level marketing company since 2012. They still say the **exact** same things (it's kind of funny in a way).

The point is that I know what I'm talking about. I'm inactive right now, but I joined because I wanted to get some financial education that they were offering as part of a licensing process. I saved hundreds of dollars doing it that way. I didn't want the license. I wanted the education. I got it and I am happy with my decision. This is what I mean by using jobs as tools to get what you want.

Now go open a brokerage account and invest in an index fund.

CHAPTER TWENTY-SIX
Your Five-Step Financial Plan

While I'm tempted to keep rambling about my life to get you to see just how much I understand what you're going through, the time for talking is over. **It's time to take action.** There's no point knowing any of this stuff if you don't do anything. So let's put it all together in just **5 steps.**

#1: Figure Out Your Average Monthly Expenses.

   ✓   This is the **MOST IMPORTANT STEP.** You **need** this number to be able to evaluate your financial health at a glance. It removes the uncertainty of wondering if you have enough money and how you're going to pay your bills. **Nothing I suggest will work unless you know this number.**

   ✓   If you don't know what your average monthly expenses are, total all the debits, withdrawals and charges from your bank account during a non-holiday month when you didn't travel. You're trying to get an idea of how much you **normally spend** without any extra stuff.

   ✓   Now do it again for **two other normal months**. Your monthly expenses should be roughly the same for normal months. Average those three months and you'll get your regular monthly expense.

#2: Figure Out How Much Money You Have Left Over Every Month.

✓   This the **SECOND MOST IMPORTANT STEP**. You **need** this number to help build your savings account, get out of debt and start investing. If you don't know this number, you can't make a plan and nothing I suggest will work.

✓   If you don't know how much money you have left every month, look at your account balance from the day **after** the last debit transaction you had in the month you used to figure out your monthly expenses. So if you figured that January was an average month with no travel and no holidays and your last debit transaction was on January 28, check your balance from January 29 and see what you had left.

✓   Now do it again for two other normal months. Your leftover amount should roughly be the same. Average the three months and you'll have your regular leftover amount. If your leftover amounts are *way* different, **choose different months**. Either way, you'll start to notice a pattern with your spending that can help you figure out ways you can save money.

✓   Once you know what your leftover amount is, **DO NOT SPEND IT. Move it to your emergency savings account every month.** Commit to using this amount every month to achieve your financial goals.

✓   **It doesn't matter how big or small your leftover amount is.** Even if it's just ten dollars, we're going to make it work. Slow and steady wins the race.

✓   If you ever receive unexpected income from a tax refund, government stimulus, gifts, or work bonuses, **DO NOT SPEND IT**. Use that money to build your emergency savings account.

#3: Use THREE Different Bank Accounts That Each Do ONE Job.

✓   Your emergency savings account has one job: to protect you against unexpected expenses and income loss. It needs **at least**

3 months' worth of expenses at ALL times, but **no more than 6 months' worth**. Use your leftover amount to build up your balance. **DO THIS FIRST.**

✓ Your checking account has one job: to pay your monthly expenses. Set up your bank's Online Bill Pay to pay all of your bills from one place. You need to keep **at least one month's worth of expenses** in it ALL times. Continue using your leftover amount to build up your balance **AFTER** you have at least 3 months' worth of expenses in your emergency savings account.

✓ Your personal spending savings account has one job: to pay for your vacations, Jordans, gadgets or whatever else you think you've got to have for your life to be enjoyable. It **should only contain** gift money and the money left over from canceling all of your unnecessary monthly subscriptions and un-important monthly expenses.

✓ **HOWEVER**, do **not** contribute more than $100 to this account per month. If you have found a way to save more than that by canceling unnecessary expenses, add any amount over $100 to your leftover amount so that you can reach your financial goals faster.

✓ That's **THREE** accounts containing at least **FOUR** months' worth of expenses and spending money for you to enjoy your life. Here's the order again:
    - Get **3** months' worth of expenses in your emergency savings account.
    - Get **1** month's worth of expenses in your checking account.
    - Then, use **half** of your leftover amount to continue building up to **6** months' worth of expenses in your emergency savings account. Use the other half to **start paying off high interest debt.**
    - Once you have **6** months' worth, **STOP** saving and focus **all** of your leftover amount on paying off high-interest debt.

#4: Pay Off All Your Credit Cards and High-Interest Debt.

✓ If your interest rate on any debt is in the double digits, it's high-interest debt. Pay it off. Most likely it's just your credit cards, but it can be other forms of credit debt like financing for purchases at stores (like furniture) or financing certain home repairs (like new windows or a new AC unit). If you have a car loan with a high interest rate, focus on the credit debt for now.

✓ Use your leftover amount and the Debt Snowball method described in the credit score chapter. Pay off the lowest credit card balances first so that you can build your "snowball" faster.

✓ After you pay off your high-interest debt, your leftover amount will be higher. Use this money to invest.

#5: Invest in an Index Fund Every Single Month No Matter What.

✓ Use your debt snowball amount (your leftover money plus the monthly savings by paying off your credit cards) and buy an index mutual fund or ETF **every month.**

✓ It does not matter what the market is doing. You are focused on the long term. Use ALL of your increased leftover money to invest every month. **Do not** spend any of it. **Do not** skip a month.

✓ By this point, you *already* have money for emergencies and personal spending. **Do not** hesitate or make excuses to delay investing. The sooner you start and commit to this, the earlier you can choose to retire. Remember, you're not *losing* your money, you're *using* your money to make money while you sleep.

✓ Choose an index fund with an expense ratio of 0.2% or **less.** The lower, the better.

✓ Choose to reinvest your dividends. This may be a setting you have to change in your brokerage account.

✓ Invest in index funds **first.** Invest in individual stocks **later** after doing your research.

✓ Buying cryptocurrency is not investing. It's speculation. Don't speculate with money you can't afford to lose.

✓ I suggest having a portfolio that gives you a good mix of security, growth, and a little bit of speculation so you don't have the fear of missing out. Here's a good place to start:
  - 70% in a low-cost Index fund
  - 25% in individual stocks
  - 5% in cryptocurrency, forex trading or any other speculative activity not addressed in this book

If you do these five steps, your financial life will seemingly work on autopilot. You won't have any late fees, NSF fees or interest charges on credit cards. You'll have a **lot** less stress and compound interest will work for you even when you're not thinking about it. Once you get to step five, you're prepared for anything life throws at you **today** while also preparing for whatever life throws at you **in the future**. When everyone else is freaking out about losing their job, the economy or gas prices, you'll be *calm* because you'll have **seven months** of income at your fingertips. You'll have plenty of time to ride out the storm and figure things out.

However, this plan is not about becoming debt-free. That is a good goal, but I don't want you to attempt paying off a $10,000 car loan or a $200,000 mortgage before you start investing. Saving and debt reduction are just *one* part of becoming financially independent. **You must invest or your money can't grow.**

Now that you have a plan to get ahead, here are some helpful tips for some of your biggest expenses like your auto loan, mortgage loan, credit cards and insurance. These are just the highlights of earlier chapters in a quick list that you can reference when you need to.

Use ONE Credit Card and Pay It Off Every Month.

✓ Once you've paid off all of your cards, pick the one that has the best perks with no annual fee and only use that ONE card.

✓ If you use ApplePay, a digital wallet or a stored credit card on sites like Amazon, only use this one card. **Remove** any other stored card from any other site or service.

✓ Cancel any card with an annual fee.

✓ Leave the rest of your credit card accounts open but take the physical cards **out** of your wallet/pocketbook and **do not use them**. Stick them in a drawer or a closet somewhere.

✓ To avoid paying interest, **never** carry a balance on this card month-to-month. Pay off your entire balance every single month. You can use your bank's BillPay service or use the card's AutoPay service.

✓ To keep your monthly bill low enough to pay off every month, **only** use your card for smaller expenses like your cell phone bill, cable, streaming services, groceries and etc. **Do not use** your credit card for large bills like rent or car payments. Use your checking account for those larger monthly bills.

Get Your Free Report from all THREE Bureaus and Check Your FICO Score

✓ Go online and get your credit reports from TransUnion, Equifax, and Experian.

✓ If you see anything wrong with any one of your credit reports, **immediately** dispute it.

✓ Go check your FICO score. Know this score before you apply for a loan. It may not be free, but it's currently the most important score.

✓ Don't assume that the "free credit score" you got is your FICO score. It may be a VantageScore or a score from one of the three agencies. These can give you a good idea of where you're at, but lenders generally ignore these scores when you apply for a loan.

✓ Freeze your credit with each of the three credit bureaus so that no one can open credit cards and loans by stealing your identity.

✓ Do not apply for additional credit cards and ignore credit card offers in the mail. Do not trust or respond to credit offers from emails.

Get Basic Health Insurance. Get Life Insurance If You Have Kids.

✓ If you have a job, get health insurance through your job. It's usually cheaper through your employer.

✓ If you are self-employed or freelancing, purchase an individual insurance plan on your own.

✓ If you ever become unemployed and receive a notice for **COBRA** insurance (Continuation of Health Coverage from your former employer), it will likely be super expensive. You're probably better off shopping for an individual plan on your own.

✓ If you're under 30 with no kids, you are not likely to visit the doctor much. Don't spend a lot of money and find a plan with a low monthly cost. A high deductible HMO plan will be fine for most of your needs.

✓ If you have a pre-existing condition, have kids or are planning to have kids, you will likely visit the doctor frequently. Find a health insurance plan with a lower deductible that you can afford to pay. It will cost more per month, but your total out-of-pocket expenses will likely be lower for the year.

✓ If you don't have kids, you generally don't need life insurance.

✓ If you do have kids, get a term life insurance policy for enough money to cover your debts and expenses for your kids. A $25,000 policy is a good start. Don't go nuts with the policy amount. You're not trying to make your family rich by dying.

✓ You don't need whole life insurance unless you're attempting to use your policy as an investment vehicle.

Buy a Cheap Car with a Small Monthly Payment or Use Cash.

✓ Forget about status and appearances. Get a cheap car that can safely get you from point A to point B.

✓ If you get a loan, it should be no longer than 60 months (5 years) and your monthly payment should be lower than $200.

✓ That means you shouldn't spend more than $10,000 on your car. It will likely be used. Get a car that has under 50,000 miles if possible. That may not be your ideal car, but you'll have far better options in the future if you sacrifice today.

✓ If you can use cash, you will avoid a monthly payment. That is good, but **do not sacrifice your emergency savings to buy a car**. It's better to have a low monthly payment than to spend a huge chunk of cash.

✓ Use your FICO score to have a good idea of what your interest rate and the monthly payment will be.

✓ Get pre-approved from a credit union or online bank before you go to the dealership. Don't tell the salesperson that you've been pre-approved until after you get the price you want for the car.

✓ Get gap insurance from your auto insurance company, not the dealership.

✓ Decide whether or not to buy an extended warranty before you go buy the car. Get quotes from the internet before you buy the car so you know how much it costs. Do not buy extended warranties from the dealership if they are more expensive than what you saw online.

✓ If there is a charge listed on the loan paperwork that you do not understand, pull out your phone and look it up. Do not trust salespeople to have your best interest.

Don't Rush The House Buying Process

✓ Think of buying your house like getting married. Don't fall in love with the first thing you see. Make sure you know everything about the house itself, its history and the area that it's in.

✓ Buying a house will likely be the most expensive thing you ever buy. Make sure you get the best interest rate and the best price you can. You'll be making payments for a long time and a small difference in the interest rate can cost you tens of thousands of dollars over time.

✓ Don't let your real estate agent or anyone rush you or make you feel like you have to make a decision faster than you're comfortable with. Nobody makes any money until you close on the house. They are incentivized to rush you to get their commissions.

✓ Research the area that the house is in. Make sure that it has decent schools and is relatively close to desirable things like shopping and public parks.

✓ Make sure there isn't a bunch of crime in the neighborhood.

✓ Read the home inspection report. If you don't have the money to fix the problems it discovers, try to negotiate the price lower. If that's not possible, look for another home. Don't assume that you'll have the money later for major repairs.

And that's it. Like I said, I'm tempted to try and cram everything I know about money in this one book, but my goal is to give you the basics that will set you up to have more success as you get older and increase your income. If you have a strong foundation, it will be easier to build wealth and you won't have to spend your middle-age years fixing the mistakes of your early adulthood.

Being 25 was stressful for me financially, but I've learned enough during these last 17 years to create a lifestyle that's comfortable and low-stress. I basically do what I want when I want to do it. I have the freedom to choose how I spend my time and where I want to work. I wish I had figured this stuff out sooner, but the perspective it has given me has allowed me to help a lot of young people who are trying to figure this out.

If I'm being honest, I hope that this book changes your life. It's my desire that this information makes your life better and saves you years of pointless frustration and needless stress. I hope that this will change how you look at finances and money in general so that you can see that it's just a tool. It has nothing to do with status or your identity. Live your life for who you are as an individual and don't allow anyone else to tell you that buying something will make you happy. It won't. Money only gives you the freedom to choose. What you do with that freedom is up to you.

God bless you and I wish the very best for you. I'll be rooting for your success!

Alex Gardener